The Missionary Oblate Sisters

McGILL-QUEEN'S STUDIES IN THE HISTORY OF RELIGION

Volumes in this series have been supported by the Jackman Foundation of Toronto.

SERIES TWO
In memory of George Rawlyk
Donald Harman Akenson, Editor

1 *Marguerite Bourgeoys and Montreal, 1640–1665*
Patricia Simpson

2 *Aspects of the Canadian Evangelical Experience*
Edited by G.A. Rawlyk

3 *Infinity, Faith, and Time*
Christian Humanism and Renaissance Literature
John Spencer Hill

4 *The Contribution of Presbyterianism to the Maritime Provinces of Canada*
Edited by Charles H.H. Scobie and G.A Rawlyk

5 *Labour, Love, and Prayer*
Female Piety in Ulster Religious Literature, 1850–1914
Andrea Ebel Brozyna

6 *The Waning of the Green*
Catholics, the Irish, and Identity in Toronto, 1887–1922
Mark G. McGowan

7 *Religion and Nationality in Western Ukraine*
The Greek Catholic Church and the Ruthenian National Movement in Galicia, 1867–1900
John-Paul Himka

8 *Good Citizens*
British Missionaries and Imperial States, 1870–1918
James G. Greenlee and Charles M. Johnston

9 *The Theology of the Oral Torah*
Revealing the Justice of God
Jacob Neusner

10 *Gentle Eminence*
A Life of Cardinal Flahiff
P. Wallace Platt

11 *Culture, Religion, and Demographic Behaviour*
Catholics and Lutherans in Alsace, 1750–1870
Kevin McQuillan

12 *Between Damnation and Starvation*
Priests and Merchants in Newfoundland Politics, 1745–1855
John P. Greene

13 *Martin Luther, German Saviour*
German Evangelical Theological Factions and the Interpretation of Luther, 1917–1933
James M. Stayer

14 *Modernity and the Dilemma of North American Anglican Identities, 1880–1950*
William H. Katerberg

15 The Methodist Church on the Prairies, 1896–1914
George Emery

16 *Christian Attitudes Towards the State of Israel*
Paul Charles Merkley

17 *A Social History of the Cloister*
Daily Life in the Teaching Monasteries of the Old Regime
Elizabeth Rapley

18 *Households of Faith*
Family, Gender, and Community in Canada, 1760–1969
Edited by Nancy Christie

19 *Blood Ground*
Colonialism, Missions, and the Contest for Christianity in the Cape Colony and Britain, 1799–1853
Elizabeth Elbourne

20 *A History of Canadian Catholics*
Gallicanism, Romanism, and Canadianism
Terence J. Fay

21 *The View from Rome*
Archbishop Stagni's 1915 Reports on the Ontario Bilingual Schools Question
Edited and translated by John Zucchi

22 *The Founding Moment*
Church, Society, and the Construction of Trinity College
William Westfall

23 *The Holocaust, Israel, and Canadian Protestant Churches*
Haim Genizi

24 *Governing Charities*
Church and State in Toronto's Catholic Archdiocese, 1850–1950
Paula Maurutto

25 *Anglicans and the Atlantic World*
High Churchmen, Evangelicals, and the Quebec Connection
Richard W. Vaudry

26 *Evangelicals and the Continental Divide*
The Conservative Protestant Subculture in Canada and the United States
Sam Reimer

27 *Christians in a Secular World*
The Canadian Experience
Kurt Bowen

28 *Anatomy of a Seance*
A History of Spirit Communication in Central Canada
Stan McMullin

29 *With Skilful Hand*
The Story of King David
David T. Barnard

30 *Faithful Intellect*
Samuel S. Nelles and Victoria University
Neil Semple

31 *W. Stanford Reid*
An Evangelical Calvinist in the Academy
Donald MacLeod

32 *A Long Eclipse*
The Liberal Protestant Establishment and the Canadian University, 1920–1970
Catherine Gidney

33 *Forkhill Protestants and Forkhill Catholics, 1787–1858*
Kyla Madden

34 *For Canada's Sake*
Public Religion, Centennial Celebrations, the Re-making of Canada in the 1960s
Gary R. Miedema

35 *Revival in the City*
The Impact of American Evangelists in Canada, 1884–1914
Eric C. Crouse

36 *The Lord for the Body*
Religion, Medicine, and Protestant Faith Healing in Canada, 1880–1930
James Opp

37 *600 Years of Reform*
Bishops and the French Church, 1190–1789
J. Michael Hayden and Malcolm R. Greenshields

38 *The Missionary Oblate Sisters*
Vision and Mission
Rosa Bruno-Jofré

SERIES ONE
G.A. Rawlyk, Editor

1 *Small Differences*
Irish Catholics and Irish Protestants, 1815–1922
An International Perspective
Donald Harman Akenson

2 *Two Worlds*
The Protestant Culture of Nineteenth-Century Ontario
William Westfall

3 *An Evangelical Mind*
Nathanael Burwash and the Methodist Tradition in Canada, 1839–1918
Marguerite Van Die

4 *The Dévotes*
Women and Church in Seventeenth-Century France
Elizabeth Rapley

5 *The Evangelical Century*
College and Creed in English Canada from the Great Revival to the Great Depression
Michael Gauvreau

6 *The German Peasants' War and Anabaptist Community of Goods*
James M. Stayer

7 *A World Mission*
Canadian Protestantism and the Quest for a New International Order, 1918–1939
Robert Wright

8 *Serving the Present Age*
Revivalism, Progressivism, and the Methodist Tradition in Canada
Phyllis D. Airhart

9 *A Sensitive Independence*
Canadian Methodist Women Missionaries in Canada and the Orient, 1881–1925
Rosemary R. Gagan

10 *God's Peoples*
Covenant and Land in South Africa, Israel, and Ulster
Donald Harman Akenson

11 *Creed and Culture*
The Place of English-Speaking Catholics in Canadian Society, 1750–1930
Terrence Murphy and Gerald Stortz, editors

12 *Piety and Nationalism*
Lay Voluntary Associations and the Creation of an Irish-Catholic Community in Toronto, 1850–1895
Brian P. Clarke

13 *Amazing Grace*
Studies in Evangelicalism in Australia, Britain, Canada, and the United States
George Rawlyk and Mark A. Noll, editors

14 *Children of Peace*
W. John McIntyre

15 *A Solitary Pillar*
Montreal's Anglican Church and the Quiet Revolution
Joan Marshall

16 *Padres in No Man's Land*
Canadian Chaplains and the Great War
Duff Crerar

17 *Christian Ethics and Political Economy in North America*
A Critical Analysis of U.S. and Canadian Approaches
P. Travis Kroeker

18 *Pilgrims in Lotus Land*
Conservative Protestantism in British Columbia, 1917–1981
Robert K. Burkinshaw

19 *Through Sunshine and Shadow*
The Woman's Christian Temperance Union, Evangelicalism, and Reform in Ontario, 1874–1930
Sharon Cook

20 *Church, College, and Clergy*
A History of Theological Education at Knox College, Toronto, 1844–1994
Brian J. Fraser

21 *The Lord's Dominion*
The History of Canadian Methodism
Neil Semple

22 *A Full-Orbed Christianity*
The Protestant Churches and Social Welfare in Canada, 1900–1940
Nancy Christie and Michael Gauvreau

23 *Evangelism and Apostasy*
The Evolution and Impact of Evangelicals in Modern Mexico
Kurt Bowen

24 *The Chignecto Covenanters*
A Regional History of Reformed Presbyterianism in New Brunswick and Nova Scotia, 1827–1905
Eldon Hay

25 *Methodists and Women's Education in Ontario, 1836–1925*
Johanne Selles

26 *Puritanism and Historical Controversy*
William Lamont

The Missionary Oblate Sisters

Vision and Mission

ROSA BRUNO-JOFRÉ

McGILL-QUEEN'S UNIVERSITY PRESS   Montreal & Kingston • London • Ithaca

ISBN 0-7735-2954-3 (cloth)
ISBN 0-7735-2979-9 (paper)

Legal deposit fourth quarter 2005
Bibliothèque nationale du Québec

Printed in Canada on acid-free paper that is 100% ancient forest free
(100% post-consumer recycled), processed chlorine free

McGill-Queen's University Press acknowledges the support of the
Canada Council for the Arts for our publishing program. We also
acknowledge the financial support of the Government of Canada
through the Book Publishing Industry Development Program (BPIDP)
for our publishing activities.

Library and Archives Canada Cataloguing in Publication

Bruno-Jofré, Rosa del Carmen, 1946–
The Missionary Oblate Sisters : vision and mission / Rosa Bruno-Jofré.

(McGill-Queen's studies in the history of religion ; 38)
Includes bibliographical references and index.
ISBN 0-7735-2954-3 (bnd)
ISBN 0-7735-2979-9 (pbk)

1. Oblate Missionaries of Mary Immaculate–History. 2.
Manitoba–Church
history. I. Title. II. Series.

BX4411.8.B78 2005 271'.97 C2005-905735-1

This book was designed and typeset by studio oneonone
in Sabon 10/13

Contents

Foreword

It was in October 1989 that Dr Rosa Bruno-Jofré had just begun teaching Educational Foundations and History of Education courses at the Faculty of Education, University of Manitoba. She felt hampered by the lack of resources available for her students to research the history of education in the province, particularly women's contributions to education. She soon set out to organize a committee called the Community of Inquirers supporting the History of Education Project at the University of Manitoba. The committee was made up of students, professors, and retired teachers. Having been in contact with the Faithful Companions of Jesus, a female teaching religious congregation in Calgary, Alberta, Dr Bruno-Jofré had developed an appreciation of and keen interest in their educational achievements. For this reason she wished to involve Sisters in the research she was initiating at the University of Manitoba. Through a graduate student she was introduced to us, the Missionary Oblate Sisters, a teaching congregation founded in St Boniface with roots linking us to the Manitoba School Question that unfolded in the 1890s. She met with our leadership team of which I was a member, shared her plan to involve us in the research, and invited one of us onto the committee. My name was suggested and I accepted the offer with alacrity, for I had a special interest in history and the renewal of our Congregation. I had delved into our archives, read and written on the subject for more than ten years in search of clues for a renewed identity and spirituality for the Oblate Sisters in the aftermath of the Second Vatican Council. We agreed that she would help us tackle the difficult task of writing our story.

This was for me the beginning of a long journey of discovery and challenging collaboration with Dr Bruno-Jofré in which she, as a secular person, supplied the tools of her expertise and I, as an insider, provided my knowledge and experience of the life of the Congregation. Little did I anticipate the shock, denial, and resistance she would encounter from many of us who had very limited understanding of what historians do and how they do it. We needed to learn about the process of thinking about and rereading the primary sources of information, peeling away the hagiographic baggage and the pious religious language in order to allow the plain historical reality to emerge. As a congregation we were not ready to acknowledge that our myth of foundation had been construed in a selective way, as all foundation myths are. We had included the data that seemed affirming to us and left out what seemed too painful or less acceptable to the prevalent social and church norms of the time and to the image we subconsciously wanted to project. We did this without being much aware of it or because we could not question the authority of our leaders and say openly that something had been wrong. Because certain data did not fit with the accepted view of the story, we downplayed or simply ignored them. This way of relating to the past led to a distortion of what certain people experienced and prevented the community from learning and thus benefiting from past mistakes. Rosa Bruno-Jofré wished to engage us in the historian's way of thinking and of interpreting our myth to help us better understand our history and develop a new vision for the future.

Progress was slow during the first four years. Gaining access to relevant documents and gathering information proved difficult. There was a sense of apprehension and distrust in the archival department. Some of the Sisters who agreed to be interviewed had only vague memories of certain significant events, or they painted too rosy a picture of their experience. On the other hand, others freely shared information and memories and enjoyed doing so. At the General Administration of the Congregation (the superior general and the council), attempts to control the outcome of the research and to contest the findings of the author were overtly expressed by some members. There were no financial strings attached to the project. We had offered to contribute seven thousand dollars at the outset to help remunerate a student for the initial research and photocopying of archival material, but Rosa found other ways to cover expenses, and she would not accept any remuneration for herself.

In 1993 Rosa Bruno-Jofré edited *Issues in the History of Education in Manitoba: From the Construction of the Common School to the Politics of Voices*, which included a chapter written by her on the early years of the Missionary Oblate Sisters. This was the first of several publications and presentations by the author on the Sisters. I was happy to contribute a five-page essay on my experience of teaching at a bilingual parochial school, École Sainte-Marie, in St Vital, Winnipeg, Manitoba, in the late 1940s and early 1950s. This write-up was included in the last chapter of the book, which was composed of recollections, reminiscences, and reflections of men and women whose life work had been teaching.[1]

During our General Chapter in 1993 we invited Rosa to make a presentation on the part of the book dealing with the early years of the Missionary Oblate Sisters. There were mixed reactions among the Sisters, as might have been expected, concerning her portrayal and interpretation of Ida Lafricain's "forced transplantation," a term used by Sister Alma Laurendeau, in her essay entitled "First Attempts," to describe Ida Lafricain's transfer from Montreal to Manitoba. There were also objections to portraying the "paternal benevolence" of Archbishop Langevin as patriarchal with regard to his role as founder.[2]

One of Rosa Bruno-Jofré's interests was to rescue the role and voice of women in history. She found that her work with our Congregation gave her an inexhaustible opportunity to do so. At a joint conference of the Historical Society of St Boniface and the Oblate Fathers in 1995, she made a presentation entitled "Lifting the Veil: The Founding of the Missionary Oblate Sisters of the Sacred Heart and Mary Immaculate," in which she dealt with the circumstances surrounding the foundation, the first two years, and the myth of foundation that developed subsequently. The text of the presentation was published in *Historical Studies in Education*.[3] The strong negative reactions on the part of the leadership of the Congregation to Dr Bruno-Jofré's exposition showed how sensitive the material she had uncovered was for many of us who were not ready to understand the painful but liberating influence of acknowledging the truth. This experience was traumatic for the author. For several years she stopped working directly on the history of the Oblate Sisters, although she was involved in other ways with the Congregation, giving us a workshop on feminism, helping me to prepare presentations on "Dualism, Ecology, and Spirituality." During those years I, Sister Lea Boutin, and several other Oblate Sisters maintained close ties with Dr Bruno-Jofré, appreciating her especially as a visionary advisor to help us develop the Aulneau Renewal Centre's counselling project. She also proved to be an invaluable contact with the Faculty of Education of the University of Manitoba regarding the project.

Meanwhile a new awareness of and desire to come to grips with our history was growing among the Sisters. In the fall of 2001 long-term planning for the forthcoming celebration of the centennial of our foundation in 2004 began and in 2002 preparations started in earnest. This and the crucial importance of our next General Chapter in 2005 were for Rosa a turning point, providing a powerful incentive to resume the work and to bring her back fully to the task, which was so dear to her. She used part of her summer and Christmas holidays in 2003 to complete the book. Writing a chapter on the Oblate Sisters proved to be a healing experience for her. In addition, she realized that the Congregation had changed. The Sisters could now deal with the content, and therefore the way was cleared to write and publish the book. Our gratitude and congratulations to Dr Rosa Bruno-Jofré for her hard work and perseverance in bringing to completion this book, which is priceless for us, the Missionary Oblate Sisters.

DORA TÉTREAULT, MO

Introduction and Acknowledgments

In 1904 the archbishop of St Boniface, Monseigneur Adélard Langevin, an Oblate of Mary Immaculate (OMI), founded the Missionary Oblate Sisters of the Sacred Heart and Mary Immaculate, a Manitoban French-English bilingual teaching congregation. Few are aware that the archbishop created the Congregation as a form of "protestation" in the aftermath of the Manitoba school question to the growing anglicization of the common school at the turn of the century. The Sisters' low profile over the years was sadly reversed in the 1990s with the denunciation of the residential schools, where the Sisters had worked as auxiliaries of the Oblate Fathers. Unfortunately, the situation emerging from the denunciation overshadowed their educational role in the building of a French Canadian identity.

Accordingly, as a way of mirroring the Oblate Sisters' own historical process of re-examining the past to support a process of renewal in the present, this book concentrates on the foundational period, from the building of the motherhouse (Maison-Chapelle) in 1902 to approval of new constitutions by the General Chapter of the Oblate Sisters' Congregation in 1929. These constitutions shifted their mission and subordinated their role as educators to the Oblate Fathers. I focus on the inner life of the Congregation as filtered through the particular experiences of the Sisters, to facilitate understanding of their lives both as individuals and as community. This inward approach opens windows to the communities in which they carried on their apostolic work. It helps to understand the workings of a male-dominated church in which the authorities represented God and uniformity and obedience led to perfection. In this context the Sisters' outward and complex relationship with Archbishop Langevin, Abbé Henri Bernard, and with Father Péalapra, OMI, the Congregation's chaplain after Langevin's death, gains lively tones.

The book uncovers the difficulties the Congregation had in developing its own "project of Community." Further, I examine differences in views, traditions, and attitudes among the Québécois, the Manitoban, and the American Sisters despite their ostensibly common French Canadian roots. Not unexpectedly, the early American Sisters nurtured a culture of transgressions to rules that became a window to common sense.

The Oblate Sisters' history is one of hard work, spiritual devotion, and internal struggles over vision and mission, a mission that was spawned in part by their view of the French Canadian issue. The Sisters' struggle to develop their own spirit as a congregation becomes intelligible in the context of an evolving relationship with the Oblate Fathers.

The book closes with a chapter that brings the Oblate Sisters' early history full circle into the present. The final chapter deconstructs the Congregation's historical process of construing official memories, in particular the myth of foundation, and analyzes its discursive components. Then it turns to the renewal process that started in 1973, within the framework of Vatican II and the desire "to live" as a community, which motivated the Sisters to revisit their memories and their interpretation of the past. The tensions between the official memories and the unofficial ones, the latter warm, subjective, and transgressive, provided an avenue to the past but also a way into the future. The chapters are separated by poems written by the Sisters and recorded in their internal and external publications. They reveal the Sisters' aesthetic sense of religious life and their lived spirituality.

The writing of this book was affected by unintended and sometimes painful interruptions but a final manuscript emerged thanks to the loving cooperation of a courageous religious, Sister Dora Tétreault. She stood by me inspite of overwhelming opposition to the research. She helped uncover materials, she responded to my urgent calls for information, she found and discussed documents, she provided internal insights, and she opened doors. Sister Dora was eager to see the results of this history even though she fully understood why it was necessary to suspend work on the project for some years. The Congregation has moved ahead in search of its future in the context of a new understanding of its past, and so the writing of this history became a welcome enterprise. Along the way, I have felt privileged to gain entry to insiders' views of the profound meaning of religious life.

Special thanks to the Congregation's general council, which allowed me to include interviews with the Sisters in the book, to use important unclassified documents, especially those I have accessed in the last two years, and to publish the photographs.

Special thanks to the Sisters, who typed some of the interview transcripts, and to Marlene Schellenberg, who helped with the transcripts. Last but not least, I would like to acknowledge Karin Steiner for reading the manuscript with profound interest and curiosity, and for making suggestions to improve its clarity. I would also like to acknowledge Dr Don Kersey, who kindly took care of the technical details of the preparation of the manuscript and who called my attention to important editorial details.

Most of chapter 1 and segments of chapter 6 of this book were published previously in Rosa Bruno-Jofré, "Lifting the Veil: the Founding of the Missionary Oblate Sisters of the Sacred Heart and Mary Immaculate in Manitoba," *Historical Studies in Education* 9, no. 1 (1997): 1-21. The editors of *Historical Studies in Education* kindly provided permission to reproduce the article in this book. The research for the article was supported by the Institute for the Humanities of the University of Manitoba.

My thanks to Don Akenson, senior editor of McGill-Queen's University Press, who expressed enthusiastic support for the book. As the manuscript moved towards publication, Roger Martin provided thoughtful advice on the publication process. At the production stage, Joan McGilvray's editorial expertise and Claire Gigantes's careful eye facilitated the process of rendering my manuscript into book form.

The author is responsible for the translations in the text, in some cases in consultation with Sister Dora Tétreault, MO.

Abbreviations

AIHM Archives of the Sisters, Servants of the Immaculate Heart of Mary
AMIC Archives of the missionary Sisters of the Immaculate Conception, Montreal, Quebec
AMO Archives of the Missionary Oblate Sisters, St Boniface, Manitoba
ASJCF Archives of Society of Jesus, French Canadian, Montreal, Quebec
CEFCO Centre d'études franco-canadiennes de l'Ouest
CSV Clerics of St Viateur
DD Doctor of Divinity
IHM Immaculate Heart of Mary (Sisters, Servants of the Immaculate Heart of Mary), Monroe, Michigan
MIC Missionary Sisters of the Immaculate Conception
MO Missionary Oblate Sisters of the Sacred Heart and Mary Immaculate (Missionnaires du Sacré-Coeur et de Marie Immaculée)
OMI Oblates of Mary Immaculate (men)
SJ Society of Jesus (Jesuits)
SM Society of Mary (Marianist Brothers and Priests)
SP Sisters of Providence

The Missionary Oblate Sisters

J'IRAI TOUJOURS!

Aller toujours! ces deux mots sur mon âme
Ont imprimé comme une cachet divin,
J'irai toujours grâce à la douce flamme
Qui désormais éclaire mon chemin.

J'irai toujours! ... les peines, la tristesse,
Ne pourront plus m'empêcher de marcher.
J'irai toujours au Dieu plein de tendresse
Qui le premier a daigné me chercher.

J'irai toujours! Oui, Seigneur je le jure,
Pleurant de joie au pied de votre autel.
J'irai toujours, mais je vous en conjure,
Ne m'ôtez pas votre appui paternel.

J'irai toujours, malgré la défaillance,
Les noirs soucis, les brisements du cœur.
J'irai toujours, c'est mon cri d'espérance,
Mon chant d'amour, mon rêve de bonheur.

J'irai toujours, malgré la lassitude,
Malgré l'ennui, les ronces du chemin.
J'irai toujours, avec la certitude
Que mon Jésus me tiendra par la main.

J'irai toujours ... quel que soit le calice
Que le Seigneur présente à mon amour.
J'irai toujours, ne trouvant de délice
Qu'à m'immoler pour lui seul, sans retour.

Chroniques des Missionnaires Oblates du Sacre-Coeur et de Marie Immaculée 2, no. 10 (December 1916). This poem is believed to have been written by Sister Marie-Joseph sometime after the death in 1915 of Monseigneur Adélard Langevin, archbishop of St Boniface, Manitoba, and founder of the Missionary Oblate Sisters.

1

The Early Years, 1902–1905

I often think about what has been said many times about your humble Congregation, comparing it to a tiny child in its cradle. Lacordaire once said, "The greatest temptation that hovers over any new endeavour resides in the newness itself, in that obscure horizon where those things without a past seem to float."[1]

On 19 March 1895 Father Louis-Philippe Adélard Langevin, provincial superior of the Oblate vicariate of Saint-Boniface and parish priest of Saint Mary's in Winnipeg, was consecrated archbishop of Saint-Boniface. He succeeded Archbishop Alexandre Taché who died in 1894. He received a diocese that included Manitoba, the district of Keewatin to the north, and northwestern Ontario to the east down to Lake Superior, as well as the district of Assiniboia to the west, which extended into southern Saskatchewan.[2] Langevin began his pastoral work as archbishop at the peak of the Manitoba School Question.

The school question refers to the school crisis between 1890 and 1896, when provincial legislation abolished the dual confessional state-supported schools in accordance with a settlement known as the Laurier-Greenway Compromise. Following the compromise the Public School Act was modified in 1897, thus setting the legal basis for the building of the common school. The Catholic church was not allowed to have its own school districts under its jurisdiction, but the new legislation allowed for religious exercises under specific conditions.[3] The Manitoba school question was not only a Catholic question but also a French one since the new legislation moved the Franco-Manitoban minority to the margins of power by denying French people in Manitoba constitutional rights and privileges they had earlier had as members of a founding nation.

Furthermore, the new regulations contradicted the conceptual basis of Catholic education sustained by the Church at the time. Catholics did not accept the so-called nonsectarian schools, which as late as the 1920s were described in publications by the archdiocese of Saint-Boniface as "a formidable machine directed against the rights of God, an almost irresistible force of de-Christianization."[4] The Church did not favour the education of children from diverse denominations in the same schools and strongly questioned the separation of morality from religion.[5] However, Langevin had to direct his actions within the parameters of Leo XIII's encyclical *Affari Vos* (1897), which declared the agreement deficient, imperfect, and inadequate but advised Catholics to accept the compromise and to make the best of it.[6]

Langevin heavily emphasized Catholic schooling for the development of the faith. In light of the arrival of Ukrainian, Polish, and German Catholic immigrants, he also worked to retain maternal languages as a countermeasure against Protestant proselytizing. In practical terms, Langevin consistently acted to organize as many private and parochial schools and to hire as many certified teaching Sisters as possible. He wanted Sisters to teach in the public system, particularly in largely Catholic communities in rural areas, where struggles over values with the Department of Education were waged through boards of trustees and in which classrooms for such schools were under the jurisdiction of elected boards of trustees.

Langevin dealt with linguistic demands and ethnic tensions in his diverse Catholic constituency by inviting various religious congregations to come to Manitoba. Among the female congregations that came were the Sisters of the Order of St Benedict (who arrived in Winnipeg in 1905 from Duluth, Minnesota, to teach eastern European children at the Holy Ghost Parish); the Ruthenian Sisters known as Sisters Servants of Mary Immaculate; and the Soeurs de Miséricorde from Montreal. Fearful that teaching Sisters might be recalled from Manitoba, Langevin exercised his full authority by Canadianizing the female congregations that provided formal education. In 1912 Langevin detached several groups of Sisters from their original houses and placed them under his jurisdiction. For example, he succeeded in Canadianizing the Chanoinesses Régulières des Cinq-Plaies-du-Sauveur (also called Soeurs du Sauveur), who had come in 1895 from Lyon, France, and the Sisters of the Order of St Benedict from Minnesota.[7] At the same time, the so-called archbishop of the "absolute solutions" began his struggle to establish a new women's congregation, the Missionary Oblate Sisters, a

French-English bilingual teaching congregation, thus providing yet another vehicle of Catholic education.[8]

Letters about the creation of the Congregation show a tension between, on the one hand, Langevin's religious concern, the specific needs of his Catholic constituency, and his fear of anglicization, and, on the other hand, his culturally dual French/English view of Canada.[9] Although several letters written between 1900 and 1902 make no reference to the French character of the prospective congregation,[10] his correspondence from late 1902 with a St Viateur priest, J. Emile Foucher, pastor of Outremont, Montreal, makes clear that Langevin was committed to the foundation of a congregation with a strong French Canadian character.[11] Langevin thought a French Canadian congregation could deal with the aftermath of the Manitoba School Question through Catholic education and through language. Thus, the first constitutions of the Oblate Sisters recommended the study of French and English and, if possible, a third language such as German, Polish, Hungarian, or an Aboriginal tongue.[12] As early as 1909 and 1910, Langevin's talks to the Oblate Sisters referred to possible undertakings with the Hungarians and the Ruthenians, among others, none of which materialized.[13]

The inspiration to create a new religious congregation can be interpreted as an act of protestation.[14] Jean Séguy used the term "protestation" to refer to acts or discourses of leaders and spiritual institutions whose effects are to reveal interests in opposition to the Church and its political stances, to the global (secular) society, or to the ways the clergy deals with secular problems. The creation of the new congregation was thus Langevin's way of denouncing the ecclesiastical politics dealing with the Manitoba School Question, and of acknowledging his own political isolation. After January 1897, Rome effectively prevented the Quebec hierarchy from exerting its political influence on behalf of Manitoba Catholics.[15] The prospective congregation was one way of dealing with anglicization and with the prevalent Protestant culture.

In the aftermath of the Manitoba School Question, Langevin's resistance was aimed at the common school and thus at the rising twentieth-century state. This is not to say that Langevin had renounced the claim and hope for "complete restitution" of a Catholic separate school system supported by public funding. That he would never relinquish. Rather, his protestation was deeply rooted in a sense of his role and his motto, "Depositum custodi – Garde le depot,"[16] and what he perceived as lack of understanding among his ecclesiastical critics of his political circumstances. Langevin would use his power and the power of the

Archbishop Adélard Langevin, of St Boniface, founder of the Missionary Oblate Sisters. Picture taken in a studio.

clergy in regulating social life in Catholic settings, and in mediating God's will to create a women's congregation.[17]

During the summer of 1902, Langevin decided to build a house that was designed as a small convent, which he called Maison-Chapelle. It was located a few metres from the bilingual Normal School that was also being built, at the corner of Masson and Aulneau Streets in St Boniface, and was to be the cradle of the new congregation. As early as December 1902, the house became the residence of two Franco-Manitobans and two pious Québécoises of poor socioeconomic background. The house provided room and board for prospective teachers who were attending Normal School and meals for several St Boniface College students. The directress of the house left amid internal conflict in January 1903. Ultimately only one woman of the original group remained. On the day the directress departed, a fourteen-year-old Polish girl, Elizabeth Storozuk, the future Sister Marie-Gertrude, entered the Maison-Chapelle.[18] Many years later she described to the Oblate Sisters her encounter with Langevin. Elizabeth, who came from Ethelbert,

Elizabeth Storozuk (Sister Marie-Gertrude) from Ethelbert, Manitoba, born in Poland. Picture taken by a professional photographer in January 1903 before she entered the Maison-Chapelle at the age of fourteen.

Manitoba, had been sick at Saint-Boniface Hospital and decided to work there to pay – as she said – "for my operation and be cured." She continued:

Archbishop Langevin had come to the hospital on January 2, 1903; he saw the Sisters [Grey Nuns], there were not so many, and nurses. Then he came to a corner to speak to the people at work; we were thirty altogether. He pointed to me and said, "Who is that little girl? I haven't seen her yet." Sister said, "She is a little Polish girl and she wants to be a nun." Langevin responded, "Oh well, then she is mine. I am taking her."[19]

The date of the first entry in the "Journal de la Maison-Chapelle," 29 July 1903, coincides with the arrival of two new candidates, Alma Laurendeau and Zénaïde Marcoux.[20] It reads: "A touching simple ceremony took place at the Maison-Chapelle, opened in St Boniface by Archbishop Langevin with the goal of preparing teachers."[21] Langevin was the source of the institution's authority, providing guidelines for

The Maison-Chapelle 1903–1910
First residents and boarders at the Maison-Chapelle built at 621 Aulneau Street, in the fall of 1902 as the cradle of the Congregation of the Missionary Oblate Sisters. Picture taken in May 1903. Miss Georgiana Bédard, Miss Laure Roy, and Miss Rose Ouimet (the first director of the house), all dressed in black, are standing with two lady boarders. Four young students are sitting on the steps, one of whom is Elizabeth Storozuk, who later became Sister Marie-Gertrude.

the rule of life, distributing tasks and roles, and indicating that the Congregation would be called Oblates of the Sacred Heart and Mary Immaculate when it came officially into being by canonical erection. The religious habit was to be distinctive in having the scapular of the Sacred Heart,[22] but members of the group had great difficulty in reaching agreement on the model of the religious habit and on several other matters.[23] There was no sense of community at that point and no leadership within the group. Differences among the members generated tensions to the point that the taking of the holy habit scheduled for 1 November 1903 had to be postponed.[24] By January 1904 there were only three women left in the house, Alma Laurendeau, Marie Laure Roy, and Elizabeth Storozuk. Alma was profoundly attached to the French Catholic culture of Manitoba. She had only four days to make her decision to enter the Maison-Chapelle, but the request had come

Sister Marie-Joseph (Alma Laurendeau) from St Boniface. Picture taken in a studio on the occasion of her perpetual vows in 1911.

from the archbishop and in Alma's understanding of religious life, he mediated God's will.[25]

Born in Quebec, Alma Laurendeau came to Manitoba with her family when she was very young. Immediately after graduating from high school, she taught in Franco-Manitoban rural communities from 1896 to 1903. Alma attended Normal School during the summer and she succeeded in obtaining a teaching certificate. She was representative of the modus vivendi created by Franco-Manitobans in rural areas after 1890. She began as a bilingual teacher in Barnsley, a poor community ten miles from Carman, taking a position offered by Father Arthur Béliveau (the future archbishop), himself sent to Alma's house by Langevin. Alma had been recommended by the pastor of the cathedral. Langevin asked her to develop the faith among her students and, through them, their parents. He thus showed his reliance on education for the preservation of Catholicism, for Barnsley had no regular religious services. The next year she went to Fannystelle, where she placed a special emphasis on religion and faith as a basis for citizenship. In

September 1898 she went to St Malo. In 1901 she taught in Lorette and then in Île-des-Chênes for two years.[26] Alma, the future Sister Marie-Joseph and later on general superior, embodied the virtues then valued by the Church in a woman: she was obedient, unassuming, and eager to accept God's will as dictated by the Church.

Langevin had been corresponding with Father J. Emile Foucher, CSV, pastor at Outremont, Montreal. His letters to Foucher show a relentless urgency to find a mature, experienced religious woman to head the prospective congregation. This request appears along with a passionate commitment to the scapular of the Sacred Heart, which was very dear to Foucher.[27] In January 1904 Langevin called Alma to the archbishop's house and, having ascertained that she wanted to stay in spite of the recent departures, placed her in charge, saying: "I lay upon you all the weight of this project that must go on ... until I release you (of the responsibility). I am convinced God wants this work."[28] Langevin needed Alma Laurendeau for his prospective congregation. He used the power of his spiritual position to persuade her of her duty to help him attain his objective, that is, to found a bilingual teaching congregation. Alma agreed to the request and carried the responsibility as directress of the group for two years.

The "Journal de la Maison-Chapelle" begins again in March 1904. New members had joined the group and the date for the novitiate to begin had been set for 24 March.[29] Ida Lafricain joined the prospective congregation on 19 March. She was the experienced, mature woman for whom Langevin had been looking.

THE QUEBEC SOLUTION: BREAKING IDA LAFRICAIN'S CALL

The way Langevin proceeded to found the Congregation shows his isolation. He looked for Québécoises to accomplish his objective. In fact, Langevin and Father J. Emile Foucher targeted Ida Lafricain and decided to bring her to Manitoba to work with the new community.

Ida Lafricain was born in Montreal in 1871. In 1894 she entered Bethany House, also in Montreal, a house of good works financed by Madame Poitou and directed by Father Almire Pichon, SJ.[30] Ida taught catechism to people with intellectual disabilities, to street children, and to other youth from poor socioeconomic backgrounds. She also helped impoverished families for eight years. Among the women who lived in the house was Délia Tétreault, who later founded the Missionary Sisters of the Immaculate Conception. Ida and Délia became close friends and one day Ida shared her apprehension regarding the future of Bethany House. Years later she reminisced: "After eight years, there had not been any notable change. Nothing indicated that we would become religious some day. I said then to Miss Tétreault, 'But I always had the idea of working in the Missions!' She [Délia] threw herself in my arms and she told me in tears: 'God has manifested his will through your mouth.'" Ida said that Délia advised her to take pharmacy at the Hôtel-Dieu hospital to prepare for missionary work overseas, while Délia herself went to the Sisters of the Congregation of Notre-Dame to learn more about religious life.[31] The testimony shows a convergence of interests, a desire to be full religious women, and a common call for missionary work.

In January 1901 Délia Tétreault received approval from Monseigneur Bruchési, archbishop of Montreal, to establish the École Apostolique to train young women for missionary work in Africa and China. Délia opened the school with the help of Joséphine Montmarquet and Ida Lafricain. In February 1902 she rented a small house at 900 Maplewood Avenue, Côte-des-Neiges, in Montreal, where on 3 June the École Apostolique opened its doors.[32] These three women formed the nucleus of the future Missionary Sisters of the Immaculate Conception. Langevin had heard of Ida Lafricain through an acquaintance of hers who visited St Boniface. Subsequently, he visited Délia Tétreault at the school. Ida accidentally overheard Langevin saying to Délia: "You will give her to me. Won't you?" After the visit, Ida recalled, Délia went to her bedroom and stayed there for a long time. Ida tells of Délia's reaction:

> Later I brought her lunch, she was all in tears. Around four, I took her a glass of milk; I found her very sad, the same at dinnertime. And since she did not say a word, I asked her [what was the matter]. Finally, after the evening prayer, she told me that I needed to know what was going on. I went to my room and I cried. I told her, "Please, tell me what is the problem? I heard something without meaning to." "I did not want to tell you," Tétreault said, "because I was afraid that you would leave, and I lack the generosity to let you go." (Such a delicate soul!) "But you know very well that I do not want to go," I replied. This response made her so happy that she threw herself into my arms and cried with happiness. On November 21, 1902, she bought me a 10 karat gold ring, gave it to me and said: "Here's the pledge, we will never be separated, will we?"[33]

This dramatic testimony clearly shows that these two women did not see Ida's "transplantation" as God's will.

In May 1903 the personnel of the school made up of nine members moved to Chemin de la Côte Ste-Catherine, parish of Outremont. There, Ida met Langevin's supporter, Father Foucher, the parish priest, who became her spiritual director.[34] Langevin was relying on Foucher to find the right person for his prospective congregation and Foucher was certainly not displeased by Langevin's offer to have the new Sisters wear the scapular of the Sacred Heart as revealed to Estelle Faguette in Pellevoisin.[35] Langevin's letters to Foucher take on an insistent tone from November 1903.[36] As soon as Langevin realized Foucher was spiritual director of the women at the school, or at any rate of the local parishioners, he asked Foucher to intervene to move Lafricain to St Boniface. Furthermore, Langevin made clear that he needed not one but two persons. He saw the school as a source from which he could draw women for his own missionary project. Foucher promised complete participation in Langevin's plans to move Lafricain. His letter contains a statement that is definitely out of line with Lafricain's testimony and with the unfolding events.

> I tell you that your proposal has struck me in an unusual manner. It is because the woman whose services you are requesting has been suffering in a strange way and for a long time, in the environment where she is; her character is not adapting to the condition in which she is living; and in spite of profound esteem and religious admiration for Miss Tétreault's holiness of life, she succeeds poorly in controlling herself and in hiding her natural oppositions. Their temperaments are too different from each other. So much so that I have already asked myself whether she was called to the apostolate in which she is presently involved.[37]

It is difficult to determine the reasons for this assessment. Apparently Ida Lafricain was afraid of being removed from the school and saddened by the prospect of having to leave, as Langevin had already requested her services. She was not inclined to be as submissive as the clergy might normally expect.[38] Foucher, on his part, seemed reluctant to frame his favour to Langevin, the transfer of Ida, within a discourse of grace and God's will. The Oblate Sisters later used Foucher's interpretation to explain the triumph of Grace in the process of founding instead of exploring Ida's testimony and her desires. The Sisters were taking their cue from the men.

Ida's account of events described how Foucher began his work of moving her to Manitoba by exerting all his power in his capacity of spiritual director. She was in charge of the class of young children taking catechism lessons at the school. On 31 December 1903 she took the children to the parish church for confession. After they were done, she went into the confessional to receive Father Foucher's blessing and to thank him for his cooperation with the school. As she was leaving he asked her if she had received a letter from Monseigneur Langevin. She replied: "Monseigneur has not written to me." Foucher then asked her if she wanted to go to St Boniface, adding, "I do not want a response now but think about it." Ida recalled: "I did not want to hear and I asked myself: 'What will I do? What will I do?' I left the confessional so upset that the children asked me what was the matter."[39]

A few days later Father Foucher asked Tétreault to tell Lafricain that he wanted them to make a novena. Lafricain responded, "If he does not want to say why he wants the novena, I won't make it. I am the one who presides over the prayers," and she forgot about it. She humorously said later that if she came to St Boniface, it was not because of the novena.[40]

Langevin's letters to Foucher made clear his need to know as soon as possible whether Lafricain had decided to come and asked for the day of her departure.[41] At the end of February, Father Foucher reminded her that he had not yet received an answer to his question and asked if she had written to Monseigneur Langevin informing him of her decision. Ida realized she was cornered. She recalled: "I came to the house, I was pensive, you understand, I felt sick. I did not eat. I did not sleep at all. I knew that they wanted to send me to a distant country among the 'sauvages' and that I would be alone. Many dark ideas came to my mind." Finally, she surrendered: "I decided to write to Monseigneur Langevin. I told him that I would leave on March 12. However, I had to postpone the trip. I arrived at St Boniface on March 19, the feast of St Joseph."[42] Monseigneur Bruchési and Délia Tétreault had given her permission to move to St Boniface. Foucher had done the work entrusted to him by Langevin. For his part, Langevin committed the Sisters to Mary, Our Lady of Pellevoisin.

Ida Lafricain was thirty-three years old at the time. Adapting to her new reality was not easy. Langevin and Foucher had decided that she was the right person for the foundation in Manitoba, without regard to her personal feelings, or to her own sense of a spiritual calling. A simple event shows the extent of male domination. She had to change her name as was customary in most congregations, so on 22 March, after the examination of candidates Ida addressed herself to Langevin:

"Your Grace, the other postulants have their names, what is going to be mine? I had thought about the name of Saint Joseph but I see that it is already taken." He responded, "You will be called Sister St Viateur." "But for what reason?" asked the postulant. "I thought," replied the Archbishop, "that it was understood and that you knew something about it: it is because of Father Foucher, cleric of St Viateur, who has directed you here. I think that is going to please him."[43]

So she became Sister St Viateur, compelled to take a name that honoured the cleric who along with Langevin had contrived to move her to Manitoba, who had helped to end her work with Tétreault's apostolate, and who had caused her to give up her chosen spiritual path. The women at the school had thanksgiving as the main characteristic of their spirituality, but as an Oblate Sister she had to embrace reparation as a central element in her spiritual life: making amends to God, on behalf of oneself and fellow humans, for sin or wrongdoing in order to restore equity. As spiritual director, Foucher had exercised great power over her understanding and discerning of God's will. One can only imagine her doubt and the fear that she would no longer follow divine guidance if she kept resisting, torn as she was between her strong inner inclination and the forceful external direction she was receiving.

TAKING THE HABIT: IDA IN THE NEW CONGREGATION

The ceremony of habit investiture took place on 24 March 1904.[44] Ida described it as both comical and sad.[45] Some postulants had to leave, either to light the candles or join the choir, and then come back for the ritual of investiture. The whole ceremony was in French. This was the beginning of the new Congregation. The main elements of the Catholic discourse of the time were there: submission, humility, mortification, and sinfulness. The document for the canonical erection of the novitiate gave as reasons for the creation of the new congregation requests coming from various parts of the diocese for religious teachers to direct schools among whites and Aboriginals. It also mentioned that the congregations of teaching women in Canada had refused, for lack of members, to start new foundations in the West. At the end of the cer-

Statue of Our Lady of Pellevoisin, decorated with a garland of roses made of tin by Sister Marie-Immaculée in 1941. The pink roses symbolize the joyful mysteries of the rosary, the red, the sorrowful mysteries, while the white symbolize the glorious mysteries of Christ's life and his mother's. The rays of sequins represent the streams of grace (favours) showered upon the earth through the intercession of Mary. The base of the statue is surrounded with clouds made in papier-maché and plaster. The background was also oil-painted by Sister Marie-Immaculée. The statue itself is carved in wood and was imported by Archbishop Langevin, circa 1912.

emony the archbishop formally appointed Sister Marie-Joseph, Alma Laurendeau, as directress and named Sister St Viateur, Ida Lafricain, as assistant. Langevin also distributed functions among the other four novices.[46] The group began a year of formation in preparation for taking vows of chastity, obedience, and poverty and promising observance of the constitutions (which were taken by Langevin to Rome in 1906).

The spirituality of the new Congregation was in the making. The Sisters shared with the Oblate Fathers the devotion to the Sacred Heart of Jesus, with reparation as the main element. Langevin, however, brought into the devotion the scapular as revealed to Estelle Faguette in Pellevoisin in 1876, thereby linking the motherhood of Mary with the spirituality of the Heart. They shared with the Oblate Fathers the devotion to Mary Immaculate. The dogma of the Immaculate Conception (proclaimed by Pius IX in 1858) meant that Mary was conceived and born without original sin and therefore did not share with other human beings, particularly women, the sinfulness inherited from Adam and Eve. The Sisters also shared with the Oblate Fathers the commitment to evangelize the poor. Bishop Eugene de Mazenod, founder of the Oblate Fathers, used the expression "âmes abandonnées," which referred both

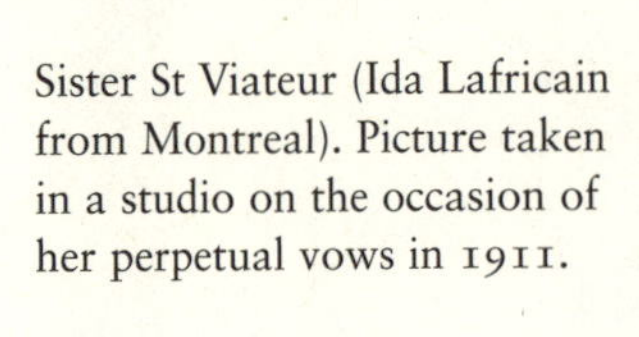

Sister St Viateur (Ida Lafricain from Montreal). Picture taken in a studio on the occasion of her perpetual vows in 1911.

to the evangelization of the unfaithful, and to the provision of spiritual help to "le petit peuple," that is, to the working classes.[47] This element of the charism,[48] an effect of the industrial revolution in Europe, was strongly, although not exclusively, present in the Manitoban missionary work. It nourished the Sisters' mission among the Aboriginal peoples as auxiliaries to the Oblate Fathers.[49] In a stricter nominal sense, the Oblate Sisters had a commitment to the poor, as stipulated in their first constitutions (1906) and as shown in their approach to parish and even private schooling.

Four days after the ceremony, Ida wrote to Foucher about her spiritual and emotional torment during the event:

People say that the ceremony was beautiful. All the guests, and they were numerous, were happy. The Archbishop was jubilant. As far as I was concerned, my heart was too sad to be able to rejoice in this celebration, but these past few days I feel somewhat better. I try to recover my spirit and to put all my worries into the Heart of Our Lord, which is not always easy. I try to reason with myself by saying that all is well since everything is led by divine Providence. However, my poor human nature rebels against suffering and is not even willing to hear about it.[50]

Langevin left for Rome and the Holy Land on 12 April 1904 for six months. It was a terrible time for Ida. She promised herself not to leave until he came back. Her letters to Foucher clearly indicated her spiritual struggle and her unhappiness. She read the signs, firmly convinced that the École Apostolique and Tétreault's project were "willed by God" and that they would succeed. Langevin wrote to say it was Providence that had led her West ("that he saw this written in letters of fire").[51] Her profound rebellion is expressed in comments about the habit, whose main features had been chosen by Langevin. She wrote to Foucher in May 1904: "I would like you to see us: we look like real towers." She found the habit "very ugly."[52] As in other congregations, it sought to desexualize its wearers in the context of an angelic asceticism conceived by men. She expressed her dislike for everything, including the priests and the devotional exercises that, she said, took most of their time. Langevin had regulated the exercises: four hours every day in the chapel. She mentioned the recitation of the office of the Blessed Virgin, the rosary, the way of the cross during those hours. "On Thursday," she continued in the same letter, "we have a holy hour from eleven o'clock till midnight. In addition, on the vigil of the first Friday of the month, the adoration began at eight o'clock in the evening until the next morning."[53] She saw very early the negative impact of the excessive amount of spiritual exercises on the life of a small apostolic congregation.

Langevin's political situation within the clergy worsened her crisis. By early August 1904 she had discovered two things: one, that the thought of Délia Tétreault's apostolate was with her day and night and that it appealed to her more than that of Archbishop Langevin; and two, that she had doubts as to the success of the new foundation in Manitoba. Furthermore, her doubts, she wrote to Foucher, were shared by the vicar general, Monseigneur Azarie Dugas, and by all the priests of the archbishop's house, except the chaplain of the Maison-Chapelle. Langevin had appointed the chaplain, Father Joseph Antoine Trudel, a young priest from Quebec, as her spiritual director but she was unable to open up to him. She found him very young "in every way" and "extremely exaggerated." She wrote, "Since the Archbishop left, he has repeated, at least twenty times, that the whole Apostolic School was to be transferred from Outremont to St Boniface, that it did not function any more and that Archbishop Langevin had convinced Miss Tétreault to leave the province of Quebec."[54] The priest, fearful that Sister St Viateur might decide to leave, repeated to her again and again the story of the amalgamation. When Sister St Viateur laughed about it, thinking he was teasing her, the priest severely reproached her for her lack of faith in his words. She then pretended she believed him to calm him down. From that day on, she became very cautious as to what she told him.[55] She remained attached to Foucher through her first year, but her isolation was already setting in. By August, Sister St Viateur could not understand Tétreault's changed disposition toward her. She said: "Sometimes I am tempted to believe that she does not have the freedom to write to me. If she could see how disappointed I am when the mail is brought in the evening and that there is nothing for me! Nonetheless, I try to accept this trial the best I can, but I often cry."[56] Her ties with Tétreault had been severed. The silence was only sporadically broken from 1905 forward.[57]

Sister St Viateur wrote a letter to abbé Gustave Bourassa, ecclesiastical authority of the École Apostolique, asking his permission to return to the school. His response contained stern words, to judge by her transcription of the letter: "If you do not succeed in overcoming these obstacles and these difficulties, I shall conclude that you are not called to religious life, and that you will have to return to your family. Make all the best efforts to identify with your house, and do not say 'chez nous' any more when speaking of L'École Apostolique, this is not befitting on any account."[58]

Despite Bourassa, Sister St Viateur had decided to leave and asked Délia Tétreault to help her to find a job as a nurse at the Hôtel-Dieu in Montreal.[59] There is no way of knowing Délia's response, or even if there was one.

In a letter to Foucher in February 1905 Langevin acknowledged the crisis during his absence and appreciated Sister St Viateur's perseverance because "Miss Tétreault's memory was haunting her day and night and that made her sad, sometimes to the point of death."[60] Langevin was grateful to Foucher because his letters helped Sister St Viateur "enormously" and "strengthened her determination to stay here till death, through obedience if not through personal taste." He added, "Peace and happiness reign in the house." He then raised the central theme of his letter. He wanted Délia Tétreault to send members of her École Apostolique to Manitoba. That would be, in Langevin's words, "a confirmation of Miss Tétreault's apostolate extending and blossoming in our regions where there is so much good to be done." Langevin insisted that he was addressing this thought both to Foucher, given his influence on Tétreault, and to Tétreault herself through

Foucher's services. Langevin added: "Sister St Viateur is thrilled with joy at the thought of this flow from Montreal" and he quoted her as saying: "This would fully reconcile me with a departure that I still have a hard time understanding."[61] Langevin also said in the letter that Sister Marie-Joseph (Alma Laurendeau) had twice requested him to nominate Sister St Viateur as the directress of the community. He quoted Sister Marie-Joseph (directress at the time): "It will be the means to attach her more firmly to our project and to make easier the relationship between the two houses."[62] There is a clear reference here to the École Apostolique. Sister Marie-Joseph understood Langevin's wish to appease Sister St Viateur without creating dissension. This practice of invisible power helped to reinforce self-sacrifice and to suppress the will, although the decision later became a source of contention.

On 19 February, Sister St Viateur asked Foucher for advice.[63] She recalled: "I wrote to Foucher and expected to receive permission to leave. How great was my disappointment when I read that he was sure of my good dispositions and that he wanted me to persevere."[64] She told Langevin what she thought about the project and expressed doubts about the profession of vows that was to take place in March 1905, to which the archbishop responded by postponing it. She stated that in suggesting that women come from Tétreault's house, she was trying to see it through Langevin's own eyes. She had shared her concerns with the vicar general, who told her that the new Congregation was not needed. She wrote, "He went as far as to say that if we commit ourselves through religious vows, we are exposing ourselves to be a source of problems for the Archbishop later on."[65] When she received Foucher's response on 19 March 1905, a letter she later destroyed, she made up her mind to let go of her sadness. She said, "I began to feel more at home."[66] Foucher had also decided that she should address her concerns to her new spiritual director and advised her to write less often.[67] She accepted that she was caught in a system whose limits she had tested in vain.

In April Langevin expressed his annoyance to Foucher, angered by Sister St Viateur's drawn-out resistance, but satisfied with Foucher's use of coercive power, a satisfaction that he masked in religious language.

> Sister St Viateur must have resigned herself to stay here, because until now she has only pitched her tent. She has shown a lot of faith and generosity after some shuffling and unyielding resistance that made me suspect, in spite of her intelligence a lack of vision and in spite of her generosity, a lack of courage ... She

has remained silent after your letter because it was the bitter chalice that the angel of the Lord was presenting to her.[68]

However, by April 1905 Sister St Viateur was the new directress. According to Langevin, she applied herself to the task more than ever. He could now count on her. Langevin and Father Camper, OMI, became Sister St Viateur's immediate directors.[69] She developed a profound sense of authority nourished by Langevin's trust. He later described her as being "of perfect obedience,"[70] although it is difficult to verify that "perfect obedience" as Sister St Viateur destroyed her letters to Langevin when they were returned to her after his death.[71]

MON CRUCIFIX

Oh! Viens, viens sur mon coeur, n'es-tu pas mon partage?
N'es-tu pas mon trésor jusqu'au dernier soupir? ...
N'es-tu pas de l'Époux, dont tu m'offres l'image,
Le plus doux souvenir?

Tu me tiens lieu de tout: de trésor, de patrie,
Tout ce que j'ai laissé, tu le deviens pour moi:
Mon amour, mon seul bien, ma liberté, ma vie,
Ma famille, c'est Toi!

Tu me suivras partout. A mon heure dernière
C'est toi qui répondras à mon regard mourant ...
Toi qui comprendras seul la muette prière
De mon cœur expirant ...

Oh! Viens, viens sur mon cœur, gage qui me fais vivre, Parle-moi de mon
Dieu ... redis-moi son amour ...
Donne-moi de l'aimer, de souffrir, de le suivre
Jusqu'à mon dernier jour!

Chroniques des Missionnaires Oblates du Sacre-Coeur et Marie Immaculeé 5, no. 5, (March 1925).
This poem, like the one cited at the beginning of the chapter, is believed to have been written by
Sister Marie-Joseph sometime after the Founder's death.

II

Institutionalizing the Early Community, 1906–1915

After the first two rocky years following Ida Lafricain's transfer from Montreal and her painful adjustment to a new environment, Archbishop Langevin was able to anchor his project more firmly. He now had two related tasks for his Congregation: to write constitutions to provide a basic organization and institutional structure, and to inculcate the principles and rules of consecrated life to its members.

Langevin began instructing the Sisters on the constitutions in 1905, although he completed the first draft only in 1906. These early constitutions had of course a lot in common with other constitutions of the time. They regulated the Sisters' life according to St Augustine's Rule, which embodied a particular approach to the Christian experience, the Congregation's vision and mission, and, in particular, its service and function within the Church.[1] The spirit of the Oblate Sisters' Congregation is described in the first constitutions. The Sisters should offer and sacrifice themselves to the Sacred Heart, through Mary Immaculate for love of God and humanity, God's love being symbolized by the Sacred Heart of Jesus.[2] They should strive to live an inner life of faith with an emphasis on prayer and contemplation and practise renunciation and reparation in their daily lives. Another important component of the spirit of the Congregation is simplicity, which is understood as transparency and humility and is linked to the Sisters' commitment to the poor.[3]

Bookbinding shop at the Maison-Chapelle, inaugurated in 1909. Picture taken in 1910. The novice, with the white veil, is operating the paper cutter while the postulant, with the short black veil, is sewing the folios together.

In the spring of 1905, when Langevin expressed his intention that Sister Marie-Joseph and Sister St Viateur should begin preparing to take their vows, they objected that it was much too early and that they were not ready since they had not had a director of novices to help them in their process of formation to religious life. Langevin then appointed Sister Agnes-Émilie, a Daughter of the Cross, to fill that role for a few months in the new congregation where she stayed from 26 June until 12 October 1905. Sister Agnes had recently arrived from France where she had been mistress of novices for eleven years. Langevin instructed her that he wanted two categories of Sisters, the choir Sisters

Typesetting shop, begun in 1903 at the Maison-Chapelle. Two novices and a professed Sister at work. Picture taken in 1910. Alma Laurendeau and her sister Alice, both postulants, first took their apprenticeship with Mr Joseph Filmens, on Selkirk Avenue, Winnipeg. The typesetting for *Les Cloches de Saint-Boniface*, the monthly diocesan review, was done by the Sisters from 1903 to 1915. Alma also edited *Les Chroniques des Missionaires Oblates*, a periodical review on the Congregation, from 1911 to 1927.

and the auxiliary Sisters. They would wear the same habit, although the auxiliaries (*Soeurs converses*) would wear theirs slightly shorter and share the same recreation room and dormitory. The justification was that the majority of Sisters (the choir Sisters) needed time to study and prepare themselves as teachers while the others were to be assigned to manual work only. Some oral testimonies disclose painful memories of Sisters feeling inferior or being perceived as different within the community.

On 29 September 1905, at their first profession, Sister St Viateur and Sister Marie-Joseph took the vows of poverty, chastity, and obedience. Poverty was related to simplicity, a fundamental virtue, which Langevin strongly cultivated in the Sisters. In his talks to them, he made it clear that poverty did not mean misery, but rather the way of life of ordinary working people. The Sisters would have to work to earn a living, not beg for it, since they were not a mendicant order.[4] "In a half joking and half serious way, he had said one day that he would come after his

Typesetting, 1910, at the Maison Chapelle. Seated is a postulant, wearing the blue-and-white striped apron that all Sisters wore for manual work. The ones standing are professed Sisters.

death to see if we remained poor in spirit and in every detail, warning us that we begin with some little extras for the Superior, then another and so on."[5]

After the profession of vows took place, Langevin decided that the council would be composed of Sister St Viateur (directress and treasurer), Sister Marie-Joseph (assistant and novice mistress) and Sr Marie de la Présentation (Parmélie Comeau, still a novice) as councillor.[6] The directress appointed in charge of the nascent congregation came under Langevin's guidance. He stated clearly that "until further notice, while waiting for your numbers to increase, I will be your superior."[7] He was the person to whom the Sisters should refer concerning matters of holy obedience and the practice of holy poverty. The Founder, who "took part even in the Council meetings, controlled everything," as Sister Louis de France said, "to make sure we followed the right direction."[8]

In 1906 Langevin went to Rome to obtain papal approval for the new congregation. He was successful. The same day that he met with Pope Pius x, he wrote an exuberant letter to his dear daughters, the entire community of six professed sisters and four novices and postulants.

> Now, the good Pius x gave his complete and wholehearted approval for our new Congregation. I told him that I was afraid because in his last "Motu Proprio," he had forbidden the bishops to set up any new communities without first asking the Holy See. The good Pope smiled and said, "It does not hold for you in the missions, it is for the dioceses here in Europe. You may continue your work, I give you my blessing." If you only had the spirit of faith and goodness of the Pope![9]

In the *Memoire* of September 1906 addressed to the prefect of the Sacred Congregation of the Propaganda, Langevin argued that there were not enough teachers religious amid a war, led by Masons in conjunction with Protestants, against Catholic schools in Manitoba, as well as in Saskatchewan and Alberta. The reason for the creation of the Congregation was the insufficient number of Catholic teachers in all three provinces. Langevin wanted to ensure the future of Catholic education in the West.

The latitude and the modus vivendi that had been reached could be wiped out, in his view, by a wave of fanaticism, and if the law was applied with rigour, all Catholic schools in Manitoba could find themselves in the same situation as those in Brandon and Winnipeg. In those cities, he wrote, parents paid taxes and yet had to pay additional fees for sending their children to a Catholic school. Langevin asserted that it would have been difficult to maintain "les écoles libres" without convents, particularly in the rural areas. The convents would be the havens of Christian (Catholic) education, "the arks that will float on the waters of the deluge." It was very important, he said, to multiply the convents. In eleven years, twenty-one convents were founded among the white population and eight among the "Sauvages."[10]

According to the constitutions, the new congregation would be devoted to education of the young, particularly among the poor, and to assisting the missionaries and the priests in all the works that were compatible with the Sisters' mandate. Therefore, studies were extremely important, especially those subjects required in the teaching programs and necessary to obtain certification. In particular, the Sisters were to study French and English grammar, mathematics, history, French and English literature. The constitutions also recommended that the Sisters be humble with regard to their studies because, according to Saint Paul, "knowledge can inflate the mind"; studies needed to be sanctified by thoughts of faith. Growth in piety and in knowledge should go hand in hand. "The Sisters shall have at heart to study in order to work more effectively at their beautiful task which consists in forming and reproducing the image of Jesus Christ in the souls of the children." In that way the Sisters would "prepare for the Holy Church generations filled with faith and love, able to fight for the triumph of truth and justice."[11] Langevin expected the new Congregation to help make known the French and Catholic heritage and preserve the French Canadian identity articulated as a collective national identity based on the notion of two founding peoples and nonterritorial cultural duality, although Quebec was a powerful point of reference.[12]

For twenty-five years, Langevin had corresponded with Sister St Charles, a Grey Nun and school principal he had known while he was chaplain in a girls' high school in Ottawa. He would discuss educational and political issues with her. In their exchanges, he freely expressed his French Canadian nationalism and his conviction of the close relation between language and faith, and language and culture. He wrote:

> Keeping the French race as is offers tremendous support for the Catholic Church, and the schools alone are able to maintain and develop its [the French race] distinctive qualities: generosity of heart, vivaciousness, clarity, and method, as well as a rare distinction which leads to abhor injustice, and disposes one to become interested in all the holy causes. If our people lose their language all those treasures are in peril since they will then acquire the English temperament.[13]

In another letter he also stated: "The Council of Quebec has well proven that the future of the Church in Canada depends upon French speaking Catholics."[14] Langevin was convinced that the best ideas for the formation of Christian children came from the teachings of the masters of the seventeenth century who were imbued with the spirit of the gospel. Langevin had strong views about the female teacher, in particular women religious who were teachers. In 1896 he wrote that "a teacher who prays badly is a bad pest and a calamity worse than the plague [*la peste*], even though she may be as learned as St Thomas and as bold as Madame de Staël."[15] In the same letter, he reveals his expected distrust of modern ideas: "The idea is not to make our girls into a kind of boys in skirts, sporting jaunty airs, having strange ideas and being full of independence and pride. It is not in [North] America, and even less in the United States than in any other part of America and the world, that we will find perfection. We must find it in the classics written on the subject, in the daily study of characters and above all in meditation and prayer in front of the altar."[16]

Langevin wrote long letters to his "dear daughters" containing decisions concerning financial matters, new houses, recruitment of new members, recommendations with a "you must do" introduction, fatherly advice, comments about little occurrences in the convent and small daily details of life, comments about his health, his friends, and his brother priest Hermas, who from Hochelaga directed recruits to Maison-Chapelle. He tried to regulate the Sisters' lives and recreate their own selves as obedient women religious, members of a family of which he was the head. Uniformity was an important criterion for unity. He had written earlier, "My dear daughters, I would like to end by saying that I strongly recommend that there be a great spirit of charity among you. This will make you into a family where the members are one in heart and soul. It is important that in these new beginnings you be scrupulously faithful in the observance of the Constitutions, so as to establish order and uniformity among you."[17] In another letter addressed in 1909 to Sister St Viateur, he said, "When I think of you I think of Sister Marie-Joseph, for you are like two fingers on the same hand, and I also think of each of your daughters, my own dear daughters, especially those who are so far away and isolated in Cross Lake (residential school). They too must be united like four fingers on one hand! Why don't they write to me? Am I no longer their father?"[18] His paternalistic power was certainly noticeable and easy to expose but it often acquired an invisible quality couched in allegorical mystical language. Langevin aimed at the formation of a consciousness alerted to possible transgressions, which might be detrimental to the cohesion and unity of the group.

As was customary in religious life, the Founder stressed obedience and training of the Sisters to watch for the "deviant," the Sister who did not follow the rules. In 1910 he wrote a letter that reveals internal tensions in the Congregation: "If you love her (the superior, Sister St Viateur, by now called Mother St Viateur), you should go to her with a great openness of heart, tell her everything about yourself, and sometimes when necessary inform her of things that happen in the community." The metaphor he uses contains a degree of symbolic violence. He went on to say, "Don't you think that anyone of you who would be aware of the presence of a serpent or of poison in the house, or who would see a dangerous crack in the wall, or something being wasted, or one of the Sisters in danger of falling sick, or of getting worse, should go to the Mother Superior and tell her what you see? Are you afraid to be accused of gossiping?"[19]

Langevin's letters to the Sisters contain the principles of pastoral power, which were aimed at setting the conditions that would require the Sisters to make the choices that were expected. Through personal admission of fault and other ways to mould the soul, the superiors would have knowledge of the inner workings of the Sisters' minds and indirectly of their consciences, which they would therefore have the ability to direct.[20] Langevin, after Christ's example, was ready to sacrifice himself for the flock and in this sense pastoral power does not have a possessive connotation like royal power. He expected the same attitude from the Sisters. He said to them, "You have faith, my dear Daughters, you believe that Christ suffered, agonized? Well the disciple is not above the master. Therefore we can expect to suffer. Get used to seek consolation in God alone."[21] This form of power, however, limits the field of action by setting conditions to ensure that the Sisters behave in a way that would lead to perfection in religious life as defined by the Catholic spirituality of the time.

The letters also show a particular pattern of discourse that aimed to create memory, continuity, and an image of religious life based primarily on the workings of God presented as Divine Providence. Particularly during the first years, Langevin marked even simple anniversaries of the Congregation such as the "monthly anniversary" of the ceremony of investiture. He placed great emphasis on coincidences that, on surface, appeared casual but that actually reinforced the notion of the event as being providential. For example, he received the coat of arms for the new Congregation on the day marking the fifth month after the first habit investiture. It was also in the same period, the previous year (August 1903) during the octave of the feast of the Assumption that he had decided to consider what name to give the prospective community.[22] In other words, the Sisters were doing the work of God and this was God's will. When the pope approved the foundation in 1906, Langevin made clear that the Sisters had received the approval of the Vicar of Christ, implying the approval of Christ himself.[23] Transgressions of the rules and even doubts about the work would then be transgressions against God himself (a father) in his almighty power. God wanted it to be when things went well as when things went wrong. In the latter case the Sisters would later joyfully harvest what they had sown amid difficulties and tears.[24]

Langevin expected the Sisters to master the appropriate discourses and practices that would make them consecrated women religious. He always stressed obedience to authority, which, in his words, represented God. This is the way he asked the Sisters to understand Sister St Viateur's authority as directress. He wrote to the community: "May you listen to her (your Superior), love and venerate her as the representative of the authority of God himself."[25] As soon as Sister St Viateur became the directress in 1905, he addressed the letters to her. On special occasions, he would address a letter to the entire community.

Disobedience was a "capital" sin,[26] a most serious offence. Obedience was introduced in the 1906 constitutions as a virtue having two dimensions: external, which refers to the way the Sisters took and executed directions (humbly and faithfully, without excuses or complaints); and internal (obeying with joy and even setting aside their own will and personal judgment when required).[27] Langevin's sermons were in line with his letters: respect for authority was the strength and glory of religious communities. "In matters of obedience, one must not consider the person commanding but the authority of God. When one has a little sorrow, if one keeps it to herself, it passes more quickly."[28]

Langevin spent time explaining the virtues, especially those defined by the constitutions and those corresponding to the three vows, the concepts of obedience, humility, external and internal mortification, mortification of the will, and meditation among other practices. He asked the novices to get in the habit, right from the beginning, of walking in the holy presence of God. In his view, the memory of God's presence stimulates us to acts of virtue and thus to avoid failings.[29] Careful internal scrutiny, a guided knowledge of the self, would help to deal with personal shortcomings and would mediate actions and thoughts.

In 1906 the Congregation opened its first mission (assignment away from the mother house), St Charles Convent, located in the rural area nine miles west of the Winnipeg city centre. It did not have access to city water, nor to electricity. St Charles was a little village with a sizeable Métis population. The convent started as a private elementary school mainly for the children of the parish, who were mostly French Canadian. Langevin was anxious to make it a boarding school, giving preference to girls and the poor. The main problem was the need to divide the Sisters' community between two locations and the need for another teaching Sister. Sister St Viateur became the directress of St Charles.

St Charles Convent, a private boarding school opened in 1906 for girls and day students of both sexes. Four novices from Quebec were studying English with Miss Kay Sullivan, a lay teacher (extreme right on the porch). Picture taken by a photographer in 1909.

The third St Charles church, a small architectural jewel, built in 1905. A view from across the river, taken shortly before it burnt down in 1928.

The "Journal de la Maison-Chapelle" and the "Journal du Couvent de St-Charles" both reveal a unique intimate side of the relationship between Langevin and the Sisters. It is clear that the two convents were for him family and home. He often went to either house for a moment of recreation. He would take a gramophone with him and would even ask the Sisters to dance a waltz or a "petit bonhomme" for him.[30] At St Charles, Langevin spent time with the children and attended their religious festivities, bazaars and concerts.

He would bring guests like Father Lacombe, OMI,[31] for supper at the Mother House. Langevin and his guests were served supper in a separate refectory from the Sisters; afterwards the directress would join them in conversation and sometimes, especially if the visitors happened to be missionaries, they would be invited to address the whole community. When dropping in at St Charles or the Maison-Chapelle, Langevin would occasionally call a short council meeting without previous notice to discuss important matters immediately. His letters and visits were received with anticipation and joy.

Langevin seemed to think of himself as a father to the Congregation in a rather complex way that went beyond his ecclesiastical role as archbishop and founder. He took the role of a Catholic paterfamilias of the time, indeed and one not devoid of emotional ties to the congregation. On 4 January 4 1909 he complained that two of the juniorists,[32] his protégées at St Charles, did not make mention of the two dollars he had left for them with Sister St Viateur. He wrote to her:

> Do I have to tell you that I do not want any unfaithful intermediaries between the Sisters, the Juniorists and myself? Last year, I was very understanding and gracefully accepted your motivation for giving my gifts to others than the intended recipients. When I enclosed a note for Sister Alice, you withheld it, because you believed that it was the best thing to do ... Did you give the other Sisters their letters when I wrote to them from Montreal? I insist in maintaining my complete absolute freedom to communicate directly with my daughters ...[33]

One day later, on 5 January, Langevin wrote a letter of apology. He acknowledged it was wrong of him to doubt Sister St Viateur's honesty when in the past she had never given him any reason to do so, and that it would have been better to express his concerns verbally rather than in a letter. The tenor of the letter provides some latitude for gauging Sister St Viateur's reaction. He added, "If I couldn't count on you a hundred percent, it would be better to abandon the whole works or to find

St Charles Convent with the original 1906 structure on the right and the 1913 addition on the left. Viewing the surrounding countryside from the bell tower of the convent was an exciting part of the tour of the premises by retreatants and visitors.

someone else to replace me. But, I must admit, I am not tempted to do either. For my penance, I will go to St Charles as soon as I have a free moment, and I am sure that you will receive and accept me as a repentant sinner."[34]

Sister St Viateur seemed to retain her flair for independence well after her first vows. A 1909 letter from Langevin to Sister Marie-Joseph clearly shows Langevin's frustration with St Viateur's tendency to make some decisions on her own. He wrote: "Once more, the fact that the Sister Directress prolongs her stay without concern for the inconvenience, proves my worries. Indeed, it was daring on my part to have wanted this trip; however, I do believe that it is God's will and that it is necessary for the future of the Congregation."[35] The tone of the letter addressed to Sister Marie-Joseph points to an unusual conversation between the archbishop and the assistant to the directress.

Beyond the complex relationship between Langevin and Sister St Viateur, there were obvious underlying internal tensions in the community. These stemmed principally from the issue of Sister St Viateur's legitimacy as directress and from the intense recruitment[36] of postulants in Quebec. From very early, some of the Sisters, like Sister Marie-Gertrude (Elizabeth Storozuk), held the view that Mother Marie-Joseph was legitimately "number one" in the community since she had

Sister Marie-Joseph, Director of Novices, with sixteen novices and seven postulants. Picture taken in 1909.

arrived before Mother St Viateur and had been appointed by the Founder as directress of the original group from December 1903 until April 1905 when Langevin appointed Sister St Viateur as directress. The internal issue of legitimacy and precedence was further compounded in those years by the presence of a large number of postulants and novices from Quebec. Sister St Viateur had gone to Montreal in 1907. In April 1908 six young postulants took the habit; five of them were from Quebec, and another postulant from Quebec took the habit in September. Upon Langevin's request, Sister St Viateur went back to Montreal in 1909 for more recruits. From 1904 to 1915, fifty-five percent of the Sisters came from the province of Quebec. This strong presence brought differences in experience. While the Sisters from Manitoba and the prairies had a pragmatic, pioneering experience of religious life, the postulants from Quebec came to the nascent community with a rather institutionalized understanding of convent life and they were more inclined to move in that direction. Strangely enough, Ida Lafricain had brought an experience closer to that of the Manitobans, since she had attended school not in a boarding convent but in a model school directed by laywomen in Montreal and she had spent ten years at Bethany House living in a fairly unstructured environment, relative to convent life. It may be inferred that Sister St Viateur would not herself have imposed stricter rules on the young community to bolster her authority had she not been influenced to do so by Langevin.

When tensions began to rise in the small group, Langevin moved quickly to apply new regulations to reinforce Sister St Viateur's authority. He unequivocally showed his strong support for her when in January 1910 he promoted her from Sister Directress to Reverend Mother Superior while the title of directress was kept only for the local superiors. The Sisters were to call her "Mother" and in their conversations refer to her as "our mother" or "mother superior"; local directresses were to be addressed as Sister Directress while the "Maîtresse des novices" had to be called "Révérende Soeur Maîtresse des Novices" and the novices would refer to her as "Notre Maîtresse."[37] Langevin had clearly attempted to regulate the relations among the Sisters, stressing the hierarchical element. In a letter addressed to Mother St Viateur in January 1910, he expressed his satisfaction regarding the change of title, which the general council had endorsed, although he acknowledged that there were dissonant notes: "I am pleased with the results of the Council meeting for despite the fact that there are differences of opinion and feeling, you are able to come to an understanding. It was up to the Assistant [Sister Marie-Joseph] to ask that a new name be given to the person who is to be at the head and heart of the Congregation and of all its undertakings."[38]

On 13 May 1910, Langevin addressed a powerful letter to all the Sisters in the four existing houses. The strong and reprehending tone along with the call for obedience makes clear that he was again dealing with a serious internal problem that he attributed to a lack of virtue on the part of some Sisters. The themes are true virtue and the role of the superior. He began by referring to the lesson given by Jesus regarding true virtue, "Learn from me for I am meek and humble of heart." To put this lesson into action the Sisters would patiently accept the loneliness, contradictions, lack of recognition, appreciation, or kindness, the unjust remarks, sharp accusations, sudden change, work that they didn't like, humiliation, a disagreeable penance, or a humiliating refusal. At the core of his argument was the notion of the suffering Christ as a model. Langevin closed the letter on an encouraging note: "On the feast of Pentecost, the Holy Spirit will enlighten each one of you to help you understand, and understand these lessons in a very practical and effective manner."

The second theme of the letter, "Your Superior," makes a strong case for trust and obedience: "Your daughterly confidence in her and your devotedness marked by submission, must know no limits either ... The head and the heart of your Congregation is your first Mother ... You should act with joy, self-forgetfulness and willingness to put aside your own preferences and personal views."

Langevin seemed to respond to internal resistance to authority on the part of some Sisters in an attempt to curb any future unruliness:

To lack confidence in your superior, to avoid her, to go to see her (for the rendement de compte) on rare occasions only and to do so unwillingly, to refrain from telling her what she should know so as to guide the community, to judge her severely, to criticize her or to withhold from her your whole-hearted support in all that she does and undoes under my authority, to say that she is guided by human motivations regarding her love for a house or work of apostolate to the detriment of the common good is to show signs of a very poor religious spirit, leading one to believe that you have lost your vocation, or that you are jeopardizing it. You must see Jesus himself present in your superiors.[39]

There is a lack of documentation to explore the situation to which Langevin was referring in his letter, although it may be inferred from other correspondence that there were disagreements between Mother St Viateur and Sister Marie-Joseph, who did not always see eye to eye with her superior. She may even have had different visions of the community.[40]

It also seems that Langevin himself was not totally exonerated from blame in the situation. He may have exacerbated it by prolonging what he called the infancy stage of the Congregation by interfering too much. At times Langevin told the Sisters they were in charge, but at other times he took back the reins of government. Balancing the amount of autonomy necessary to allow the Congregation to grow proved difficult. For example, regarding acceptance of the mission at Fort Pelley (St Philippe) upon which the council was supposed to decide, he wrote: "My desire to do good and the continuous requests I received from my priests make me want to urge the Congregation to develop quickly. I see that there are certain inconveniences to this, and I do believe that you are now able to be on your own. Naturally I will always be there to protect you and to help you whenever you need but I think it would be better to leave you greater freedom."[41]

The already fragile internal situation was compounded by the arrival of a young woman of good family whom Henri Bernard, a friend of the Sisters, had recruited in Montreal with all good intentions in 1908 but who after the novitiate proved to be of contentious nature, extremely critical of any form of authority, and harmful to the peace of the houses where she was sent. She was finally dismissed in 1916 after all means to produce amendment had been exhausted.

The circumstances surrounding the foundation of the Congregation had set the stage for a potentially difficult situation. Sister St Viateur came from Montreal "after leaving her first nest" – an emotionally loaded point that Langevin occasionally kept referring to as late as 1913[42] – while Sister Marie-Joseph had arrived at the Maison-Chapelle earlier and she was a Manitoban. At the beginning Langevin relied on Sister Marie-Joseph to follow up and facilitate Sister St Viateur's process of adaptation. But once Sister St Viateur was fully into the work as directress after her first profession of vows in September 1905, and after he named her as mother superior in 1910, he obviously wanted everyone to give her their full obedience. The disagreements between the two were then resolved by appealing to higher authority, following the religious practices of the time.

The application of spiritual principles outlined in the constitutions was dependent on the development of and compliance to rules. A spontaneous sense of family had developed during the early years of the Congregation along with a degree of informality. Thus, in 1911, Langevin prepared a directory, as was customary in religious congregations, complementing the basic guiding principles with detailed regulations to generate stable traditions and keep the Sisters united by the same rules, the same discipline, and the same customs. Presuming that holiness would develop from internalizing the outlined principles, ways of regulating the inner self and ways of behaving, the directory aimed to create a sense of self as religious women. It included regulations concerning visits, journal, correspondence; rules regarding solicitude for the Sisters, persons in authority, accountability for external conduct, spiritual direction; a list of items for the trousseau; practice of the vow of poverty (visiting the wardrobe, books the Sisters may keep, writing supplies, gifts received by the Sisters); obligations of the Reverend Mother Superior and of the Reverend Sisters Directresses (general remarks, relations with persons outside the convent, order of precedence).[43] The *coutumier* (a daily life manual), which aimed to take care of daily life rituals, would take shape later on. The creation of a religious woman implied an aesthetic ideal and the willingness to internalize limits about how she might act, or what she could know. If the disciplinary techniques pursued perfection and increased the aptitude of the Sisters for religious life, they also risked draining the Sisters' own selves of power.

Langevin was always attentive to the role of the mother superior. He expected her to be strict and demand obedience but also to be motherly. He advised Mother St Viateur to let her Sisters know that she recognized and appreciated their good qualities. He was concerned with the negative influences with which the young Sisters could be in contact during the fulfilment of their missionary work after they left the novitiate to begin their direct involvement with the apostolate. These negative influences could have a double effect: "the interior life diminishes, the faults (negative tendencies) become more prominent while the qualities are strengthened and developed." For that reason, he stressed the importance of the novitiate formation.[44]

Less than a year before his death, Langevin, who was already sick, presented the second part of the constitutions to the Sisters, the one dealing with the governance of the Congregation.[45] Langevin was certainly aware that some of the rules and regulations were premature and impossible to carry out at the time. The tension between the more monastic contemplative way of life at the mother house (Maison-Chapelle) and that of an active missionary and teacher, compounded by the lack of established traditions, made natural a pragmatic approach. The community was small and the work required many Sisters in the field. There was no complete separation between the novices and the professed Sisters until 1915 and even then it was difficult to observe. Several of the novices spent a substantial amount of time in the missions although it was preferred that they be at the Maison-Chapelle under the direction of the mistress of novices. Also the composition of the Congregation generated different attitudes toward tradition. The Sisters from Quebec were predisposed to stress the rules. They had some acquaintance with religious life in one way or another. The Americans – Amanda Laberge (Saint-Jean-Baptiste) who joined the Congregation in 1904, and her sister Albina Laberge (Louis de France), who joined in 1911 – took a more relaxed approach toward the rules and the quest for uniformity. Their contribution and leadership were too valuable to call into question their transgressions, which were an important window on wisdom and common sense. There are no references to Langevin's reaction to the two Sisters' pursuit of their own identity as women religious.

In 1914 the Congregation was ten years old. There were fifty-seven members, eleven of whom had taken final vows while forty-six had temporary vows. There were also nine novices and five postulants. The members were distributed among the following houses: the Maison-

Southside view of the Maison-Chapelle. Picture taken in 1910, after the first extension was built in 1908. Sister Marie-de-la-Présentation (Paméla Comeau), the director, is seated. The others are Sister Sainte-Thérèse, Sister St-Philippe, and Sister St-André.

Chapelle (1903) contained the mother house with the novitiate (1904) and the Jardin de l'Enfance (1909), and also provided room and board to Sisters from other congregations and to laywomen attending the bilingual Normal School; St Charles Convent (private boarding and day school, 1906); Cross Lake (residential school, 1909); St Philippe (residential school, 1910–13); Norway House (mission, 1911) where the Cross Lake students and personnel were transferred temporarily until 1913; Fannystelle (convent and public school, 1911); Dunrea (boarding convent and parochial school, 1912); Pembina, North Dakota (private day and boarding school, 1913–14); and Fort Alexander (residential school, 1914).

THE RELATIONSHIP WITH FATHER HENRI BERNARD

The Sisters were not supposed to cultivate particular friendships among themselves. They were not accustomed to talk to other women about their spiritual life either, since they looked to a male spiritual director. The superior (Sister St Viateur) appointed by Langevin in 1905 turned to him and to Henri Bernard for advice. Bernard, one of Langevin's

Henri Bernard, friend and benefactor of the Sisters, originally from Laus, France, who had ultramontane ideas while supporting the Sisters' autonomy. He was ordained in 1908 by Archbishop Langevin and became his corresponding secretary in Montreal where he lived until he retired in St Boniface in 1936. Picture taken in a studio shortly after ordination.

"spiritual sons," had been from the start closely related to the community. They shared the core of ultramontane Catholic thought and a nationalist French Canadian ideal based on the notion of two founding peoples. Bernard often acted as a mediator between the Sisters and Langevin, helped the Community financially with low-interest loans from his personal resources, and provided recruits, usually from among his spiritual directees and retreatants in Montreal. The Sisters benefited from Bernard's financial contributions and moral support for many years after Archbishop Langevin died.

Bernard was ordained priest after Langevin accepted him in his diocese in 1904. He remained on the margins of the priesthood, for his poor health precluded work as a parish priest, and also entry to the church hierarchy. He had migrated as a young man from France to Montreal, where he was taken under the wing of a wealthy couple who had no children, Dr François Desmarchais and his wife. Desmarchais's two sisters, Elise and Philomène, became his Canadian "mothers" and their benevolent influence reached the Oblate Sisters. As a young free-

St Charles Convent chapel, 1914. Above the altar is the statue of Our Lady with hands extended to welcome all her spiritual children. The antependium, hanging in front of the altar, was embroidered by Sister Marie-Estelle (Véronique Chartrand).

lance writer, Bernard thought he had a mission to critique the state, the Freemasons, and the Church itself. Bernard and Langevin shared a commitment to the triumph of the world spiritual kingship of the Sacred Heart of Jesus and both promoted the spread of the flag of the Sacred Heart in Catholic churches and processions, as a symbol of the recognition of the Lordship of Jesus Christ in Canada. Langevin supported Bernard in his struggles against the Ligue de l'Enseignement de Montréal, created in 1902, which favoured public education, and against the Freemasons.[46]

Mother St Viateur consulted with Bernard and shared pains and problems, even some concerns with Langevin's ways of making decisions for the Sisters. Bernard was inclined to give the Sisters their space and was sensitive to their views and desires. He wrote regarding a candidate who had not made the proper request to the general council but whom Langevin wanted in the community nonetheless: "Mgr (Langevin) scares me!! ... I myself understand your reasons and I approve you totally ... and I insist absolutely that my grain of salt (my advice) be sifted, like anyone else's, through the sieve of your illustrious council before whose enlightened decisions I bow down deeply."[47] Bernard's adopted family, and in particular Elise, his "second mother," also a benefactor of the Sisters, influenced his way of relating to the Oblate Sisters. In an interesting letter to Langevin, he communicated Elise's observations:

Miss Elise, however, made this remark to me regarding the daily program of the Oblate Sisters. As a former teacher and Sister, even a Superior, she finds that for teaching Sisters, the Oblates have too many spiritual exercises, and that this can harm the goal they pursue, which becomes ever more difficult and requires on the part of the teachers a more thorough preparation: this demands time. At the Congregation [Sisters of the Congregation of Notre Dame], the spiritual exercises are shorter, and the teachers have more time to prepare their classes and to do some personal studies. She tells me that the Office of the Virgin Mary might be replaced by the shorter Office of the Immaculate Conception, for example. I'm telling you that, Monseigneur, in all simplicity, for I know nothing in this matter.[48]

Bernard had many contacts in Quebec and became instrumental in facilitating Mother St Viateur's recruitment efforts and her vision of missionary work after Langevin's death, a vision, partly inspired by Langevin's understanding of Canada and French Canadian nationalism, that motivated her to have foundations in Quebec as well as in the diocese of St Boniface.

LANGEVIN'S DEATH

It is with a profound grief that we have to record in our modest Chronicles the death of our beloved Founder and Father, His Grace Archbishop Louis-Philippe Adélard Langevin, OMI, of St Boniface. We can rightly say in

> our case that *great griefs are silent*. In fact, how can we express the painful loss that we have just endured? If this death is a great bereavement for the whole diocese and for the Sisters' communities, how much more it must be for us, the daughters of his heart and his apostolic zeal, who are left orphans after eleven years of existence.[49]

The death of Langevin had a tremendous impact on the young congregation. Afflicted by diabetes, a disease that proved fatal, Langevin had gone periodically to various health resorts to regain his energy. In the fall of 1914, he went to his fellow Oblates in Texas expecting that his health would improve. Before leaving on 8 October, Langevin handed the last part of the constitutions to the Congregation and he made internal appointments. On 16 May 1915, a month before his death, Langevin visited the Sisters as usual. This was to be his last visit. In choosing to talk about the foundation, his feelings, his pain, the external trials, his intimate persuasion that the Congregation was called to make an immense contribution, he was announcing his death. His words resonated for many years in the Sisters' collective memory. Once more, Langevin reminded them of the presence of the Holy Spirit in their work: "If I examine the vocations of the Sisters, I notice that two thirds of them cannot be explained from a human point of view ... It is therefore a duty for you, my daughters, to continue the work with the supernatural spirit that must direct your whole life."[50] On 2 June 1915, Langevin went to Quebec City for the golden jubilee of the priesthood of Cardinal Bégin, archbishop of Quebec. There his health deteriorated quickly. He developed an erysipelas and died in Montreal's Hotel-Dieu hospital on 15 June 1915 at eight o'clock in the morning. He was fifty-nine years old. The sorrow of the Missionary Oblate Sisters is difficult to describe. This event marked the beginning of a new phase in the life of the young Congregation that had lost its Founder. It also initiated a new reality for Mother St Viateur.

NOTRE MÈRE

O Mère à l'âme grande, au cœur brûlant de zèle,
Tout bénit votre nom, chante votre grandeur!
Dans ce petit berceau à l'ombre de vos ailes
Nous passons notre vie sans crainte, sans douleur.

Recevez en ce jour de nos âmes fidèles
Les prières et les vœux, les souhaits de bonheur.
Que l'Enfant-Dieu réponde à vos soins maternels
En inspirant à toutes une sainte ferveur.

Humble petite barque, oh! vogue vite et fière,
Ouvre grandes les voiles et fais connaître au loin,
L'œuvre ici cultivée; dis le bien qu'elle opère.

Et dans un prompt retour ramène bien des âmes!
La sainte charité de son feu nous enflamme
Toutes, nous voulons Mère être votre soutien.
Vos enfants (Les novices Oblates)

L'Écho 3, no. 2 (20 April 1919).

III

Moving Ahead, 1916–1927: Mother St Viateur's Leadership, the Power of the Deinstitutionalizing Voice, and the Redirection Set by the New Constitutions

The death of Archbishop Langevin deeply affected the community, which had relied on the wisdom of the Founder as a cohesive and integrating force. Authority derived from Langevin.[1] Mother St Viateur expressed her profound anguish to Father Henri Bernard and told him fifteen days after Langevin's death that she often talked to the latter asking for advice as though he were still alive.[2] She was quoted as saying, "I have to command in darkness, how difficult I find these moments."[3]

However, Mother St Viateur moved the Congregation ahead by building on Langevin's foundations, while trying to manoeuver at the intersection of the Oblate Fathers' agenda and her own interpretation of the Congregation's mission. She furthered the process of institutionalization of the community by requesting strict uniformity of life and observance of the rules. Mother St Viateur's leadership of the Congregation was inspired by Langevin's vision of its place in Canada as part of the French Canadian national community and according to its role in supporting the Oblate Fathers. She struggled, however, to realize her priorities and to keep Quebec as an important point of reference. During this period, Sister Louis de France, a deinstitutionalizing voice, gained a high and lasting profile. Meanwhile the Congregation became involved in the difficult process of rewriting their constitutions in accord with the new code of canon law under the guidance of Father Louis Péalapra, OMI.[4]

KEEPING THE RULES

As head of the Congregation after the Founder's death, Mother St Viateur tried to model the new Congregation after the long-established ones, particularly those in Quebec. The "Journal de la Maison-Chapelle" of 6 January 1916 states on the occasion of the separation of the novitiate from the professed Sisters, as later required by canon law, "We will imitate more closely the older communities in being rarely in contact with the Novices." Keeping the rules became the foundation of her leadership, not an unusual approach. In the analysis of the Congregation of the Immaculate Heart of Mary, Nancy Sylvester shows that at the beginning of the century, the Congregation's first general superior to govern without male supervision, Mother Mechtildis McGrail, chose to prove her governing skills by enforcing strict compliance with the Rule.[5] The rules included not just the fundamental precepts of religious life – the Rule, as adopted by founders, in this case the Rule of St Augustine – but also the laws contained in the constitutions, in the practices pertaining to the particular institution recorded in the directory, and in more detailed form, in the *coutumier*. Incidentally, the Sisters did not refer to the Rule of St Augustine at all.

The council was the site where decisions were made concerning details of daily life, contact and visits with family, annual assignments and postings to the various houses, additions or alterations to the prescribed prayers, directions on how to accomplish a variety of work such as sacristy, sewing, and tending to the clothing. Decisions concerning missionary work were also made in council. The minutes, in a way, became the means to build the *coutumier*, to complete and update the directory, and to secure uniformity as requested by the constitutions. It was determined in 1921 that the constitutions, the directory, and the *coutumier* were to be read four times a year.[6] The minutes also show the continuation of the attempt to make the Congregation more hierarchical and to base it on precedence. For example, in July 1916 it was determined that, in time, a choir Sister, not an auxiliary Sister, should be at the head of all the departments, including the kitchen.[7] The attachment to rules, which was an integral part of a Catholicism based on rites, prohibitions, observances, and permissions, was stressed as a means to spiritual perfection. Kierkegaard's ideas about becoming subjective come to mind, in particular his challenge to conforming patterns of institutionalized Christianity, and to the tendency for people to lose their individuality in the process of identifying themselves with sanctioned roles and duties. The result may be construed as pseudo-objectivity, or a form of self-deception.[8] The female congregations, in Micheline D'Allaire's view, had a disposition to interpret the rules so strictly because of their poor theological formation. Without theology, in her view, the soil was fertile for blind obedience.[9]

The Sisters, in retrospect, remembered Mother St Viateur as being too strict. However, obedience to the rules, not subservience to her, was at the core of her leadership in her particular style and manner. Uniformity, it was hoped, would lead to strong community life. Blind obedience, simplicity, and poverty were her pivotal principles. She was naturally a firm person who was described as a "femme d' affaires" (business woman).[10] In order to develop perfect obedience in the Congregation, she requested that all permissions originate from the highest authority. At the Maison-Chapelle, she personally undertook the granting of permissions. In the other houses, she reserved the main directives for herself. There were three categories of permission: special permissions to be requested each time; ordinary ones that covered in general all the authorizations needed to fulfill one's duties or to be exempt temporarily from certain rules; and, finally, small tacit permission granted in bulk, such as permission to drink water between meals or to speak to someone during hours of silence. These last two kinds of permission had to be renewed periodically at the "rendement de compte," the accounting for one's transgressions.

Mother St Viateur firmly believed that if novices were thoroughly indoctrinated with the principle of dependence on superior authority, they would be less likely to wander away from the fold when they were sent out to work in the field.[11] Mother St Viateur believed that the perfect union of the directresses of missions with the Reverend Mother General was supposed to save the community, to give it the strength of a wholesome body and the perfect harmony of the members with the head. She feared divisions in religious families. The local directresses were never to make decisions of any importance without taking the advice of the supreme authority, no matter how long they had to wait for a reply.[12] Mother St Viateur herself had turned to Langevin for advice but she was also apt to stand her ground, though this latter approach was often obliterated or even altered by the Sisters who were eager to leave a written record of the community. Such seems to be the case with Sister François-de-Sales who around 1921 or 1922 wrote the only notes

Mother St Viateur, while on a visit to Dunrea, Manitoba, in the summer of 1913, is in the backyard of the convent, dancing to the beat of music from Archbishop Langevin's phonograph, which a novice, Sister St-Camille is cranking to her heart's content.

Mother St Viateur also was remembered as a happy person who loved the outdoors.

available about Mother St Viateur based on conversations with her.[13]

Mother St Viateur was also remembered as a happy person who loved the outdoors and laughed a lot, an image that was somewhat fixed in the many spontaneous photographs of picnics with Sisters, often with students, beside the river at St Charles or under the trees in the missions. However, the most contradictory feature of her leadership in terms of strict compliance with rules was her close working relation with Sister Saint-Jean-Baptiste (Amanda Laberge), directress at St Charles Convent from 1910 to 1914 and Mother St Viateur's general assistant from 1914 until the Sister's untimely death in 1924. Originally from North Dakota, Sister Saint-Jean-Baptiste had joined the Congregation very early, in 1904; her sister Albina Laberge (Sister Louis de France) came later, in 1911. Amanda was an extrovert, a warm person, known for her common sense and open mind and for her love of the

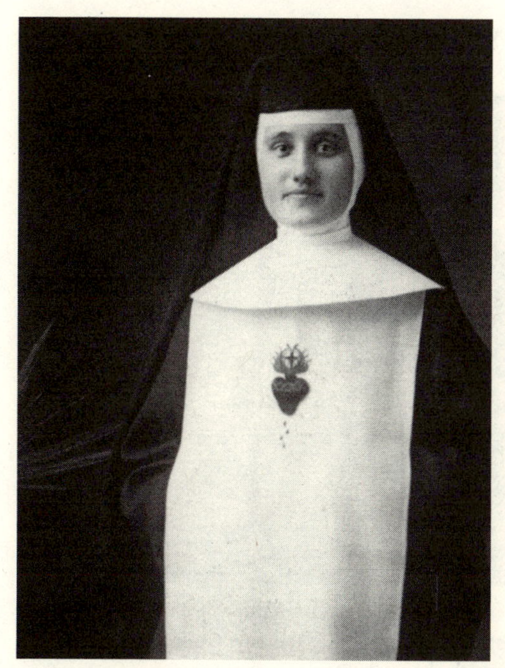

Sister Louis de France, Albina Laberge, came to St Charles in 1910 to help her sister Amanda and stayed to become an Oblate Sister. Picture taken in a studio in 1913 on her first profession of vows.

Sister Saint-Jean-Baptiste (Amanda Laberge from Grafton, North Dakota) replaced Sister St Viateur as directress of St Charles from 1909 until 1914. Picture taken in a studio in 1911.

Mother St Viateur, visiting the Sisters in Gravelbourg, Saskatchewan, in 1920. The Sisters began doing domestic work in 1918 at the new Collège Matthieu, run by the Oblate Fathers, with the understanding that the following year the Sisters were to open primary classes.

students. She had no secondary education but was very creative and pragmatic. Interestingly, her relaxed approach to rules and to the quest for uniformity caused no controversy. She was described as somebody who, like her sister Albina (Louis de France), did not follow the rules, did not get up for meditation, went to bed after midnight, helped students until late, and let the Sisters get away with small transgressions.[14] The lack of established traditions in the early days allowed for a spontaneity that the two American sisters fully embraced.

Mother St Viateur committed herself to high standards and hard work. She opened every new house herself and did all kinds of work along with the Sisters. This happened in St Charles Convent, a private school, the very first mission; in the missions with the Aboriginal peoples; and with the white missions in Saskatchewan and Quebec. She was always there. She worked extremely hard although she was not obliged to do so. She was aware that she was not from Manitoba, that she had been brought from Montreal by Langevin and appointed by him as head of the young Congregation. In addition, she had the difficult task of enforcing the rules and creating a stable life while being involved in missionary work with few Sisters and meagre financial resources. The journal of the houses left testimonies of her visits to the missions. The journal of St Philippe, a residential school in Saskatchewan where the Sisters arrived in 1910, describes Mother St Viateur busying herself in the kitchen:

Wednesday June 18, 1910. Owing to the vast amount of hard labour, the fast was not kept. Mother Superior spent all day alone in the kitchen. She cooked many things, among which was an immense bread pudding, for the children who thought she gave them a feast. The truth was that she made use of the currants and raisins she had found, for fear these would later on be unfit for use. Mother Superior also washed and dried again several pounds of these fruits.

Tuesday, June 28. Mother Superior commenced the unpacking of the trunks and the placing in order of all the things for the Sisters who would come in September.[15]

Mother St Viateur was remembered by the older Sisters in the same vein as a woman of action.

NEW DIRECTIONS AND TENSIONS IN THE MISSIONARY WORK

A few years before Archbishop Langevin's death, the archbishop of Quebec, Cardinal Bégin, had invited the Sisters to open foundations in Quebec.[16] Mother St Viateur in cooperation with the Oblate Fathers and with the support of Archbishop O.M. Mathieu of Regina, proceeded to establish the Congregation in Quebec. In 1919, the Oblate Sisters opened their first school there, the École St-Alexandre, a coeducational day elementary school, among the working-class families in the parish of St-Sauveur, Quebec City. The Oblate Fathers, who were in charge of the parish, had obtained its establishment from the Province, which meant that the teachers received a salary.[17] They had the support of Cardinal Bégin. Father Lortie, an Oblate, also supported young women's retreats organized by the Sisters, which proved to be a rapid source of recruitment for the Congregation, and a source of attraction for benefactors.[18]

There was a convergence of interests, although the Oblate Fathers had a strong agenda. Mother St Viateur was eager to find recruits for the young Congregation and have a presence in Quebec, a position that had full support from Father Péalapra, OMI, the Congregation's chaplain. Potential candidates were disheartened by the distance to

Mother St Viateur, leaving for Quebec in 1919 to open the first house in "la belle province." Notice her umbrella and her gloves. Having a foothold in Quebec was part of her vision for the Sisters.

Manitoba, so entering as postulants in Quebec would facilitate the process. The Oblate Fathers were extremely interested in helping the Congregation to recruit prospective Sisters in Quebec who could teach in the Jardins de l'Enfance in the large diocese of St Boniface and beyond. The Jardins were the Catholic primary French schools that prepared boys for the French classical colleges. They were described by Father Péalapra as being of "prime necessity, since without it, our French classical colleges will find themselves grievously paralyzed, since the young people follow the courses in the language they learned in the little school."[19] The Oblate Sisters, who ran the Jardin in the Maison Chapelle in St Boniface, had the needed experience to undertake this special area of education in Quebec.

At first glance, then, it is not surprising that in the fall of 1920 Mother St Viateur bought a big old mansion, the Villa Montcalm at Giffard, on the heights of Beauport overlooking Quebec City where she intended to open a Jardin de l'Enfance, a private elementary boarding and day school for boys. It was only in the spring of 1921 that the Sisters moved in and prepared to receive students for the following September. Father Péalapra had exchanged correspondence with Father Lortie in which he questioned the wisdom of a new foundation in terms of the availability of Sisters and the prospective financial debt for the Congregation. Péalapra argued strongly that the foundation had to be postponed, although he wrote, "it is well determined that the aim of the Oblate Sisters is the Jardins de l' Enfance, consequently when circumstances allow they will found others of this type."[20] Lortie, who feared that the aging Cardinal Bégin might die before the Oblate Sisters could obtain canonical existence in the diocese, got his way.

In a letter to Péalapra, Mother St Viateur shared the hardships of this enterprise. She had to deal with a shortage of Sisters, other requests from various dioceses and new foundations that could open avenues for recruitment. Opening Giffard proved to be difficult. The house was somewhat dilapidated, yet the parishioners were ready to send their sons to the Jardin de l'Enfance St-Joseph while basic repairs were carried out. She wrote to Péalapra from Quebec, "It is always the thought of not having enough Sisters that stops me. Perhaps I could hire some lay teachers for St Charles and get paid by the Director of Otterburne (Manitoba) for the work we are doing for the Clerics of St Viateur."[21] Three years later, in 1924, the school in Giffard was moved to a brand-new building higher up on a second hill above the villa. The archbishop of Regina, Monseigneur Mathieu, presided over the blessing ceremony.[22] This private school, one of the Jardins, was the longest-lasting mission of the Oblate Sisters in Quebec. In 1944 it was relocated as a day school to St-Cyrille Boulevard next to the Jesuits' Collège Garnier and was finally handed over to the Sisters of Charity of St Louis in 1985.

In September 1921, under the auspices of Archbishop Mathieu, the Congregation opened the Jardin de l'Enfance Notre-Dame-du-Rosaire, a day and boarding preparatory school for boys, grades one to seven, in Gravelbourg, Saskatchewan, near the Oblate Fathers' Collège Mathieu.

It was not without regret that in June 1925, Mother St Viateur and the council decided, upon a request from Cardinal Bégin, to close the house in St-Sauveur in order to accept a five-year contract at the elementary parochial school in Stoneham, a Donacona pulp-and-paper company

The first Jardin de l'Enfance (elementary school) in Gravelbourg, Saskatchewan. The building belonged to the Oblate Fathers. In 1920 it was leased to the Sisters.

town in the Laurentian Mountains, sixteen miles north of Quebec City. The president of the company had himself asked the cardinal for Sisters and he paid fourteen thousand dollars to cover the cost of installing electricity and a heating system.

During the 1920s, Mother St Viateur appears as an assertive leader who took care of her Sisters even as she had to say no to the clergy. She did not display the motherly qualities some Sisters expected from her, but she had an understanding of what they were going through and she cared deeply for them. Whenever she could, she also personally nursed back to health the sick ones who returned from the missions. A letter to Péalapra, which she wrote from Quebec in 1922, reveals the tension between her projects in Quebec, where she had placed Sisters, and the demands from the Oblate Fathers for the missions with the Aboriginal people, which were not her primary interest or within her vision of the Congregation. The letter contains powerful words:

> I am surprised that Father Provincial insists that we go to Camperville when he knows very well that at the Maison-Chapelle we are short of personnel. And we do not have enough professed Sisters to train our novices for the work of missions. I find that for the Provincial it is not difficult to pick one Sister here and there but I find it hard to force our Sisters, in addition to their own work,

to do that of those who will be removed. With this way of doing things, I fear that the Sisters would be pushed to the limits of their strength and they would not enjoy their vocation anymore. I am glad that I was not in St Boniface to give Brachet an immediate response to his request and probably, not be more discerning that I am now to make a decision on this important question.[23]

Mother St Viateur and the council decided to reject Father Brachet's request as they had refused Norway House some time before. However, during this period the Sisters agreed to be in charge of a parish bilingual elementary day school, the École de l'Assomption, in Transcona, Manitoba. They taught there from 1924 to 1973. A situation generated in Transcona in 1927 shows that the Sisters found creative ways to resist the clergy's imposition and to obtain what they wanted. We read in the minutes of the council: "The principal [a Sister] proposed to refuse boys who were 15 years or older. We cannot impose this decision because the school is under the authority of the priest, but we will try with discretion to make clear our reasons. The same discretion will be employed to try to obtain the salary of the fourth Sister and also a salary for cleaning the classes and the parish church."[24]

During this period, the Sisters agreed in 1925 to go to the residential school in McIntosh, Ontario, which was then part of the diocese of St Boniface but was later transferred to the new diocese of Thunder Bay. From 1918 to 1921, the Sisters had agreed to provide temporary domestic services to the Collège Mathieu in Gravelbourg on the understanding that they would be able to start teaching in the near future. Beginning in 1915 and up till 1920, Sister St Viateur and her council also accepted housework at La Maison St-Joseph, an orphanage run by the Clerics of St Viateur in Otterburne, Manitoba. This post, although not the kind recommended in the constitutions, was accepted at the pressing request of Father Ducharme, the provincial Father, who was in dire need of finding a replacement for another community of Sisters, the Dominicans of the Child Jesus, who had been recalled abruptly by their general superior. Archbishop Béliveau had told the provincial: "Ask the Missionary Oblate Sisters, this is an exceptional case; aren't there exceptions to the rule?"[25]

Mother St Viateur led the Congregation amid tensions and contradictions generated by the influence of the Oblate Fathers in the Congregation and her own desire to set its priorities and direction. The tensions between the commitment to residential schools on one side, and the work in Quebec and the establishment of the Jardins on the other, marked her period as leader. In addition, she had to deal with requests that were beyond the mission of the Congregation. She and the council sometimes refused, or figured their way around what they considered to go against their interest.

MAKING ST CHARLES CONVENT A QUEBEC CONVENT SCHOOL MODEL

In 1915, after Langevin died, the diocese of St Boniface was divided to create the diocese of Winnipeg. Saint Charles Convent became part of the new diocese. The division was the culmination of persistent discontent among anglophone Catholics, in particular the Irish, who saw Langevin as too committed to French and ethnic issues. Langevin had confided in a letter to his Grey Nun friend Sister St Charles that he had touched up "a memoir on the Irish delegation of December 2, 1906, and I am obliged to protect myself against a few Irish laymen who have succeeded in getting the interest of Mgr le Délégué [the pope's representative] in their audacious and unfair complaints."[26] Henri Bernard's later comment in a letter to Mother St Viateur speaks for itself: "Poor dear Mgr [Langevin], what must he think of the division of his diocese and of the coming of an Irishman, specially this one [the first bishop of Winnipeg, Archbishop Alfred Sinnott]. Happily he is in heaven, but I'm not and I have to confess a great anger that is still going on [in me]."[27]

In 1916 the Manitoba legislature approved changes to the Public School Act that ended bilingual instruction in schools, made English the only language of instruction, and approved the School Attendance Act. The same year, the Franco-Manitobans organized L'Association d'Éducation des Canadiens-Français du Manitoba. In 1922, within the context of a peculiar modus vivendi with the provincial government, it developed French programs, prescribed textbooks, and in 1923 created "les visiteurs des écoles" [French inspectors] and provincial exams.

In 1919, acting on her own inspiration, Mother St Viateur introduced to her general council the idea of transforming the Congregation's private school, St Charles Convent, into a French Catholic elementary school on the Quebec convent model rather than following the Manitoba school curriculum. This proposal, the minutes recorded, would also make the convent into an elementary school as was mentioned (or rather implied) in the constitutions.[28] That desire, the minutes of the council also recorded, was therefore the desire of the

Founder, although Langevin had actually promoted the program the council was now trying to replace at St Charles. All the councillors but one, Sister St Jean-Baptiste, were from Quebec.[29] There is no motion recorded in the minutes although the oral tradition is that the decision was not unanimous. There is a paucity of information on this initiative. The journal of St Charles made it clear that sacrifices would be necessary but also that the new approach was agreeable to God, and that Heaven would come to their help.[30]

Having a private school following the Quebec model was a challenge in Manitoba, and some Sisters thought that Mother St Viateur neglected to consider the uniqueness of the West. There was vocal opposition from outside as well but Mother St Viateur did not take it into consideration. The convent had debts, the parents had serious concerns, and of course the archbishop of Winnipeg, under whose authority the parish of St Charles was placed, was not pleased with the change. However, Inspector Roger Goulet, regarded by the Sisters as a long time friend of Langevin's, was recorded as saying, "Voilà un beau geste, il est digne d'une fille de Mgr Langevin [This is an honourable deed worthy of a daughter of Archbishop Langevin]"; he sent his daughter to St Charles Convent.[31]

The new program began in September 1920. Sister Marie-Joseph was sent to St Charles as directress (superior and principal) to implement the changes, which she personally did not support since they not only abandoned the Department of Education programs in favour of those of the Quebec convents but they also stressed the elementary level to the detriment of the secondary. As a consequence, St Charles lost a large number of students. However, Mother St Viateur did not have much interest in the high school level given her view that ensuring a good basic religious and French education was the right thing to do. She saw the high school program as a problem because the convent had to admit girls who were not French and Catholic in order to have enough student boarders to make the high school viable.

Sister Louis de France (Albina Laberge), who was the senior high school teacher and local assistant, was extremely disappointed with the decision because it would destroy everything she had tried to accomplish since 1911. Albina had gone to St Charles to teach school and had decided to stay and become a Sister mainly because she saw that the need to develop the high school corresponded with her aspirations to become a religious and educator. The attempt to pattern St Charles after the Quebec model failed. It had lasted three years. Sister Louis de

France, who strongly opposed the change, was involved in a long drawn out struggle with Mother St Viateur while trying to repair the damage done to St Charles's reputation and to reverse the trend of poor enrolment. Sister Louis de France's profile as a source of reasonableness, and her erstwhile disregard for rules became firmly established as part of the oral memory of the Congregation. She inspired a latent counterculture.

THE PRESENCE OF SISTER LOUIS DE FRANCE, THE POET

Sister Louis de France (Albina Laberge) first came to the community as a laywoman at age nineteen after finishing high school in Grafton, North Dakota, in 1910. Her sister Amanda, Sister Saint-Jean-Baptiste, was already at St Charles Convent. Without certification, Albina taught grades seven, eight, and nine that year with three grades in one room and ten to twelve students in each class. In an interview in 1993, she remembered that during her teaching years she did everything she could to make things interesting both in the classroom and outside. Her former American public school teachers were her models. When she decided to enter the community, her goal was to teach high school and to work towards improving the Sisters' education. She had a deep love of knowledge, which she actively pursued, and she believed strongly that education was a means to empower the Sisters. From very early, she worked hard with those who needed to pass examinations to complete high school and prepare for Normal School.[32] She took courses in chemistry with the Holy Names Sisters at St Joseph Academy in St Boniface, and later she studied at the University of Manitoba. After she obtained her BA from the University of Ottawa and her permanent professional teaching certificate, she lost interest in continuing her own formal education and instead chose to concentrate even more of her energies on helping the Sisters with their studies.

Sister Louis de France believed in the need to have a broad foundation of knowledge, including the classics and Latin, which she taught to the Sisters. Her views on what the Sisters needed to know sometimes contradicted their personal inclinations. Education was, in her view, the key to progress. Her concern with equalization and education as empowerment, especially for women, seems out of keeping with the Catholic church at that time. In 1925 she created the library for the young women doing the novitiate at the Maison-Chapelle. Later on in the 1940s she played a central role in reorganizing the Bureau des Études for the Congregation. As former superior general Jeanne Boucher said, "Louis de France thought that if we were going to be teachers and educators, we would have to be equipped for it. She had vision, that woman."[33]

Sister Louis de France was respected by the Sisters as a unique and wise woman with a tremendous moral authority, to whom the Sisters, including the superiors, went for advice and to whom they owed the push for education in the community. Her moral authority was not based on her obedience to rules but in her wisdom, her love of knowledge, and her empowering understanding of education. The Sisters called her the saviour of the community.

However, Sister Louis de France was to an important extent a deinstitutionalizer. She paid attention to the quality of life and chose to live, for periods of time, on the margins while remaining perhaps the most powerful leader in the community. The Sisters remember that from the early days following the rules was not Sister Louis de France's forte. She was rarely seen in the morning because she got up late and therefore often did not attend the community prayer. One of the Sisters recalled:

> We saw her at mealtime. She studied (and read magazines and journals) late at night and often she was not at mass in the morning. That was none of our business, eh. And later in the dining hall we would see her. Other than that she was always in her room studying, preparing classes, helping other Sisters probably. I know that before noon she would always have coffee in the kitchen. She enjoyed talking with Sister Marie Gertrude [the cook]. It seems to me I would see her around 10 am.[34]

Sister Louis de France responds by and large to the characterization of the poet of religious life as developed by Evelyn Woodward, as someone open to the nuances of life and to the movement of human spirit, able to illuminate what is seen as darkness and to disregard masks and pretentions.[35]

Religious life as conceived at the time posed a tremendous challenge to Sister Louis de France's liberal mind as she struggled to reconcile her ideals and make sense of her life in community. The letter she wrote to Mother Marie-Joseph in 1949 while she was seriously ill in the hospital reveals her inner crisis when confronting death and realizing that she had not always followed the rules. It also shows the compelling influence of a strictly regimented environment:

I have placed myself in the face of death many times these last few weeks, especially these last few days. I realize that if I were to start over there are many things that I would do differently and especially I would better use the graces and light that God lavishes on us in religious life. Mother, I regret in particular and I hope that you will forgive me my many failings in matters of poverty; for having spent more on house repairs than the sums allocated. It seems to me now that I spent too much money for prints of masterpieces to use in the classrooms. It was I believe $37.50. I covered the expense with the gift of $50 from Mr McDowell but this bothers me now.

Mother, I am happy for this occasion to thank you for your goodness on my behalf and also for what my community has given me for thirty-eight years. I regret not having served it better. I hope I do better in the future in particular to give a better example [to follow the rule] if God heals me.[36]

Sister Louis de France recovered and lived to be one hundred and two years of age.

Testimonies from the Sisters reveal Louis de France's wisdom in dealing with rules and penances. Elizabeth (Bessie) Donaldson-Maguet came to St Charles in 1926 as a boarding student even though she was from a Protestant family. She had vivid memories of Sister Louis de France's dealings with rules:

In the dormitory on Saturday night, we had a big sheet of tin on which the girls polished their shoes and Sister Louis de France was there and we were polishing our shoes and we were talking. We weren't supposed to talk in the dormitory. That was one of the places where it was complete silence. Sister Louis was talking too and Mother St Viateur came in like a storm and right in front of the girls she reprimanded her and I remember how Sister Louis did not say a word ... and I was ready to jump to her defence.

Another time we were preparing for Christmas and Sister Louis had allowed us to draw a Santa Claus on the blackboard, and Mother St Viateur was angry and she erased the Santa Claus, and didn't we know that Christmas was the feast of little Jesus and had nothing to do with Santa Claus. Little things like that, you know. I always remember Mother St Viateur as a strict disciplinarian, asking for obedience all the time and the rules were more important than the person in many cases, I felt.

As for Sister Louis, she was always ahead of the Sisters. She came from America. She had a completely different attitude. I think she was terribly kept in and held back. I don't know yet how she managed to carry on as she did and did the things she did. But she was a wonderful thing for the Oblate Sisters' order, a wonderful person.

So anyway we had study from 4:30 to 5:30 P.M. Everybody was in a big room and I remember at the beginning, well, I wasn't going to have anything to do with this "Catholic business, the papist business and the scarlet whore of Rome" and I had my King James Bible and after study, just before supper, I would always take it out and read a chapter. I remember once, Sister St Alfred was supervising the study and she saw me reading this and she came over and, oh, what a crime to be reading a Protestant Bible during the study! And she reported me. At that time Sister Louis de France was the Sister Directress. So I was reported to her and God bless her soul. My! She was a wonderful woman. She explained to me the difference and at that time we didn't read the Bible very much in the Church, you know. And she said it was very admirable of me to read the Word of Scripture and so on. But she said, "I have to punish you to satisfy Sister St Alfred." So she gave me a poem to memorize, or a verse of it.[37]

SPIRITUALITY, FATHER PÉALAPRA, AND THE CONSTITUTIONS

The spirituality of the Oblate Sisters was based on an ambivalent image of God as a powerful demanding God on the one hand, an image that was linked to legalism and rigidity, and on the other hand, as a tender, loving, and merciful God as strongly reflected in the gospel. The process of institutionalization was bound to reinforce obedience to rules as a means to attain a state of perfection, and therefore a static understanding of religious life. The Missionary Oblate Sisters worked closely with the Oblate Fathers whose missionary work in the North and West, so well analysed by Choquette, embodied the ultramontane conquering theology. The Oblate Fathers were a regiment doing battle to conquer the world for the Catholic faith. Obedience to the Church was at the core of the ultramontane thinking that saw the modern world as "the devil's playground."[38]

During this period, spirituality became more institutionalized and remained that way until the impact of Vatican II, when the loving and compassionate side of God's image emerged as a liberating force. The Sisters had understood obedience as a way to become a good religious and obedience to the superior remained for a long time equated with obedience to God. Marie-Anne Fillion, who entered the convent in

1943, illustrates the persistence of this understanding in the following comments: "To be a good religious, one had to be obedient to the Superior. The Superior had all the answers, and if I said 'no' to the Superior, I was not a good religious. Therefore I could not say 'no' ... If you obeyed your Superiors you obeyed God ... because I wanted to be a good religious. Today when I look at it, I would add, those are not my values anymore. This is no longer my way of living my religious life."[39]

Jansenism, although condemned by the Church, was never fully eradicated and continued to influence the behaviour of clerics and many Catholics from the seventeenth century on. It contained a disregard for freewill and a reliance on predestination along with a downplaying of personal responsibility and initiative. It was reflected not only in the image of a distant God who inspired fear but also in reliance on the rules to define spirituality. Jansenism permeated religious life in many Franco-Manitoban communities. Mother Marie-Joseph's memories of her first communion as a nine-year-old are revealing. She recalled in her later years: "In spite of all those celebrations, I did not enjoy it as I could have on that happy day ... I recognized later that a kind of Jansenism, inherited from some ancestors, had held me in the fear of God. The priest who had prepared us had caused this [fear] through the terrifying stories he told. I believe now in God's love for us and for me in particular, and all I desire is that this love grow more and more."[40]

As women, the superiors or other Sisters could not be spiritual directors. In line with the male-oriented structure of the Church, the director and confessor had to be a priest. For matters that dealt with the external aspects of their lives (the external forum), the novices were accountable to their directress, while the professed Sisters went to their superior. The rule required that this encounter, or "rendement de compte," take place in a relation of subordination every two weeks during the novitiate, and once a month thereafter. Kneeling was the external expression of this subordination. The Chapter of Faults, presided over by the superior, was a public accounting of minor external transgressions of the rules and the Sisters received a penalty or penance that was usually lenient, such as having to pray the "Our Father" with arms extended. The idea was to raise awareness, strengthen the will to strive for perfection, and develop humility.

Regarding the internal forum, that is, matters of conscience, the inner life and prayer, the Sisters, as a matter of fact, referred not to their superior but to the male spiritual director, or the confessor. The observances regarding both forums took a stronger tone after the enforcement of canon law in 1921.

Langevin had written the constitutions within the context of the dominant traditions but before the codification of canon law, therefore the early norms had a Western, pragmatic, and even historical flavour. The aims of the Congregation responded to what Langevin perceived as the urgent needs of his diocese, mainly the provision of Catholic education to children and young people, especially among the poor, and support to parish priests and missionaries, in particular the Oblate Fathers, in the vast western regions of Canada.

Father Louis Péalapra was appointed chaplain and confessor of the Oblate Sisters at the Maison-Chapelle in 1917, a post he held intermittently until the early 1940s. Many Sisters developed close ties with him as a spiritual director. From 1924 to 1927, in cooperation with the Congregation's council, he led the task of drafting the new constitutions according to the 1917 canon law.[41] Under his guidance and the influence of the new decree from Rome, the constitutions acquired a more formal and legalistic tone. The aims of the Congregation were restated in such a way that they appear to incline the vision of the Congregation towards an emphasis in support of the Oblate Fathers' missions with the Aboriginal Peoples: "To assist [*seconder*] the priests and missionaries in the evangelization of the poor of the missions and parishes through the devoted accomplishment of various works within their jurisdiction, and firstly, through education of the youth."[42] The Congregation's original mission to educate young people was restated in the second constitutions, but it lost the original connotation that had been coloured by the aftermath of the Manitoba school question. Instead, the emphasis was on evangelization of the poor, according to the Oblate Fathers' motto, "He has sent me to evangelize the poor" (Isaiah 6:1), thus reflecting a preoccupation with conversion of Aboriginal peoples. Sister Dora Tétreault concluded in 1996 that the second constitutions had altered the mission of the Oblate Sisters by subordinating their central role as educators of the young to the role of supporting the priests (the Oblates). Making the work of education the privileged way or means to help the priests and missionaries represented a subtle shift from the clear mandate of the first constitutions.

Tétreault also found that love of the Church and respect for the priesthood as an institution had also moved to first place among the recommended virtues in the 1931 constitutions, whereas in the early

Father Péalapra, chaplain of the Maison-Chapelle (1917–26 and 1936–44). Picture taken in 1938 in the Catholic Action office at 210 Masson. He preached retreats for young women from 1923 to 1943. He also helped the Sisters to revise their constitutions in the 1920s.

constitutions, "a spirit of faith, patience, humility and charity" were at the head of the list, followed by "a family spirit and zeal for the good of souls."[43] In the 1906 version, the rules regarding love of the Church and respect for the priests were expounded separately in the last section of first chapter.[44] The implications were wide-ranging. There was a shift from the original vision and mission and a loss of autonomy on the part of the Congregation. The 1931 constitutions eliminated the biblical quotations and New Testament references and the inspiring commentaries and teachings from Langevin and emphasized faithfulness to the Rule, obligations, and observances. Uniformity, not love, became the criterion for sanctification. Tétreault also argued that the womanly aspects of spirituality that were initially present, such as the virtues of mercy and compassion, were excluded in the second constitutions.[45]

The new constitutions were approved by the missionary Oblate community at an extraordinary General Chapter in 1929, by Archbishop Béliveau in 1930, and by Rome in 1948. The new constitutions (published in 1931) symbolized the end of a vision for the Congregation of the Oblate Sisters, such that the new configuration of power strengthened the connection between the work of the Sisters and the work of the Oblate Fathers. In part, the shift could have been motivated by

Péalapra with the first three generals superior in 1941. From left to right: Mother Marie-Joseph (1939–45); Mother St Viateur (1905–27); Mother François-Xavier (1927–39 and 1945–51).

changes in priorities and needs as anticipated by Langevin in 1906. The replacement in 1927 of Mother St Viateur, who was voted out of office, closed an important chapter in the life of the Congregation.[46]

Even as he was removed as chaplain by the Oblate provincial superior in 1926, Péalapra remained influential for almost thirty years in guiding the Oblate Sisters. After 1927 he continued to work closely with Mother Marie-Joseph, the first elected general superior. The provincial father, Josaphat Magnan, had advised Mother St Viateur verbally that the Sisters had been taking too much of Péalapra's time in regard to spiritual direction. Péalapra was at the time master of the Oblate Fathers' novices in St-Laurent, Manitoba, and was perceived as being absent too often from his post. In a letter of February 1926 to Mother St Viateur, Péalapra notified her of the provincial's decision to remove him from his duties as chaplain, though he was to remain the extraordinary confessor, performing this function four times a year. Péalapra quoted some paragraphs from the provincial's letter. One of them is puzzling: "I am grieved and I know that you will also be, but in view of the remarks and complaints I received, I have not deemed it possible to maintain you in the responsibility of chaplain of our Sisters, which responsibility, I must admit seems quite contrary to Canon Law."[47]

Péalapra asked the Sisters to pray and not to be saddened. He did not believe that the decision was God's will because of the work he still had

Father Péalapra and the boys of the Jardin de l'Enfance Langevin in 1921 on their annual picnic at St Charles along the Assiniboine River.

to do. For instance, the explanation of the Holy Rules (the new constitutions), the manual of prayers, and the directory, all had to be updated in line with the new canon law. He made it clear that he would continue with his ministry, but under new circumstances. In fact, that is what happened. He came periodically to work with the general council.

Beginning in September 1939, Péalapra gave monthly talks to the Sisters, commenting on the revised constitutions, up until his death in February 1944.[48] It is significant to note that under his direction, chastity was listed as the first of the three vows in the 1931 constitutions. Although he presented Jansenism to the Sisters as a heresy, his dualistic view of body and soul and his emphasis on mortification of the body had strong Jansenist overtones. He explained chastity in relation to the Latin word "castigare," meaning to "restrain, correct, discipline." In his words, "the human body has instincts of wild beasts. What must discipline it?" he asks, "It is the soul, whose task it is to tame it, to submit it (as a superior being to an inferior)."[49] The language of fear and temptation, the emphasis on distrust and being on one's guard towards any form of entertainment because "the promiscuity of people exerts certain animal magnetic action of one sex over the other," and the language of mortification obviously contained coercive elements. It was a way to induce coercion over the body, gestures, tastes, behaviour through the application of disciplinary techniques. Although the approach was not new, Péalapra's teachings, somewhat idiosyncratic in the use of metaphor, represented the way the Church used power at the time to create the religious subject, in this case, the female subject. These teachings were the traditional teachings as found in the catechism of the vows, which most religious congregations used in the novi-

Father Péalapra with the first five directors of novices, from left to right: Mother François-Xavier (1920–26); Mother Marie-Joseph (1905–13); Mother St Viateur (1913–20); Mother St Adélard (1927–33); Sister St-Dominique (1933–53). Picture taken in 1941.

tiate. The vow of obedience, which implied denial of self and suppression of desire (the will), and the notion of authority as coming from God were central to the ideal of the woman religious.

Péalapra distinguished between two types of authority that superiors have. One is the ecclesiastical authority that comes from being legitimately appointed by the Church. The second is the domestic authority to whom the inferior should obey. Péalapra stressed that God established the paternal (*sic*) or domestic authority over the whole household, including the mother's role. The superiors had to be obeyed even if the constitutions did not envisage the particular point in question.[50] As Langevin had done before him, Péalapra asked the Sisters to see God in their superiors. By submitting their will to the superior, they submitted their will to God.[51] The vow of poverty, by which the religious could not acquire or dispose of personal or community property without proper authorization by the rule or the superior, was closely linked to obedience and was meant to lead to poverty of spirit or detachment from anything, not only material, to which humans cling unduly. The practice of poverty was relevant to the spirit and mission of the Congregation and applied to all aspects of life. In theory all three vows were aimed at freeing the religious in order to attain the perfection of love of God and neighbour, but in practice people were often caught in legalism and they lost sight of the end for which they were intended.

The new canonical constitutions along with the teachings of Péalapra gave the Congregation new levels of rigidity that would last until the early 1960s; the humanizing aspects can only be found in little stories of transgressions and internal rebellions, and in experiences where the common sense and inner freedom of the local superior or individual Sister prevailed as a moral guide for personal decisions or behaviour. However, it was acknowledged by the authority of the Congregation that the immensity of the task in the missions and the closer contact with the outside world was bound to generate a more relaxed environment than at the mother house.

Particular friendships had always been censured; close friendships were threatening as they undermined the authority of the hierarchy and were seen as a potential source of sexual encounter. Friendships were also viewed as a selfish desire to hold to something of emotional value for the self. The second constitutions, in line with the canonical requirements, specified that particular friendships were prohibited. As happened in many congregations, the inability of the Sisters to share pain and open themselves to other Sisters generated pain and problems of communication. Péalapra when teaching the constitutions described particular friendships as "a seed of hell, a pest for a community; they unite two or more subjects by separating them from the others; they lead to sins against charity, humility, obedience ... and often end up with sins against chastity and the loss of vocation."[52]

Some Sisters were careful not to cultivate personal friendship. Other Sisters developed strong relations as part of their efforts to deal with the complexities of governance or with the challenges of missionary work. Mother St Viateur, as we saw, had worked closely with Sister Saint-Jean-Baptiste (Amanda Laberge), her general assistant since 1914. The Sisters recalled the pain Mother St Viateur experienced when, in 1924, Sister Saint-Jean-Baptiste died at the age of thirty-seven as a result of an anaesthetic error while undergoing an appendectomy. Mother St Viateur cried intensively and looked from the back door with incredible pain when Sister Saint-Jean-Baptiste's body was taken away for burial. She had once again lost a religious partner and friend (the first being Délia Tétreault, from whom she had been separated in 1904). After being replaced as general superior in 1927, Mother St Viateur shared her pain, albeit in a veiled manner, through correspondence with Sister St Charles (Edith Hennessy), also a strong woman in the community.

In general, the Sisters had a close spiritual relationship with Father Péalapra. They referred to him as their second father (the first being Langevin) and found in him motherly qualities. However, the Sisters' spirituality was constrained by the preoccupation with rules, and by an understanding of community that was based on external uniformity, with emphasis on observance of prescriptions regulating daily life and the practice of formal spiritual exercises. Certain practices, such as divesting oneself of small personal possessions and family pictures, which were kept in a common album, tended to erase personal tastes and freedoms. During her leadership, Mother St Viateur tried to assert her authority by appealing to the rules, which were not always observed. According to the analysis made by Dora Tétreault, the new constitutions, even before their approval in 1931, set the tone for "a greater stress on the letter of the obligations to fulfil rather than on the spirit to live by, with a resulting loss of emphasis on a living and life-giving spirituality. On the other hand, a careful rereading of those constitutions reveals a rather successful effort to clarify and hierarchize the concepts and constitutive elements of religious life as the new code required."[53]

By the time of the general chapter in 1927, it was clear that Mother St Viateur's leadership had come under question, although there was no clear understanding of the Oblate Fathers' influence on the identification of the aims of the Congregation at various points. The community distrusted her authority as a cofounder for it had been imposed by Langevin; furthermore, she had been "transplanted" (a term used in the narration of her move to Manitoba)[54] from Quebec, and so she had great difficulty understanding the uniqueness of the West. Many of the Sisters from the West and the American Sisters did not share Mother St Viateur's approach to or her views on education. In particular, those Sisters did not appreciate Mother St Viateur's emphasis on elementary Catholic education. A few Sisters, even some from Quebec, did not see Mother St Viateur as the legitimate authority. As noted earlier, they believed that Sister Marie-Joseph should have been first in the order of precedence since she had been a member of the community before Mother St Viateur. There was also a health issue, a loss of memory, that is not clearly documented but that apparently began to affect Mother St Viateur towards the end of her leadership and that became accentuated later on.[55] The first general chapter in 1927, in effect, was to open a new phase in the life of the young Congregation.

COMMANDEMENTS DE LA NOVICE

Aimante et dévouée tu te montreras,
Envers tous indistinctement.
À la chapelle tu ne dormiras,
Jamais, jamais impunément.
À la vaisselle toujours te rendras,
La première assidûment.
Ton ménage tu feras,
Tous les matins fidèlement.
Point de minous tu ne laisseras
Se promener impoliment.
Les escaliers tu monteras,
Marche par marche seulement.
L'eau chaude dans les plats ne mettras,
Jamais une heure auparavant.
Aucune traînerie sur ton passage ne laisseras,
A la cave particulièrement.
Des affaires des autres tu ne te mêleras,
Jamais, jamais étourdiment.
Tout cela tu le feras,
Par le Sacré Cœur uniquemment.

C.D. Conseils (pen name of a novice) *L'Écho* 3, no. 2 (April 1919).

IV

The Crisis, the First General Chapter of 1927, and the Extraordinary Chapter of 1929

THE GENERAL CHAPTER OF 1927

The code of canon law promulgated in 1917 mandated that the sisters hold their first General Chapter with representatives from the entire Congregation. As Marguerite Viau recalled in an interview held in 1994,[1] Archbishop Béliveau, Langevin's successor, found that it was time to have a chapter. Langevin had talked about it in 1914 but he had been too ill to press for it. Mother St Viateur's first circular letter, dated 25 July 1927, announced that the first General Chapter of the Congregation would open on 18 August 1927, in her words, "to elect a new general administration, keep religious discipline and the spirit of unity, correct abuses and impose faithful observance of the holy rules and constitutions."[2]

The circular provided instructions to the various houses regarding the procedure for selection of delegates to the chapter and its terms of reference. Membership would be constituted by: i) ex-officio delegates, who would include the members of the general administration and the directors of houses that had at least twelve professed sisters; ii) elected delegates; and iii) four appointed delegates, to be selected at large by the general superior on the basis of needs and expertise (article 292 of the constitutions). The procedure for electing delegates was as follows.

In houses with at least twelve professed Sisters, one sister with perpetual vows, other than the director, would be elected delegate. Houses with fewer than twelve Sisters would be grouped to a total of at least twelve professed Sisters to elect one of the directors of these houses and one other Sister as delegates.

If an elected delegate could not attend, the first runner up would take her place. The chapter would elect a new general administration, receive and discuss various reports, deal with issues pertaining to the chapter, and in particular, examine the new constitutions.[3]

In a brief report presented at the General Chapter, Mother St Viateur gave an account of the work of the community. The total number of professed Sisters during the twenty-two years between 1904 and 1927 was 129, fifteen of whom were deceased (and eleven of whom had left the community). In 1927 there were fifty-seven choir Sisters, forty-eight of whom had made their perpetual vows, and thirty auxiliary Sisters, twenty-three of whom had also made perpetual vows.

The report provided statistical information on the houses by order of foundation:

i) Maison-Chapelle (the mother house) in St Boniface, "the cradle of the Congregation," housed twenty-seven professed Sisters, twelve novices, and four postulants.

ii) The Convent of Our Lady of the Sacred Heart (St Charles Convent), founded in 1906 in St Charles, Manitoba, was a private boarding school for girls and day school for students of both sexes (until 1909 a few boys were enrolled as boarders). The convent housed fourteen Sisters. Since the opening, 1,266 students had attended school. In 1906 the school had started with seventy-seven students and for the academic year 1926-27 it had 146 students.

iii) Le Jardin de l'Enfance Langevin opened in St Boniface in 1909. From the Jardin's opening date to June 1927, a period of eighteen years, 1,122 boarders and 230 day students had been registered.

iv) The Mission in Cross Lake, Manitoba, accepted in 1909, transferred to Norway House in 1910, and returned to Cross Lake in 1914, was an "Indian Residential School." There were ten Sisters, and approximately 303 boys and girls had attended since its foundation.

v) St Joseph's Convent in Fannystelle, Manitoba, opened in 1911, had six Sisters, four of them teaching at the public school administered by a local school board. From 1911 to 1927, 402 students were enrolled, of whom sixty-three were boarders and sixty-one non-Catholics.

vi) Nativity Convent founded in 1912 in Dunrea, Manitoba, housed four Sisters who taught at the parish school where 227 students had enrolled, of whom eighty were boarders.

vii) Fort Alexander Indian Residential School (1914) had nine Sisters and 131 students, fifty-nine boys and seventy-two girls.

viii) Le Jardin de l'Enfance of Giffard, Quebec, founded in 1921, had eight Sisters and 144 students.

ix) Assumption Parochial School of Transcona, Manitoba (which opened in 1924) had four Sisters; 186 boys and girls had enrolled since the school opened and 250 public school students had attended catechism classes given by the Sisters on Sundays.

x) The Indian Residential School of McIntosh, Ontario, accepted in 1925, had five Sisters and sixty-eight students, thirty-eight girls and thirty boys. The report stated that twenty-two of those students, "heathen or protestant" had been baptized.

xi) Parochial day and boarding school of Stoneham, Quebec, founded in 1925, had five Sisters.[4]

Mother St Viateur did not report on the work of the Sisters in St Philippe, 1910–13, at Fort Pelley, Saskatchewan, diocese of Regina, where the Oblate Fathers ran a residential school. Neither did she mention Gravelbourg, Saskatchewan, where the Sisters had performed domestic work at Collège Mathieu from 1919 to 1921, before they opened Le Jardin de l'Enfance Notre-Dame du Rosaire, nor Otterburne, Manitoba, where they had worked from 1915 to 1920.

Often in conjunction with the Oblate Fathers' own objectives, Mother St Viateur expanded the community's work in new directions, such as the establishment of elementary schools and a Jardin de l'Enfance in Quebec, and another in Saskatchewan. However, the missionary work with the Aboriginal People, in an auxiliary (subordinate) role to the Oblate Fathers, had already become an important component of the life of the Congregation. Langevin had initiated that process although he had not conceived of it as central to the mission.

Mother St Viateur's report went on to say that the Sisters in general fulfilled their assigned work with much zeal. In most missions they had received expressions of satisfaction and praise from the Oblate Fathers, parish priests, and parents of the students, for which they should be thankful to God. For it was through faith-filled behaviour and fidelity to the observance of the Holy Rule that the Sisters would obtain His (*sic*) favours (in order to continue the mission entrusted to them). Within this context, Mother St Viateur referred to infractions to the rules, in her words, "abuses," that she had observed in a few of the houses. Among them were: i) lack of regular observance of the daily timetable, especially when hours of work were extended to late evening to the detriment of the Sisters' health; ii) failing to observe the vow of poverty (article 487 of the constitutions) such as when Sisters wasted electricity or water, were careless with clothes and other items, or made changes in equipment without proper authorization; iii) in certain places, flawed obedience as manifested in comments, critical remarks about the superior's words and actions – disobedience that led to a lack of respect for the authority in charge; iv) the failure to observe silence: Sisters talking everywhere, even on regular premises and during strictly decreed hours of silence; v) lack of mutual forbearance regarding minor personal flaws; and vi) failure to help with housework (lack of charity). On the other hand, the Sisters had given proof of tremendous virtuous generosity, she concluded, and she expected the weaknesses to be remedied. The transgressions, which also revealed tensions and unhappiness, as expressed in oral memories, were construed by Mother St Viateur as abuses.

The General Chapter elected a new superior, Sister Marie-Joseph (Alma Laurendeau, a Manitoban) who, like Mother St Viateur, had a close spiritual relationship with Father Péalapra. The newly elected general superior sent a letter to her sister, Marie-Anne Laurendeau, a Grey Nun, hinting at the tensions that preceded and accompanied the change of superior and implying her own reluctance to talk about these internal matters to her sister. The letter reads: "I see that at Ste-Anne the news arrived through the regular channel. However, the last events [the General Chapter and Mother Marie-Joseph's election as successor to Mother St Viateur] that took place in our house were themselves brought about by the course of events and were not destined to shake the country. I was not in a hurry to make the results known."[5]

The acts of the chapter recommended corrections to all abuses mentioned by Mother St Viateur.[6] Order and trust in the leadership needed to be restored. They also included detailed interpretations, discussed and agreed upon, of expressions and of entire articles of the new constitutions, the writing of which were left to Father Péalapra, OMI. It seems evident from the document that the rules reached every aspect and every moment of a Sister's life and regulated even further a Sister's relation to her family and friends. The Sisters were expected to convey the idea that they preferred not to receive visitors at all.[7] Well into 1928, the general council devoted a large part of its meetings to regulating details of daily life and delimiting potential transgressions (abuses). The new regulations dealt with the time to get up during holidays,

First General Chapter of the Missionary Oblate Sisters, August 1927. The elected delegates with the new general administration (seated) from left to right, front row are: Sister Louis de France, general councillor; Sister François-Xavier, general assistant; Mother Marie-Joseph, the new general superior; Mother St Viateur and Sister Agnes-Emilie (Mabel Ramsey, a Métis from Ste-Amélie, Manitoba), new general counsellors. Picture taken by a professional photographer.

permissions to take a nap after hours, the number of presents to give the superior on the occasion of her patron saint's feast day, titles to use when addressing the authorities, observance of silence, and supplementary recreation, among other items. The Congregation moved to a strongly regulated life in line with the developing new constitutions and the new canon law, amidst a climate of dissatisfaction and even dissension that had characterized the years prior to the General Chapter.[8]

The crisis of leadership had developed during the 1920s on various grounds. The constitutions (drafted between 1924 and 1927, discussed at the 1927 chapter, approved by a special chapter in 1929 and by the archbishop in 1930) set the stage for an important change of direction in the life of the Congregation. The constitutional changes led by Father Péalapra during the 1920s redirected the vision of the Congregation and virtually subordinated it to the Oblate Fathers'. It also set the basis for a different kind of leadership. Mother St Viateur's attempts to generate a vision grounded in Langevin's legacy did not work or were curtailed. The Congregation had already started to develop its profile, in tune with the Oblate Fathers' vision and other diocesan projects, and within that framework, to search for the characteristics that distinguished this particular religious family.

The failure of the school changes at St Charles Convent, with their aim of shaping it after a Quebec convent, had further accentuated discontent among western and American Sisters. Mother Marie-Joseph had had a difficult time as Directress of St Charles Convent when the new program was implemented. She had opposed the proposed changes but later had the unpleasant task of carrying them out. Meanwhile, Sister Louis de France, who had strongly questioned the move, emerged strong from the failure. Her wisdom, transgressions of the rules, and her vision of education as a way to empower the Sisters nourished a counterculture with dissenting overtones. There had been in the community a growing sense that Mother St Viateur was aloof, not only from the vigorous internal and external opposition to her project in St Charles but also from the social and political developments in Manitoba.

The context had changed at various levels. Although there was a national institutional network sustaining the French Canadian national project, there was a sense of difference based on the history of the various communities and regional conditions across western Canada. Manitoba was developing its own solution. After Langevin's death, his successor, Archbishop Béliveau, would not fight to regain religious and language rights in the way Langevin had done, but he urged the clergy to support parents, trustees, and teachers to secure a Catholic and French education within the system. He had told them, the Sisters said, "If you want French, it's up to you to have French in the schools."[9] Encouraged by this new self-reliant directive, the lay leaders of the francophone community marshalled their resources and launched l'Association d'Éducation des Canadiens-Français du Manitoba. Since its inception in 1916 the association worked towards the development of a parallel educational system for francophones. It provided a sophisticated infrastructure for the modus vivendi that had existed, in school districts heavily populated by Franco-Manitobans, where the Church played a powerful role. The Oblate Sisters and the Sisters of the Holy Names of Jesus and Mary, among other congregations, collaborated with the association in various ways although the Holy Names Sisters seemed to have been more directly involved, especially regarding high school education.

Very early in her leadership, the new general superior, Mother Marie-Joseph, a Manitoban, built a connection with Langevin's vision and the work of the association. She wrote:

With regard to French, we would not be the worthy daughters of our venerated Founder, Archbishop Langevin, if we did not put our whole heart and [use] all our means to teach French in our houses. A favourable occasion to show our devotedness to the cause is to prepare the children the best we can for the exams of the Association d'Éducation, at least for the houses that are not exempt for reasons deemed good by the competent authority.

Every year for the past three years, we have been asked for a series of questions to use for the exams. In spite of the additional work which this requires from us, just like the task of marking the papers, I consider the fact as an honour for our young Congregation and an occasion to collaborate to the work that is, so to speak, our raison d'être as a community.[10]

A FEW WORDS ABOUT MARIE-JOSEPH

The change of leadership in the Congregation was the result of a slow process of dissatisfaction nourished by a model of community in which the role of Mother St Viateur had been defined by Langevin's vision and rooted in his paternal benevolence. The long resistance from Mother St Viateur, and her occasional desire for autonomy had been mere nuances colouring Langevin's role as the father of the community, and as the source of knowledge and authority. The Oblate Sisters were his Sisters, his dear daughters. After his death, Mother St Viateur furthered institutionalization and tried to build upon her own vision and what she interpreted as Langevin's inspiration, within new constraints set by the Oblate Fathers' needs and desires.

The crisis of leadership had also to do with uneasy feelings with the internal structure established by Langevin, in particular the division of the Sisters into choir and auxiliary Sisters. Mother St Viateur's attachment to rules had created a rigidity that invited small transgressions and generated a tense environment. She had suppressed her pain and early resistance and cultivated a zeal for obedience, in her words, "the master of all virtues." The new constitutions reinforced that approach to obedience and the observance of the rules. The Sisters also tried to have a voice in the organization of the Community, although in 1929 they voted for and carried out the changes in their new constitutions, without much understanding of the consequences.

In the eyes of some Sisters, the source of Mother St Viateur's authority had derived from Langevin's personal trust in her. It did not rest on the legitimate choice of the membership as expressed through election. Langevin's last circular letter[11] (written in September 1914 on the tenth anniversary of the Congregation, and less than a year before his death) dealt with several important matters, including part two of the first constitutions on the governance of the Congregation; confirmation of the "supreme authority of the Most Reverend Mother St Viateur and naming her (officially) the first General Superior"; the nomination of Sister Saint-Jean-Baptiste (who was held in high regard by all the Sisters) as general assistant; and creation of a formal order of precedence that recognized that "since Reverend Sister Marie-Joseph du Sacré-Coeur took part in the founding of the community and that she was the first assistant and the first novice directress, she will have first place at Maison-Chapelle after the Most Reverend Mother St Viateur." Sending Sister Marie-Joseph as directress and principal of the new mission in Pembina, North Dakota, while she was still on the council seemed to have been the Founder's way of reducing the friction arising from diverging views between the two and of quelling the partisanship among the Sisters.

Péalapra's influence in helping to stabilize the community after Langevin's death should not be underestimated. Péalapra was close to the Sisters, who trusted and loved him. He was close to both Mother St Viateur and to Sister Marie-Joseph. It is clear that he was not only aware of the internal crisis but that he also advised both Sisters. The Sisters saw him as filling Langevin's role. Sister Marie-Joseph's letters to him in the early 1920s indicate that she construed his participation in the life of the community in a spiritual way more than as an advisor in internal matters of governance. In 1921 she had asked Péalapra to be her spiritual director.[12] In her 1920 Christmas letter she had thanked him for his solicitude for the Congregation, comparing it to that of the Founder.[13] In her view, Péalapra interceded with God through Langevin on behalf of the Congregation the latter had founded.

After the General Chapter of 1927, Mother St Viateur was assigned to St Charles as directress, or local superior. Previously the positions of superior and principal were held by the same person. Sister Louis de France, who was to remain as school principal, had to step down as local superior to accommodate the decision from the general council, a decision that proved to be counterproductive. Mother St Viateur took her disappointment to St Charles, even though she seemed happy to return to her first mission. To compound matters, there was some confusion regarding roles. Mother St Viateur interfered in school matters. Sister Louis de France had been the principal for a long time and was

Mother St Viateur, enjoying a moment of relaxation by the riverbank, summer 1928.

knowledgeable in educational matters. The tensions between the two Sisters were discreetly hinted at in letters and kept alive in the Sisters' memories. Mother St Viateur expressed her pain when writing to Sister St Charles who was working in Fort Alexander at the time: "What shall I say about St Charles? Should I admit that the spirit which reigns in the house gives me a certain cause to fear? You have lived here long enough to understand what I mean. All what I wish, my dear Sister, and which I beg you to grant me is the help of your good prayers as well as those of your Sisters and your children, so that God ... may come to my assistance."[14]

Mother St Viateur experienced profound hurt and sadness for some time. She had felt extremely tired for years and complained in her letters in 1929 and 1930 that she was too old for her sixty years of age.[15] The conflict dragged for a long time. She mentioned in one of her letters written in May 1929 that since August there had been seven different cooks, a true procession of Sisters at St Charles Convent.[16] The great depression of the early thirties also reduced to an all time low the number of boarders whose fees were the main source of revenue. This had a disastrous effect on the school, which could barely survive, and so added another source of pressure on the Sisters.

Mother Marie-Joseph confided in Father Péalapra, her spiritual director. In a letter written to him shortly after the 1927 chapter, she refers to Sister St Charles, a friend and a confidant of Mother St Viateur, who was stationed in Fort Alexander: "About Fort Alexander Sister St Charles is not saying anything that is much good. She seems distraught and at the end of her means; she seems to me not yet recovered from the painful impression produced by the late events [the results of the chapter]. God be her helper! Again this is all that I can do."[17]

In the same letter she refers to the pervasive uneasiness at St Charles Convent and the problems with Mother St Viateur. The tone of the letter gives a feeling of an ongoing conversation on the matter with Father Péalapra: "As she used to do here, Mother St Viateur wants to see to every detail and disapproves of everything that is being done, so much so that the Sisters would be disposed to band together to defend their former Directress. I do not believe that things can carry on for long this way. From what I hear Mother St Viateur has already threatened to come back here (to the Maison-Chapelle). So then what should I do!"[18]

The situation was difficult for both Mother St Viateur and Mother Marie-Joseph. Mother Marie-Joseph was very explicit about her feelings in her letters to Péalapra, who seemed to be receptive to her words. She wrote in November 1927 while Mother St Viateur was away visiting the houses at her request: "I hear that the sun is slow to shine at St Charles in spite of the absence of the one who seemed to darken its rays. The latter is enjoying her trip as though it was a delightful dream from which one is afraid to awaken too suddenly. The rest that she is taking should renew her completely, but after that, what next? ... So many problems to solve!!"[19]

The crisis of leadership had been profound and it had lasting effects that became evident much later, in 1931. In the summer of that year, the implementation of changes in the organization of the Mother House by Mother Marie-Joseph, mainly the separation of the Jardin Langevin and the Maison Chapelle in two communities, generated resistance and disarray.[20] In July 1931, just before leaving Manitoba where he had spent six weeks, Henri Bernard (priest and friend of the community) wrote a letter to Father Péalapra, OMI, to whose care he entrusted the Sisters. He thanked him for the paternal affection he had for "nos petites Soeurs à nous deux" and the important services he delivered with affection and tact. He saw Péalapra as continuing Langevin's work with the Sisters as their present father even as Péalapra had been removed as official chaplain of the Congregation. This trust, although within the context of the passing crisis, contradicted Bernard's former expressed views on the undue influence of the clergy on the Congregation. Indeed, Péalapra had been instrumental in shifting the mission of the Congregation towards the Oblate Fathers. This time, Bernard was concerned with the internal upheaval. He went on to say:

I am absolutely persuaded that all, all of them from the first to the last are inspired with the best dispositions, the best goodwill and ardent desire to work for the glory of God and the general welfare of the Community. What they lack, for the time being, as the community leaves its childhood and its inevitable period of adolescent guardianship, is to know where to stand so as not to step on one another's toes. They have to learn how to use their freedom, to have a better understanding of their constitutions, the rights and duties of each category (the superiors and the membership). For this they need your wise counsel, which is the fruit of your experience and prudence. I count on your dedication and your charity to continue the work of their Founder. Courage, then and always![21]

The tone of the letter and the words chosen reflect the perceived immaturity of the Sisters as a cause of the internal crisis, rather than a complex process to which the Oblate Fathers themselves were not alien. The lack of theological background and the extreme dependency on the clergy became evident in the aftermath of the crisis. Bernard also wrote to the community on that occasion. He asked the Sisters, whom he addressed as "mes chères enfants," "mes chères petites soeurs," to pray to Mgr Langevin, to develop a devotion for their saintly Founder, to sing His name (God's praise) at all times.[22] He wished them to pray to Langevin to intercede with God for them. Bernard asked the Sisters to love one another, to support and help one another. He continued:

You have to expect this, you must prepare yourselves, you will be tossed about, shaken just like a young man, a young woman of 18. It's in the order of things. You will have like them the inner storm, now that you have passed the childhood crisis. Beware, be on your guard for everything will be broadcast from the rooftops. Avoid dissentions, help one another, support one another. I beg you, pray to Archbishop Langevin, love one another, help one another, support one another, be ready.[23]

The rules, following the revised constitutions, when interpreted literally, tended to become more stringent and pervasive than before, aiming to penetrate and direct the Sisters' consciousness. However, Sister Marie-Joseph was not moulded into the leadership role as Mother St Viateur had been by Langevin. She had a very different temperament and character and was less pragmatic than her predecessor. Mother Marie-Joseph needed to rely more on other Sisters and was inclined to share authority more easily, and as a result the relationship between the general superior and the local superiors changed considerably. Her correspondence with them had a warm tone. She affectionately addressed them as "mes grandes (soeurs)," and considered them more like collaborators than subordinates. Her style of governance was not rigid. She was more inclined to laissez-faire. Sisters recall her as very human, yet she could be firm when necessary.

After her appointment, Mother Marie-Joseph visited the different houses and explained the preliminary version of the new constitutions, including the interpretation of articles and expressions used. It was necessary, however, to hold a special general chapter in July 1929 to approve the final draft of the constitutions, which took into consideration the remarks of the bishops from the other dioceses where the Sisters worked.[24] The agenda for the chapter also included the question of the two categories of Sister, the choir Sisters and the auxiliary Sisters. Mother Marie-Joseph referred to the opinion of reliable priests and bishops who considered that having two categories of Sister was not desirable in a small congregation like the Oblates. She also referred to the nature of the work, the spirit of the population that was being served, and the social milieux from which candidates came as reasons to consider abolishing the categories. These divisions had been more or less imposed by the Founder as a way to favour studies for the teaching (choir) Sisters by releasing them from much of the manual work, which would be performed by the auxiliary Sisters (the less well educated).

Other items on the agenda of this special chapter had to do with the contemplative aspects of the Sisters' life, finding ways to generate balance between their prayer and their work, "finding the way to do the work that should be done without leaving aside the prescribed spiritual exercises."[25] Many of these items would form part of the directory and the *coutumier*.[26]

The extraordinary chapter of 1929 approved the new constitutions and eliminated the two classes of Sister. These were fundamental changes in the life of the Congregation because they set new parameters to the spirit of the Congregation and to the characteristics that would distinguish this religious family.[27] Mother Marie-Joseph named those characteristics: the inner life of faith, simplicity, and dignity.[28] Father Péalapra developed the theme of the inner life of faith. Mother Marie-Joseph elaborated on simplicity and dignity. The Oblates, in her words, were "des soeurs à tout faire" (Sisters that were ready to do anything that needed to be done). She tried to find a middle ground between presumption and narrow-mindedness ("étroitesse d'esprit"). "Dignity is not arrogance but justice that respects and commands respect for the sacred gift (dépot) that God has entrusted to us."[29] However, it was not until 1996 that the Congregation, informed by Sister Dora Tétreault's research on the constitutions, realized that their central role as educators had been subordinated to the role of supporting the Oblate Fathers' mission.

LA CHANSON DU JARDIN

(Hommage à notre saint Fondateur)
O Monseigneur! Gloire à toi dans les cieux,
Reçois les chants de tes enfants joyeux.
Bénis ce Jardin de l'Enfance,
Où grandit notre foi,
Où l'Hostie donne la vaillance,
Où Jésus-Christ est Roi!
Enfants jaloux de ta couronne,
Nous nous donnons à Jésus comme toi!

O notre Père! Noble et vaillant soldat!
Toujours ton nom nous excite au combat.
Jadis tu disais de nos Pères les glorieux exploits,
Tu retrempais nos caractères
Aux accents de ta voix!
Et tous unis en petits frères,
Nous proclamions notre langue et nos droits!
Et maintenant ton clairon a sonné,
Et le réveil a surgi spontané
Ton drapeau sans peur ni faiblesse
Vole aux nobles conflits;
Il entraîne notre jeunesse
Aux devoirs accomplis!
Et sur tes pas, pleins d'allégresse
Nous marcherons sous ses glorieux plis.

Amicus Parvulos (Friend of the Children – a novice's pen name)
L'Écho 1, no. 5 (1916)

V

Experiencing Apostolic Life

ENTRANCE IN THE COMMUNITY AND LIFE CYCLE

The foundation of the Congregation of the Missionary Oblate Sisters was not the result of a mystical experience but a response to needs that Archbishop Adélard Langevin had identified, especially with reference to the Manitoba school question. The uniqueness of the prairies, most particularly the historical, ethnocultural, and socioeconomic conditions in Manitoba (including its changing demographic reality), gave the work of the mission a special connotation. There was a clear understanding that the Oblate Sisters were not meant for the upper classes, and the Congregation did not place emphasis on the dowry as some other congregations did.

With few exceptions, the majority of Missionary Oblate Sisters came from French Canadian communities in Manitoba, Quebec, Saskatchewan, and Ontario, though some came from French Canadian families that had moved to the United States (see appendix A, Table 1). The Congregation enjoyed a steady growth in membership from 1904 up until 1964, after which time the rate of new membership declined. By 2004 the total number of Sisters who had taken vows in the Congregation reached 396 (see appendix A, Table 2). Approximately thirty-four percent of the total number were from Quebec. Throughout its history, the main cause of attrition has been the death of a Sister, or a

First retreat organized at the school by the Sisters for young women in St-Sauveur, Quebec, on Ash Wednesday, 1920. Five of these young women became Oblate Sisters.

Sister's decision to leave the Congregation, whether after taking temporary vows or after final vows (appendix A, Table 2). In the early years, few Sisters left after taking temporary or final vows, though after 1964 a greater proportion of Sisters who had taken final vows left the Congregation. Initially, the majority of candidates came from Quebec. However, over time the percentage of candidates from that province who took vows declined steadily. The percentage of candidates from Quebec ranged as high as 66.7 percent for the period from 1904 to 1915, to a low of 17.3 percent from 1940 to 1951, to no candidates from Quebec between 1964 and 1994 (appendix A, Table 3). Much of the total membership of the Congregation originated from rural village areas, so it is not surprising that farming was consistently listed as the father's occupation (appendix A, Table 4).

In the early years, Mother St Viateur travelled to Montreal in search of candidates with the help of Henri Bernard and Langevin's friends. By 1919 the foundations in Quebec provided a permanent base from which to identify vocations. Mother St Viateur was a careful recruiter and she did not hesitate to reject candidates that had been put forward

St Charles elementary classroom students. Picture taken by a professional photographer in April 1909.

by the clergy. Meanwhile, St Charles Convent (a girls' boarding school) had become a source for membership in the new congregation. In 1908 Henri Bernard suggested the creation of the juniorists, a designation to be given to high school students, particularly boarders, who were considering becoming Sisters. The juniorists were adolescent girls, fourteen to eighteen years old, who followed special regulations and met with the director of juniorists who taught them about prayer and religious life. After completing grade 11 or 12, several of these girls went to the Maison-Chapelle to become postulants. The juniorate existed until the late 1930s. The process of deciding whether or not to enter the community was always coloured for those students by the characteristics of Catholic family life on the prairies, and the influence of the Church. Sister Germaine Cinq-Mars described the process that led to her decision to become a Sister:

I had a big sister [Léontine], Sister Saint-Luc who was a religious. When she left (in 1912) I was five years old. She had gone to see Father Jolys (the parish priest in St Pierre). She was going to get married but had changed her mind during a retreat at the Oblate Sisters' (Maison-Chapelle). And so she entered the Oblate Sisters. After that the time came for her to take the holy habit (to become a novice). It was evening and Archbishop Langevin was there. The next day there was a Mass and I went and made my first communion. After the Mass, he came to the parlour with my parents. My father and mother were both there. Monseigneur Langevin sat me on his knees and asked me what I myself would do.

And you know ... I had seen my sister so I certainly was going to become a Sister too. So I told him I would become a Sister. That always stayed with me. He traced a large sign of the cross on my forehead. I continued to grow up and go to school. I went to St Charles as a boarder in 1914. I was eight years old.[1]

Others made the decision after attending a retreat at St Charles. The retreats had begun in 1923 and they attracted young women from Franco-Manitoban communities. For some of these young women it was a way to find a place in life within the context of a close-knit French Catholic community where the women's role was circumscribed. A large number entered as a result of efforts at recruitment in Quebec. At times, Archbishop Langevin personally brought young women from Montreal directly to St Charles to become juniorists.[2]

The narratives show that the imagery of Sisterhood and the lives of saints strongly attracted young women. Sister Annie Trohak, a Hungarian who spoke English and made French her daily language in the Congregation, entered in 1916 when she was fifteen. She was inspired by the example of St Theresa of the Child Jesus, who had to ask the pope for permission to enter the Carmelite Order at the age of fifteen. Annie went to her parish priest who said, "I'll give you permission if your parents are willing." She replied, "Yes, they are willing."[3] Most of these girls admired the nuns and their garb. The mystical aura emanating from the habit and its flowing movements was a sign of separation from the world. Many of the prospective Sisters had admired a particular Sister for her demeanour in school, in chapel, or in other situations.[4] Sister Gisèle d'Amour attended mass at the Maison-Chapelle when she was a child and she "loved very much to see Sister Marie-Estelle, a Métis from St-Laurent, playing the organ."[5] Another Sister, Marie-Anne Fillion, recalled, "The first thing I saw was the photograph of my [two] great aunts who were my grandmother's sisters. I saw their photos and I said to myself, 'It's a Sister like that, that I want to be.'"[6] For outsiders, the habit was an inspiring, mysterious component of religious life but for insiders, it had a formative ascetical function for the body and the soul, which was far from being romantic.

The missions were also part of the imagery, often with exotic overtones and conquering language; young Catholic women were eager to be part of the missionary contingent to save souls. Raised in a French Canadian cultural environment or in Quebec, for them the French Canadian cause was their cause as well as that of the Congregation. There were very few Sisters who were not of French-Canadian origin.

Out of the 396 Sisters who took vows between 1904 and 1994, eleven had Polish or Hungarian as their first language; they also spoke English and learned French in the community (Table 4). Sister Annie Trohak was one of the Hungarians who upon entering in 1919 did not know French. During her postulate and novitiate, the directress taught Sister Annie and gave her a small dictionary, which she kept in one of her big pockets. From time to time she would open the dictionary, then try to make up a sentence. The process was somewhat dramatic as she was wont to use phrases facetiously, knowing of course that the novices would welcome the occasion to laugh at her incongruous translations. Annie described one such humorous incident to Sister Dora Tétreault. Annie was in the refectory with another Sister, Germaine Lord, from Quebec, who would eat after the others because she was in charge of answering the doorbell during the meal. After eating she washed her dishes while Annie was cleaning the tables. Annie said to her in English, "Please leave your dishes in the water, I will wash them for you. When I finish washing the tables, I will empty the dishpan." Sister Germaine did not understand. Annie then tried French, "Alors, j'ai dit, 'ma soeur, quand je me vide, je vous viderai.'" ("So I said, 'Sister, when I empty myself, I will empty you'"). Germaine had a good laugh and left the dishes in the pan.[7]

Novices from Quebec often did not speak English. They were sometimes sent to St Charles Convent, for eight months on one occasion in 1910, to learn the language while doing student supervision during the study periods and in the dormitories. There were daily communications by telephone (installed in 1908) and frequent visits to and from the novitiate in Maison-Chapelle. Archbishop Langevin visited St Charles regularly, although not as often as the novices would have desired, and gave them talks on religious life.[8] The candidates were postulants for six months; the postulate (from the Latin word *postulare*, which means to ask) was a preliminary period of gradual initiation to religious life. Thereafter the postulants took the habit as novices and began their formal religious training. After two years they took temporary vows and were sent to the missions for five years; at the end of that time they made their final profession of vows. The general superior assigned the Sisters to the various missions according to the perceived needs of both the houses and the Sisters. There was rarely any consultation and assignments were known as obediences. Normally novices stayed in the novitiate at the mother house during the two years before their temporary vows, but some were sent for a stage in

This picture was taken in front of the church before a group of postulants from Quebec left for Manitoba in July 1920. Retreats, which the Oblate Sisters started in St-Sauveur in 1919, were instrumental in recruiting members.

the missions if it was felt necessary to test their aptitude and vocation. However, increasing needs in the small community sometimes forced the superior to send some novices to work in the missions to relieve a temporary shortage of Sisters due to illness or other circumstances.

In the oral history of the early Sisters, memories of the novitiate are sketchy and rarely detailed. The novitiate provided religious formation. Some Sisters found it hard and strict, and they still remember that the community was poor and that food was scarce. Others, like Sister Annie, did not find it so hard but she found Mother St Viateur too strict in her attempt to instill perfection in the novices. From 1911 to 1921 Mother St Viateur was both general superior and officially directress of novices, while Sister François-de-Sales was acting directress and as such spent more time with the novices. On Fridays Mother St Viateur came to preside at the Chapter of Faults. Annie recalls that she always found fault with one thing or another. "She would have me climb the stairs (again) because I went down too fast. Then when I was up, she would tell me, 'Ma petite fille, descendez lentement maintenant' (come down slowly now)."[9]

The Maison-Chapelle provided the cultural and physical space that complemented the building of the novices' identity as women religious living in community. Each postulant was given an "angel," a senior

Weekend retreat at the school in St-Sauveur, Quebec. Retreat master in the centre is Father Joseph Guy, OMI. The retreatants wore the symbolic white tulle veil on the day of their initiation into the sodality of Mary. Notice the picture of Archbishop Langevin on the wall above the chalkboard.

Postulants and novices from Quebec. The picture was taken in 1921 to send home to their parents.

The new chapel at the Maison-Chapelle, in 1911. Two Sisters are kneeling in prayer during their hour of adoration before the blessed Sacrament of the Eucharist, which was exposed daily on the altar. They are wearing white tulle veils over their black veils. The lilies on the altar, hand-made by the Sisters, are part of the Easter decoration. Picture taken by a photographer.

novice as a companion to initiate her into the little practices and routines of life in the novitiate, a peer to whom she could go for help and advice. This served at the beginning to create a sense of connectedness with the group and sometimes a lasting bond of friendship between the two, even though particular friendships were strongly discouraged by the rules. The practice of short invocations to Jesus and Mary on the hour was aimed at developing a spirit of prayer and intercession for the world. Framed holy pictures and spiritual mottos hanging on the walls were also a reminder and invitation to cultivate a sense of the presence of God. The daily schedule of the novitiate was rarely interrupted and periods of prayer and silence were more strictly adhered to than in the missions.

The physical environment also played a part in the religious and ascetic formation of candidates. The lower pane of the windows was translucent to allow sunlight through and ensure privacy while shutting out the world of distractions. The frosty effect was obtained by dabbing white enamel paint thinly and evenly all across the pane with a ball of cotton wrapped in a thin cloth. A paper monogram of Mary or the emblem of the Sacred Heart of Jesus was placed in the middle of the window pane before applying the enamel, so that when removed they were "etched" on the panes. This also helped give the building a

Front view of the Bilingual Normal School, built in 1902 as part of the Laurier-Greenway reparations; closed in 1916, it was purchased in 1923 by the Missionary Oblate Sisters. That same year the Jardin de l'Enfance was transferred from the Maison-Chapelle to this building, which continued by extension to be called Maison-Chapelle, although its official name was Jardin de l'Enfance Langevin. Picture taken by a professional photographer.

"sacred character." In the early days all the interior walls of the house were whitewashed periodically. The bare wooden floors were scrubbed regularly and oiled once a year. Tidiness and cleanliness were instilled as important means to create a peaceful, wholesome atmosphere and an inner climate leading to the higher virtues and holiness. The outdoor path shaded by rows of maple and elm trees led to a Lourdes grotto and stone benches where the novices could go and spend the noon recess in the summertime. Going outdoors for at least fifteen minutes each day to get fresh air and exercise was mandatory throughout the year. Hanging clothes on the line and weeding the garden were two-in-one tasks that fulfilled the obligation.[10]

The novitiate set the basis for obedience as regulated by the constitutions and the directory and became more and more formalized with time. Eva Dégagné, a Sister who had been a juniorist in St Charles and entered immediately after completing grade 10 left a testimony of the negative aspects of her days in the novitiate between 1913 and 1916 at the Maison-Chapelle.[11]

Novices and postulants from Maison-Chapelle at a picnic in St Charles in 1910. This was one of the few outings the Sisters and novices had. It was a great annual event.

Sister Eva pointed out that all the letters the novices received and all those they wrote were opened and read by the directress. In Eva's view this created a barrier between the novice and her family. The frugal meals were served by a Sister from the end of each table. When the novices were given too much, they had to eat it; when they did not get enough it was embarrassing to ask for more. They never had fresh fruit and when a family sent some, it was reserved for the priest who had breakfast at the Maison-Chapelle after the mass. When the novices received candies or chocolate, they were kept and shared at a community feast. Sometimes other personal presents were also kept. The snack in the afternoon was also frugal and, during the war years, 1914–18 was accompanied by cold water because it was too expensive to boil water. Except for the directress and the superior, the novices shared common dormitories, which were locked all day. The key could be obtained only under special circumstances.

Sister Eva also recalled that the biweekly "rendement de compte" was the "point névralgique" or *bête noire* for all.[12] During the "rendement" the novices had to kneel until the directress invited them to sit down. They could not cross their legs, nor were they supposed to look outside the window "à la belle nature"; to do so showed a lack of self-discipline and was a distraction from their task of inner recollection. When a novice took the habit, she had to set aside her personal possessions such as "medals, chains, even a little thimble received as a present." Eva continued, "Unbelievable, but the corsets were done away with!" The novices had to keep silence (at breakfast) in the refectory except on Sundays and festive holidays. During recreation time in the evening, everyone had to do some work with their hands, such as sewing, mending, or knitting. The community was poor and Mother St Viateur was extremely severe in matters of poverty; nothing escaped her attention, broken dishes, burnt linen, wasteful use of water or electricity.[13]

Sister Eva wrote that talents were not cultivated. "It was blind obedience!" According to her, many young women left because of that; there was great richness among them that could have been useful for a Congregation in its beginning years. She also mentioned that candidates who were not willing to teach but were capable of other work such as caring for the sick, had to accept the placement (obedience). Therefore, Sisters with little preparation or experience had to take care of the sick.[14] This testimony is in line with other recollections. However, Sister Eva's experience was compounded by a deep wound resulting from a painful rift between her family and the Church over the obligation of parents to send their children to a distant Catholic school rather than to the nearby public school.[15]

In 1917 the novices created *L'Echo*,[16] an internal handwritten magazine presented quarterly to Mother St Viateur, to keep her informed of their activities. It was a work of art and a labour of love that revealed a refreshing sense of simplicity and spontaneity and showed a search for balance within the bounds of the rules. In other words, the magazine offered a creative outlet that alleviated some of the Sisters' existential hardships. *L'Echo* is a testimony to their calligraphic skills, artistic inclination, sense of humour, and poetic bent. The poetry, which separates the chapters of this book, embodied the novices' aesthetic sense of religious life, albeit with some mischievous undertones that showed how the Sisters could negotiate their felt experiences in the context of the strict foundational core principles of their formation. During the war years, the novices offered their prayers for peace, expressed their love for France (la mère patrie), and prayed for the children in France.[17]

Obediences were the assignments (places and tasks) given annually to each Sister by the general superior in consultation with her council. This was done each summer at the end of the annual retreat. Some Sisters stayed a long time in the same convent while others moved more often depending on what was needed. Changes in assignments had to be made at times, as in cases of illness or other circumstances. In such cases, the Sister herself was seldom advised ahead of time about her

Left: Early Artwork of the Sisters: *L'Écho du Noviciat*, 1917–20, the novices' journal, which they presented quarterly to Mother St Viateur, was a work of art that gives a glimpse into their life. Right: The novices' ink artwork and poetry recorded in their journal *L'Écho du Noviciat*, 1917–20.

Left and right: The novices' ink artwork and poetry recorded in their journal *L'Écho du Noviciat*, 1917–20.

new assignment and often she had to prepare in a hurry. Sister Annie Trohak was sent to St Charles in 1923 after completing her novitiate. She relates the peculiar way she learned about her new destination:

Mother St Viateur was sending me to St Charles in the middle of the year and I didn't know about it. In the evening I came (to my cell) and all my clothing was gone from my dresser. How could that be? I went to the wardrobe and my dress was gone. The next morning, as I was not too shy with Sister Saint Jean-Baptiste [Amanda Laberge, General Assistant], I went to see her and asked, "How come? Last night, I came and all my clothing was gone from my dresser". Quite surprised, she said to me: "Didn't Mother Saint Viateur tell you anything?" I replied, "No!" "You are going to leave for St Charles." Then she added, "When she tells you, just pretend that you don't know. She was supposed to tell you. She forgot."[18]

The Sisters were assigned to the missions where they lived and worked. These postings were annual but were usually renewed for a number of years. In some cases, having acquired expertise and being very successful in her work, a Sister practically made her career in one place; such is the case with Sister Louis de France who remained at St Charles as a secondary school teacher and principal for many years, as well as several other Sisters whom she had helped prepare and specialize to teach in the high school.

As noted earlier, the Congregation had two classes of Sisters, auxiliary and choir Sisters. The auxiliary Sisters provided the support system, especially in the boarding schools, for the work of teaching that was carried out by the choir Sisters. The life of auxiliary Sisters was not easy. The division was eliminated at the General Chapter in 1929. In practice this elimination did not make a great change, although it had an emotional and psychological effect on many of the auxiliary Sisters. Sister Zélia Auger (Sister St-Donat) knew she was going to be an auxiliary Sister because she had entered with a grade 8. She first went to the missions after completing her novitiate in 1929, the same year that the two classes of Sisters were eliminated. She could not remember how she felt; to her it did not make much difference. What's more, even before the change everyone shared to a point in the household chores. She recalled, however, that Father Josaphat Magnan, the Oblate provincial, came to talk to the novices as he did occasionally, but this time he addressed the issue of the two classes of Sisters. He made an interesting argument:

As for us men, we understand the necessity of having [auxiliary] brothers because for those who want to become religious but do not have the required health or aptitude to study in order to become priests, well, they can still become religious, and belong to the community and participate in the prayers but not do [priestly] ministry. Now, for the Sisters, it's not the same. There is no reason to have two classes of Sisters.[19]

In other words, none of the Sisters could minister, thus subdivisions of Sisters were unnecessary. The novices became aware of the impending change when all the new habits made for the novices who were going to take their vows had the wide sleeves on their dresses (a former distinction of the choir Sisters' habits). According to Zélia, those novices who were to become auxiliary Sisters thought, "It's coming! We will all be in the same class of Sisters among ourselves."[20] The Sisters were happy with the new arrangement. Zélia also recalled that when she worked with the Sisters of Jesus and Mary of Sillery in Gravelbourg, Sakatchewan, she had observed before entering that in other communities that had two classes of Sisters, the auxiliary Sisters were separate from the choir Sisters. The written sources do not refer to the status of the auxiliary Sisters in the Oblate community, but from the interviews it is evident that they did manual work only and did not sit at the same table with the choir Sisters; moreover, there were two lists of "order of profession" numbers used to identify each Sister's belongings, the auxiliaries having an "A" before their number. Otherwise they all prayed together and shared the same community room and dormitory. There was also a difference in the ability to participate in the business of the Congregation, for the auxiliary Sisters could not participate in the General Chapter or in governance in general. The dress was the same except for the width of the sleeves and length of the skirt, narrower sleeves and shorter dresses being more convenient for manual work.[21] In 1927 there were thirty auxiliary Sisters, twenty-three of whom had perpetual vows, and seventy-five choir Sisters, forty-eight of whom had perpetual vows. In other words, 28.5 percent of the Sisters were auxiliaries.

Historian Marta Danylewycz argued that convents provided women with a choice and an attractive alternative to marriage and motherhood or spinsterhood. Convents opened the possibility of exercising leadership and influence or of escaping the fate of their mothers.[22] While this may have been the case for the choir Sisters, the convent did not provide the auxiliary Sisters with an alternative life to that of their hard-working

Hand-made adornment of the altar at Maison-Chapelle, Easter 1919. Notice the backdrop of the altar: the royal mantle of the Sacred Heart of Jesus, surmounted by a crown.

mothers, women who often raised ten to twelve children on the farm. Although the pursuit of spirituality in a communal living environment did set the auxiliary Sisters' experience apart from that of their mothers, they worked as hard for the mission as their mothers had worked on the farm. Sister Zélia Auger, who entered the convent in 1926, shared in a memory circle memories about her work after the novitiate:

Z: I went to St Charles. I was with Sister Marie-Gertrude in the kitchen.
R: Lots of work?
Z: Yeah! specially because we did not have all what they have in the kitchen now. We did all by hand. This was a boarding school (in St Charles), Sister Marie-Gertrude was in charge and I was just a helper then.
R: At what time did you wake up and at what time did you go to bed?
Z: In St Charles, I woke up at five o'clock and we went to bed at nine o'clock. We followed the bell.
R: What did you do from five until breakfast?
Z: We had to go to chapel to do our meditation, and our prayers after mass. After that we went down for breakfast. After breakfast we started to work.
R: Did you have to prepare breakfast also?
L: Yes, this is why we had to go to the kitchen between morning prayer and the mass.

Z: We made the coffee. When I was on the farm I woke up early to send the children to school. My life didn't change that much after I entered.
D: After breakfast you went back to the kitchen?
Z: Of course! We worked all morning to prepare dinner (the noon meal). After dinner we washed dishes and then it was the particular examen (a spiritual exercise in the chapel). We'd go back to the chapel to say the prayers. At half past one, we had the "lecture."
D: That was the spiritual reading (in common for half an hour). At two o'clock you went back to the kitchen?
Z: Yes, first to prepare the afternoon lunch (snack and coffee break) and then to start our supper.
D: Did you have to peel the potatoes?
Z: At first we had to peel the potatoes by hand but later [in the 1950s] we had a machine.
D: Did you get help from the girls [the boarders]?
Z: Not much, not much ... After the meals they came to help to wipe the dishes but after that the students had to be in school. It was just the boarders who helped.[23]

The auxiliary Sisters had physical work to do but they also had to comply with the numerous rules that disciplined the body and the mind. They were even taught to do manual work in a certain way and at a certain time.

The choir Sisters, as explained earlier, were teachers, although few of them were certified. Some had completed grade 10 or 11, even grade 12, before entering. Many taught without a permit and without the benefit of Normal School. Sisters who did not have certification had to wait their turn to obtain a credential from a Normal School as they were needed in the classroom and there were few resources to pay for their continuing education. Several, including Sister St Viateur, exchanged a Quebec diploma for a teaching certificate from the Manitoba Department of Education. The agreement meant that the Sister was required to follow summer-school courses in agriculture at the bilingual Normal School in St Boniface. Once such courses had been completed, the Manitoba second-class certificate became permanent.[24]

Sister Louis de France helped many Sisters upgrade their academic records, in some cases from grade 9 up. She prepared many, particularly those from Quebec, for the departmental exams. Some of these Sisters were in their forties and a few in their fifties when they attended Normal School, after much nudging and encouragement from Sister Louis de France. In principle, after 1929 all the Sisters could aspire to

Grotto of Our Lady of Lourdes on the grounds at Maison-Chapelle, designed and built by Sister Marie-Immaculée (Cecile Leclecq from Minneapolis, Minnesota).

Christmas crib in papier-maché made by Sister Marie-Immaculée.

Bilingual Normal School built in 1902 at the corner of Masson and Aulneau, St Boniface. The picture shows Sisters attending an agricultural summer course in 1911. The Oblate Sisters are shown wearing a white collar or "guimpe" and a veil with a flat headpiece. The other Sisters were Grey Nuns, Sisters of the Saviour, Holy Names Sisters, Sisters of Our Lady of the Missions, and Daughters of the Cross. Inspector Adrien Potvin is lecturing.

further their education, although Mother Marie-Joseph (who had replaced Mother St Viateur) did not place great emphasis on diplomas until the late 1940s.

TEACHING: "A MINISTRY OF ANGELS"[25]

In their early days, the Missionary Oblate Sisters did not have extensive formal education. However, they cultivated a desire to put into practice the ideals of Catholic education as explained to them by Archbishop Langevin. He often instructed them not only on educational aims but also on pedagogical matters such as child development and teaching. Chapter 5 of the first constitutions (1906), written by Langevin, reads, "It is said that teaching is a ministry of angels because the divine messengers are in charge of bringing to men the light of eternal truth. To

Bilingual Normal School, agricultural course. Student teachers were taught how to make vegetable gardens. The building in the background is the Maison-Chapelle. Picture taken in 1911.

teach children is to imitate Jesus himself. Each child is a moral and social source which will have its influence in the world."[26] Therefore the Sisters should teach children with great care. Religious teaching could only be done under the authority of the Church for only the Church could provide the true sense of the sacred texts.[27]

Visiting priests gave the Sisters lectures on education and the role of women religious as teachers. One of them was Father Beauregard, parish priest of St Charles from 1921 to 1923. He contended that "by working for the Church at forming saints, the religious teacher would prepare excellent citizens, faithful wives, mothers and daughters who would be for families a sweet consolation and a beautiful ornament."[28] The Sisters should aspire to be catechists, the role of teacher being subordinate, because it was the heart and the soul that they wanted to reach. The core of the argument was that the Sisters, having freely and entirely dedicate themselves to God, had received as a special gift of grace a way of being that permeated their discourses and actions.

In the same way that vigilance (*surveillance*) was central to the making of a religious, Beauregard saw it as a condition for education. He made reference to demons that as rapacious birds would devastate the house of education if the sentinels fell asleep. Beauregard referred in this way to worldly ideas that opposed Christian ways. But teaching Sisters had to exercise vigilance over their passions and distractions, and that demanded devotion and obedience. The uncontested authority of the teacher religious would be rooted in her own respect towards her superiors, whom she would blindly obey in whatever she was asked,

Wedding scapulars made by Sister Marie-Estelle (Véronique Chartrand), who had previously entered a religious congregation in France where she had learned to develop her artistic talent in a variety of art forms.

Below: Close-up of a brocade medallion of the Virgin Mary painted on silk appliqué embroidered with metallic thread, done by Sister St Veronica (Géraldine Nolin) circa 1921.

as well as in her daily reflection (self-study) in order to learn to behave and talk as the repository of divine authority.[29]

The Sisters developed their own understanding of teaching. At times, their understanding – as manifest in journals, narrations, oral histories, and obituaries – seemed to be at odds with the Church's views and the priests' lectures in an almost intrusive way. On the death of Sister Saint-Jean-Baptiste in 1924, the Sisters wrote: "Like our revered Founder, with whom she shared more than one character resemblance, it is to the children that her gifts of intelligence and tenderness went. Her profound sense of motherhood led her to watch constantly over their conduct, their health, their studies, games, etc. And occasionally these young ones who were thus privileged would not spare her their tributes of affection and filial trust."[30]

The internal manuscript journal written by the students at St Charles Convent between September 1911 and October 1913 not only confirms

Bilingual Normal School classroom. The school closed in 1916 when the new Manitoba Public School Act abolished the right to teach French in elementary schools. Picture taken in 1911.

Bilingual Normal School, agricultural course. Sisters taking notes are wearing their full garb on a hot summer day. Summer 1911.

that portrait of Sister Saint-Jean-Baptiste, who was directress at St Charles from 1910 to 1915, but also opens a window into the life in the classroom at the high-school level. There was political passion over the French Canadian issue and the French class sometimes relocated to the cafeteria to debate the issues separating Montrealers and Manitobans. The journal reveals a very caring relation between the students and the Sisters, in particular Sister Saint-Jean-Baptiste.[31] The Sisters tended to teach in the way they were taught. While most had attended public or convent schools in Franco-Manitoban communities, the Quebecers had for the most part attended convent schools. Those from other provinces, who were a minority, had similar experiences to the Manitoban Sisters. The Americans, like Sister Saint-Jean-Baptiste and her sister, Sister Louis de France, although of French Canadian and Catholic origin, had attended public schools and had been taught by Protestant teachers. The emphasis on sharing experiences (in lieu of formal professional development) was important, for many of the Sisters lacked sufficient professional preparation.

In August of 1921, the Sisters inaugurated a pedagogical conference after the annual retreat as a means to explore ways of teaching. Sisters shared their experiences with regard to teaching methods and problem solving. At the 1921 conference, for example, one of the Sisters showed how she taught reading to grade 1 students using a phonetic method. She explained that the phonetic method could be combined with the syllabic to enhance reading and spelling simultaneously. Select topics presented by the Sisters included reading for the intermediate classes, lesson preparation, review, calculation for beginners, arithmetic for intermediate grades, methods for teaching decimals, French and English composition, and catechism.[32]

The Sisters' school work was certainly influenced by the Association d'Éducation des Canadiens-Français du Manitoba, an organization that was created in 1916, with headquarters in St Boniface. Its mandate was to protect the interests of French Catholics in Manitoba. Although there was a national institutional network, the Société Saint-Jean-Baptiste, to support the French Canadian national project, there was a sense of difference based on the various communities' history and regional conditions. For their guidance, as was the case with all similar institutions sustaining the French Canadian project, the association drew upon ultramontane tenets that had gained dominance in the Catholic church worldwide and upon the Québécois agriculturalist ideologies. The ultramontane influence on the Church in the prairies was reflected in the promotion of religious renewal through private and public devotions, such as the devotion to the Blessed Sacrament, thus making the parish priest central to religious life and school life. These shared and individual practices generated a sense of community identity as well as a strong personal experiential bond with the supernatural.[33]

Furthermore, Franco-Manitobans felt themselves to be the victims of injustice. A strong desire for recognition and action, channelled through the association, took the form of a collective challenge to the Manitoba Department of Education. Language and faith and attachment to tradition were central elements of identity; in the Manitoba curriculum French was treated as another "foreign" language, which strengthened the belief that the French were far from being partners in Confederation.[34] The influence of Franco-Manitobans and the Catholic church on school life, particularly in francophone rural areas, was facilitated by the fact that the administrative structure of public education in Manitoba was based on small school districts that could exert local control. As late as 1945 (and in fact until consolidation in the 1960s) there were 1,875 school districts with 2,098 school buildings and 1,450 one-room schools.[35] The trustees controlled almost all aspects of school administration including the hiring and firing of teachers, and in Catholic districts they worked with the priests, who had tremendous power in the community, to ensure that language and religion were not neglected.

The Oblate Sisters and other congregations collaborated with the association in various ways. The Programmes de l'Association (later on programmes d'études françaises) were created in 1922. Many schools that were run by the Sisters used programs or initiatives developed by the association. The public school in Fannystelle, the parochial schools in Dunrea and Transcona, as well as the Congregation's private schools such as St Charles Convent and the Jardin de l'Enfance Langevin all undertook programs created by the association. For example, a French program with accompanying books, annual competitive exams (*concours de français*), the hiring of competent teachers, and the creation of the inspectorate (*visiteurs d'écoles* as in the Québécois tradition) was applied widely.[36] In practice, the program worked as a parallel curriculum with reference to French and to the values inculcated in the schools, while the history of Canada as dictated by the department was taught in French instead of in English in the elementary grades. The *visiteurs d'écoles* ensured the implementation of the program. At the same time, Franco-Manitobans and the association were not opposed to their children being fluent in English. The association encouraged teachers to teach the official curriculum along with their program. This was certainly contrary to Mother St Viateur's failed project at St Charles (1920–23), which provided a Quebec program. Religion was a central part of both the overt and the hidden curriculum in public, parochial, and private Catholic schools although religious teaching took place early in the morning or after the non-Catholic students were dismissed at 3:30 P.M.

The Church, school, community, official curriculum, and parallel curriculum generated in the children a sense of being French Canadian. Their identity developed within the overlapping parameters set by the state and the Church. The point of reference was the claim to the right to teach and learn French and to practise the Catholic faith in the schools.[37] The *Bulletin des Institutrices* (1924), published in St Boniface by the Ligue des Institutrices Catholiques de l'Ouest, was the means to provide curricular and pedagogical information, and to maintain contact with the teachers from one French convention to the other, which took place following the English conventions during Easter week. *La Liberté*, the French weekly founded by the Oblate Fathers in 1913, also played an important role in education among Franco-Manitobans. It published the list of schools and marks of students that participated in the *concours de français*. It also contained many articles and news concerning education and life in Franco-Manitoban communities, as well as reports of the *soirées* of the Association d'Éducation, which were held locally approximately once a month on Sunday evenings.[38]

THE MISSION IN WINNIPEG

St Charles Convent, Notre-Dame du Sacré-Coeur

The Convent of Notre-Dame du Sacré-Coeur was located in St Charles, a village that is now part of Winnipeg. St Charles was opened in 1906 to provide education and boarding facilities for girls in the St Charles parish, which had a mainly French speaking population. This was a primary and secondary school. Until 1909 it included a Jardin de l'Enfance, an elementary boarding school and day school for boys. It has been the most representative and durable contribution of the Oblate Sisters to French and Catholic education in Manitoba. In 1962, after a new wing was built, the school was renamed St Charles Academy at a time when lay involvement gained prominence.

A view of the ferry and St Charles Convent from the south shore of the Assiniboine. Notice the windmill on the right behind the convent. Picture taken circa 1910.

Langevin, who was anxious to open a school in St Charles parish where he perceived a serious need, authorized the building of the convent, which was entrusted to the Oblate Sisters and which became the Congregation's first foundation. The Oblate Fathers of Manitoba transferred to the Roman Catholic Archdiocesan Corporation of St Boniface the land requested for St Charles Convent. This property, located across the road from the new church, was bounded on the south by the Assiniboine River, on the west by St Charles Street, on the north by Augier Avenue, and on the east by the lane adjoining the property of Mr Buchanan, which later became the Glendale Golf Course. Langevin also authorized the expenditure of $13,500 to cover building, heating, and lighting systems. It is interesting that in 1906 he thought it would be possible to have the St Charles Public School transferred to the convent. In that case, the trustees would have paid salary and rent sufficient for the Sisters to make payments on the interest and capital of the debt.[39] The transfer never materialized. The Sisters had to pay the interest on a $3,400 loan that the diocese had borrowed from outside sources.

Langevin wrote in his letter of September 1907 that religion was the first reason for the Sisters to open this private school: "The programs should be the same as those in public schools. But since English is the only language taught in those schools, we must make the necessary

The feast of St John the Baptist, at St Charles convent, 24 June 1909. The shy-looking little boy on the right portrays John the Baptist as a child, wearing a fleece and sandals, and holding a cross. The lamb is a symbol of Christ, the Lamb of God. On the left, the girl with wings represents Gabriel, the archangel.

modifications so as to allot the time for teaching French grammar, composition, spelling and literature. You must teach the students religious hymns and national hymns."[40] Langevin asked that "The Maple Leaf Forever," "Nearer My God to Thee," "Vive le peuple canadien," "God Save the King," and "L'ombre s'étend sur la terre" (an evening hymn to Mary) be taught and sung at school.[41]

Langevin wanted the Sisters to have certificates or at least teaching permits. He thought that Sister St Viateur, who had a teaching certificate from a model school in Montreal, was sufficiently prepared to teach with the help of the other two Sisters assigned to St Charles; beyond that, it was in God's hands. God would send her capable Sisters. "After all," Langevin said, "you will be doing this work for God, not for vanity's sake or fame, nor for purely human knowledge."[42]

The school, which had both boarders and day students, was a private school. Boarding and tuition fees were set at six dollars per month and music lessons at three dollars; a dollar was requested for laundry and mending, and an additional dollar per month for bedding. If there were two children from the same family, prices were reduced. At the request of the parish, boarders could be admitted with little or no charge

Convent boarders at St Charles convent. Picture taken by a professional photographer at end of the school year 1922–23. Note the black dresses and stockings worn on Sundays. The ribbons and medals were part of the system of incentives and rewards.

under special circumstances. Parents had to pay in advance. Parents of day students who were able to pay were asked for a monthly contribution. Archbishop Langevin instructed the Sisters to be accommodating "without yielding too much," particularly with families that had several children in the school. St Charles school did not ask for money from children of poor families. Langevin wanted to have a large number of day pupils whether or not it brought financial benefit.[43] In 1906, seventy-seven students (both boarders and day pupils) were enrolled. In 1927, the year of the first General Chapter, the enrolment had increased to 146.[44]

Langevin made clear that the goal of the convent was not to receive young girls from outside of the area, especially if they were already attending a Catholic school or a convent, but to give preference to those girls in the parish who were poor. Until 1909 boys who needed to be accommodated as boarders to attend a Catholic school were accepted.[45] There were no uniforms at St Charles. On Sundays and special occasions the boarders wore black dresses that did not have to be of a uniform pattern, and black stockings. Sister Louis de France (Albina Laberge) recalls that in the early days the children attending the school came from

Piano students posing for a picture taken by a photographer after their music exam in 1913, at St Charles convent. On the right one can see Sister St Alfred's framed diploma from the University of Montreal.

Sister Marie-du-St-Esprit (Antoinette Caron from St Charles parish) is seen standing by her mother. Picture taken in 1918 while stopping to see her family who lived across the road from the St Charles convent.

Sister Saint-Jean-Baptiste (Amanda Laberge) holds a bag of crab apples, a gift from Mr Buchanan, a neighbour, and Sister Rose-de-Lima carries a bowl of popcorn, a treat for the girls. Fall of 1914.

St Charles parish; they were mostly French-speaking Catholics, although there were some English Catholics. She remembered the Métis children who were poor and could not pay. They came from a little settlement known as Le Faible, which was situated upstream, along the Assiniboine River. "They kept apart from the French and were looked down upon by them. They were a class in themselves. They did not mix at the social level but at the school they were all together."[46]

The "Journal du Couvent St-Charles" starts in 1911. The entries, sometimes only a few lines, tells of a life structured by routine work, visits, and special activities. There were lots of picnics in the woods with the students and particular celebrations such as the Fourth of July to honour the two American Sisters, Sister St-Jean-Baptiste and Sister Louis de France. Mother St Viateur, as recorded in the journal, did not miss an opportunity to prepare natural medicines such as ginger wine to be included in the medicine cabinet. Langevin often visited the convent, interacted with the children, and distributed pictures of saints. He took distinguished visitors, such as Bishop Charlebois from northern Manitoba, to the convent for supper. The concerts and student presentations were colourfully depicted in the journal. Religious festivities were very important in the lives of both the Sisters and the children.[47]

Sister Louise de France eating lunch with the primary school girls in the grove by the river, 1925.

St Charles provided Sister Saint-Jean-Baptiste, local superior from 1910 to 1914, with a space to express her love of life. In the case of Sister Louis de France, who was local superior at various times, St Charles embodied her intellectual inclinations and spiritual vision. The classroom became a very special world for many Sisters. The journal kept by the students at St Charles for the years 1911 to 1913 provides some insights. A student wrote on Saturday, 13 April 1911: "At three o'clock the French Canadian students had a meeting in the classroom and created a literary club. We call this club, 'Cercle littéraire Saint-Jean-Baptiste'. Its motto will be 'duty first'. The honorary president is Sister

Statue of Notre-Dame de Pellevoisin erected in the garden at St Charles, circa 1911. Each year on 31 May, the senior girls celebrated the Crowning of Mary with garlands of flowers. Picture taken in 1937.

Saint-Jean-Baptiste ... Let us love our language. Let us be French Canadians."[48] The journal was written by enthusiastic students with a strong commitment to the French Canadian cause. Some entries are eloquent:

At 2:00 p.m. the six students of the French class go to the small refectory, where after the lesson, a hot discussion begins between the girls from Montreal and those from Manitoba. Patriotism sparks from both sides and the fire is strong in both camps, and it is fun to hear the quick rebuttals that follow each other gracefully and rapidly, as wit is also present with the ones as well as the others. After this, we go back upstairs for more serious work.[49]

Constance Franzmann, a non-Catholic boarder taking grade 11 in St Charles in 1925 (ten years after Langevin's death), recalled episodes of her school life there:

Upon dismissal at noon we had to line up to go to the washroom – in silence – and we went in, one or two at a time. Then we walked in line to the refectory for the noon meal. This was a large room in the basement furnished with long

Young women from St Boniface, at St Charles for the first retreat preached by Father Péalapra in June 1923. Five of these became Oblate Sisters. Retreats were hosted each year until 1937, after the students left for the summer holidays.

tables covered with oil-cloth and wooden benches on either side. We all had to stand for the blessing, then the nun in charge dinged a bell and we all sat down. Another ding and we pulled out a little drawer in front of us and took out our table napkin which was rolled in a napkin ring, our cutlery, and a small pat of butter or spread in a little dish. The food was passed from the kitchen through an opening [a wicket] in the wall, and brought to the tables by girls who were designated for that purpose. Another girl arranged slices of bread on trays and brought them around.

Older girls sat at each end of the tables and acted as servers, being careful to see that each one received a fair share. The meals were very plain, but they must have been nourishing because many of us managed to put on a few more pounds. After the meal, basins of water were brought around and the cutlery and small things were washed at the table. Then to the dinging of the bell we were dismissed in reverse order … When the weather permitted we had to go outside at noon, otherwise we went to the recreation room in the basement. Some days we were taken for walks – two by two – in an orderly manner accompanied by a nun …

On Sundays we were all marched two by two to the local church, but weekdays we all had to attend mass in the chapel. I soon learned to say some

Sister Léonard-de-Port-Maurice (Marie-Ange Béchard) with the junior high girls at St Charles convent. The Saturday afternoon walk came to a halt when one of the girls caught sight of a snake in the grass. Picture taken in 1925.

of the prayers in French but the nuns never tried to impose their religious views upon me.[50]

In a letter home dated 16 April 1925, Constance describes a concert at St Charles which was put on twice, once for the mother superior, and the second time for the public: "In the last scene of our English play, 'The Emperor's Slave', the stage is all draped in red. This is where the Emperor stabs his slave who is a young girl, and gets ready to kill two more people when the curtain is drawn. –Not the usual convent entertainment, I would think!"

In another letter Constance wrote about the retreat:

November 1925. It has been very quiet here during the latter part of the week because of the retreat. On Thursday, Friday, and Saturday, we all had to keep silence except when talk was necessary. We did not have any classes or music, but read books and sewed and went to the chapel six times daily. I am anxious to get down to work again. I also mentioned the nuns putting on a whist drive for us with the girls playing piano solos for entertainment and having candy for refreshments. So it wasn't all work and no play.

Constance Franzmann did not regret her year at St Charles, but "it was not altogether an easy one." Sister Louis de France was the principal in 1925. Constance describes her as a "soft-spoken nun with kind brown eyes and a high colour in her cheeks."[51]

There are testimonies of the continuity of the initial commitment to accept children of poor families, even as boarders, even if they were not able to pay. One of these testimonies is from Elizabeth (Bessie) Donaldson, a Protestant girl who had remained in Scotland with her father, who had been blinded by melting steel and who was not allowed to enter Canada, while her mother moved to Winnipeg with other siblings to escape poverty. When her father died, her mother sent her the money to join the family:

I arrived here in Winnipeg at 12 years of age. I was twelve in May and I arrived in August 1924. I think I was a rather difficult child. Mother had to work to support me and she had to find a place for me to stay. I think I was in and out of various homes. I can tell you about many experiences of that. But anyway, she lost her position at that particular time and went back to her old trade of midwifery. She was one of the first graduates of the school of midwifery in Glasgow, Scotland. So she was called to a place on Lipton Street. I remember the number, 849. There was a Catholic family and they already had nine children; my mother helped to deliver the last baby. It did not have a very long life. Anyway, my mother was sharing her sadness that I wouldn't behave and that I was in that place and so on. So finally Mrs McDonald said to her: "Why don't you put her in the convent?" We were not Catholics, you know. My father was an Orangeman; he was a ragged anti-Catholic. I mean he felt he was doing God's work to harass the Catholics. We were never allowed to walk on the street if there was a nun or a priest. We had to cross on the other side. My father had attended the famous Orange Day Parade on the 12 of July and all that. So that was just terrible when it was suggested to me that I get put in a convent. So, mother went to St Mary's Academy. And of course, she was just a simple poor woman and she was earning her living by cooking at that particular time. The Superior said: 'Well, Mrs Donaldson, I don't think that this is the right school for your daughter because it is for more wealthy people and so on. Why don't you just try St Charles Convent.' So that was the first that we learned about St Charles Convent.[52]

The Sisters have memories of hard work at St Charles. After making her temporary vows Sister Zélia Auger went to St Charles, where for seven years she was in charge of the manual labour, working mainly in the kitchen, milking the cow, and gardening. In an interview she explained how she came to realize that other Sisters felt as she did:

Sister St Claire was maîtresse des emplois [co-ordinator of work assignments]. She did the house cleaning. She came from Fannystelle where she had taught

Coat of Arms of St Charles Convent painted in oils on rayon cloth by Sister St Veronica in 1932. Each grade 12 graduate received one as a souvenir of her alma mater.

and completed her term as Superior [in 1928]. One day she was painting the parlour and varnishing the floor. Sister Marie-Gertrude [the head cook], told me: "Why don't you take a snack to Sister St Claire?" I went to give her some coffee and cookies. When I went in, I found her all in tears. She was crying. I was so surprised! I said: "Sister St Claire, what's the matter?" She said: "Ah, I'm so lonesome for Fannystelle! It was so clean. I come here and the house cleaning has not been done yet." I gave her the coffee and told her: "Here, take this, it will help you." And I left. I was so glad to know that I was not the only one to feel lonely. I had thought I was the only one to find it hard at St Charles. It comforted me so much that I forgot about my own pain. I said to Sister Marie-Gertrude: "She finds it hard [here]. She left Fannystelle all clean. Here the house is big. Everybody has to do some house cleaning."

I even saw Sister Louis de France washing the floor in the dormitory [at the end of the school year to prepare for the vocational retreat for young women which took place in early July].

Dora: "She was washing the floor with the boarders?"

Zélia: "Yes, with the students. Sister Gabrielle Viau, Sister Louis de France and others would place themselves between two students, one Sister between each to wash [on their knees] all in a row so that it would go well and be well done. This was on top of their class work. They were young, but did they ever do lots of work!"[53]

The presence and influence of Sister Saint-Jean-Baptiste and Sister Louis de France made St Charles a unique place. In the classroom Sister Louis de France remembered that she did everything she could to make her teaching interesting. Her own former American public school teachers became her models. She found in the school a space to express liberal views and creative abilities. She said in an interview that she never used the strap and did not remember punishing the children, or putting them in penance, away from others. She said: "I was teaching pupils not subjects." The Sister tried to engage parents in the life of the school, although the Métis parents tended to stay away. She cultivated her freedom in the school. She candidly recalled, "I was for progress, forward going, I wanted girls to go for what was open to them."[54] Many of her former students kept in touch for years. They even returned occasionally to Manitoba to visit her from various regions in Canada.

Transcona

In 1924 the Congregation accepted responsibility for a new elementary parochial school, the École paroissiale de l'Assomption in Transcona, a town that was six miles east of St Boniface, known as the location of the Transcontinental Canadian National Railway shops. The parish priest, Father Clovis Paillé, had been raised in St Charles so it seemed normal that the Oblate Sisters be asked to come to Transcona. The school was set up first in a public hall, which had been purchased by the parish, and then moved next to the church. The parishioners built three classrooms and set the Sisters' quarters on the second floor. The school opened with 105 students. Ninety percent of the students were francophones who had never received schooling in French; therefore, they required basic instruction in reading and writing in their maternal tongue. In this parish school the Sisters provided, in their words, "an education more in conformity with the beliefs and ethnic traditions of the French population which is practically drowned by the English protestant majority."[55] At the end of the first school year, parents came for the public oral exam and expressed their pride and satisfaction by awarding numerous prizes to acknowledge the progress of the children. They encouraged staff and students to continue.[56]

Jardins de l'Enfance: Preparing Boys for the Classical Course

In September 1909 the Sisters opened elementary bilingual classes for boys aged five to twelve at the Maison-Chapelle in St Boniface; the boys who boarded at St Charles were transferred there. This was the

Jardin de l'Enfance in Gravelbourg, Saskatchewan, 1923. The day students came from the town of Gravelbourg and the boarders mostly from the neighbouring farms and other rural communities.

The Jardin de l'Enfance Langevin (formely Jardin Maison Chapelle). Picture taken by a photographer after the renovations and extension of 1928. The part of the building in the foreground, left, is the former Normal School to which a full third storey was added and a new wing on the west side. After grade six many of its students proceeded to the Collège Saint-Boniface or to the Juniorat de la Sainte-Famille; several of them later became priests, doctors, politicians, lawyers and even judges.

Picture of the Maison-Chapelle taken in 1911 by a professional photographer after the completion of a new wing (on the left) to the south-west of the original convent (on the right). It contained a kitchen, a refectory, and the book bindery in the basement, a two-storey-high chapel, and a dormitory on the third floor. The vacated attic floor of the older section housed the two classrooms and dormitory of the Jardin de l'Enfance, with elementary classes for boys, ages five to twelve, from 1911 to 1923.

beginning of the Jardin de l'Enfance Langevin. One of the aims was to give boys a good solid foundation (especially in French) for the classical course at St Boniface College where students started to enroll in grade 7. The Jardins were described later in 1919 by Father Péalapra as the breeding-ground from which the French colleges would recruit to fill the ranks of the clergy and the liberal professions or those who would hold positions of influence in their milieu.[57]

During 1910–11, an addition was built at the Maison-Chapelle partly to accommodate the growing number of boys. In 1923 the Jardin was moved to the former bilingual Normal School, which had been closed in 1916 and remained vacant for several years but had finally been bought by the Oblate Sisters.[58]

The Jardin opened in 1909 with sixteen children. By 1927 there were 178 registered pupils (125 boarders and 53 day pupils). Over the course of eighteen years, 1,222 boarders and 230 day students were registered, and the total number of students rose to 1,352. For several years, most of the children came from outside towns and surrounding rural areas; several were orphans or from broken families. At first few families from St Boniface sent their boys to the Jardin, for they had the Provencher School, a public school in the vicinity, which was operated by the

Marianist Brothers. The people of St Boniface also had apprehensions about this new Congregation of Oblate Sisters, and they regarded it as a questionable and unstable institution. The reservations had to do with Langevin's unsuccessful attempts at establishing the congregation between 1902 and 1904. The women who joined the early groups were the laughing-stock of neighbours who called them "Les Filles de Dieu seul" (Daughters of God Alone), and even more derisively, "Les Filles Sans Dieu" (Daughters without God).[59] The Jardin therefore had to earn the trust of the people as a sound and even superior educational institution, particularly as it related to French and religious formation. The Sisters devoted special efforts to achieve high standards in all subjects and to make this preparatory school and the other two Jardins in Gravelbourg and Giffard places where children received a well-rounded education that met the requirements of the Departments of Education.

In 1921 the Congregation started the Jardin de l' Enfance in Gravelbourg, Saskatchewan. Although independent from the College des Oblats de Marie-Immaculée (for which, at the request of Archbishop Mathieu of Regina, the Sisters had provided domestic service since 1918), the Jardin prepared boys for admission to the classical program of studies at the college. At the end of the first year, fifty pupils were enrolled. Those fifty joined their parents, the Sisters, members of the college, and friends of the Jardin for a picnic to commemorate the opening of the school. During the 1920s the Jardins had an important place in the teaching mission of the Congregation.

THE MISSION IN QUÉBEC

Oblate houses in Quebec represented a meaningful and almost natural enterprise, in St Viateur's understanding of the place of the young Congregation in Canada. Quebec provided Sisters for the Congregation and helped maintain a connection with an important source of the Oblate Sisters' identity.

In 1919 the Congregation opened a coeducational elementary school, École St Alexandre, in the parish of St-Sauveur, in Quebec City. As explained in chapter 4, the Sisters' presence in Quebec was facilitated by the Oblate Fathers, who were in charge of the parish, by Archbishop O.M. Mathieu of Regina, and in particular, Father Lortie, an Oblate advocate for the Sisters.[60] The Oblate Fathers had a special interest in primary education, and for the Jardins for boys in particular.

The four Sisters appointed in 1919 to open a co-educational elementary day school in St-Sauveur parish located in a poor district of Quebec City in 1919. From left to right, Sister Marie-Madeleine and Sister St-Adélard (from Quebec), Sister Marie-de l'Incarnation (from Massachusetts) and Sister Catherine-de-Sienne (from St Boniface, Manitoba).

St-Sauveur, Quebec. Ms Pelletier with her class in 1923, all dressed in their Sunday best for the photo. Notice two girls are wearing pinafores over their dresses while two boys in the back row are wearing ties and not the traditional white collar and bow usually worn on Sundays by boys under twelve years of age.

École St-Alexandre was set up in an old vacant building at St Sauveur, Quebec, 1919.

Mother St Viateur experienced difficulties initiating the work in St-Sauveur. She went with four Sisters and found upon arrival that they did not have a place to stay. Students had been enrolled, but the facilities were not ready. Mother St Viateur, who carried on a regular correspondence with Father Péalapra, talks in her letters about the stress of the situation. She wrote: "I haven't been in a good emotional space and I was waiting to feel better before writing. Today my heart feels less constrained thanks to an hour spent before the Blessed Sacrament. Praise God!"[61] In spite of these difficulties, on the first day there were 125 children who were divided among three classrooms; by November of the second year, the school remained filled to capacity with 124 children. The school board had to open another classroom that was soon filled by forty-two children. The school was closed in 1925 when Cardinal Bégin

Sister Jean-de-la-Croix (Marie-Jeanne Arcand, from Quebec) with her class at St-Sauveur in 1924.

asked the Sisters to open an elementary parochial school in Stoneham, a town north of Quebec City and west of St Anne de Beaupré.

The Jardin de l'Enfance that was opened in Giffard in 1921 (as part of Father Lortie's project) became the central point for a strong and lasting relationship between Sisters, clergy, and parents, as revealed in many activities registered in the journal of the house.[62]

THE MISSION IN THE FRANCO-MANITOBAN RURAL COMMUNITIES

Fannystelle

In 1911 the Congregation began work in the public school in Fannystelle, which was administered by a local school board. Mother Marie-Joseph later said of Fannystelle: "This school in the midst of a French Canadian majority was the kind which Archbishop Langevin had in mind when he dreamed of new foundations for the Missionary Oblates."[63] After the changes to the Public School Act in 1916 that allowed the teaching of religion and French only after school hours, the Sisters found ways to teach French and to maintain the Catholic faith; they even hired a special teacher to teach French in a room that was set apart from the other classrooms. In September 1913, the growing number of students made it necessary to open a third class; at that time there were seventy-five students registered, a few of them boarders.[64]

The Congregation had its own house in Fannystelle, St Joseph Convent, which contained boarding facilities. The journal of the Congregation in Fannystelle shows the Sisters completely integrated into the life of the community in all its social dimensions: the parish, the village, and the school. The Sisters took time to visit the sick and the dying. There were instances when the board could not find a janitor and the Sisters and the trustees made a joint effort to clean the school. The community of Fannystelle showed its appreciation by rendering a variety of services to the Sisters, such as repairing the furnace, the roof, and the chimney or ploughing their five-acre field. The gifts from the townspeople and farmers included chickens, turkeys, wild ducks, rabbits, strawberries, cakes, cream, and butter, among other things.[65]

Constance Franzmann attended the school between January and June 1925, where she took grade 10 before going to St Charles. A Protestant, she recalled being one of the six or seven boarders. They shared the convent routine in the morning: "There was a chapel in the convent and a priest used to come every morning (on week days) to say mass. All boarders were required to attend – protestant included. Most of the service was in Latin so it seemed very strange to me as I didn't understand the ritual. Sometimes for a special mass we would all be marched to the church – a fine edifice which is still in use today."

Constance remembered her piano teacher, Sister Marie-des-Anges (Lucie Gagné, a former student and juniorist at St Charles), as lighthearted and very pleasant; in her long habit she seemed to float into the music room, which was really a little parlour in the convent. Her classroom teacher was Sister St Claire (Mary Wery), "a very capable nun and a strong disciplinarian. She kindly coached me some evenings in some of the work I had missed the first term. She had a pet cat, and as we sat in the nuns' refectory the cat would come and jump up on her lap and I can still see her stroking it as she discussed British History with me."[66]

The Sisters and the students took part in all the church activities including the parish bazaar, choir, Sunday school, even the cleaning of the church. Priests from surrounding parishes, including St Boniface, would drop in for mass and for meals. They visited the children and distributed candies and prizes. The parish priest also visited the school regularly.[67]

The visits of the inspector from the Department of Education were duly registered in the journal, sometimes motivated by complaints from Anglo-Protestants about French. In fact, for many years, as normally happened with schools in rural Franco-Manitoban communities, inspectors were the political mediators between the Department of Education (the inspector represented the department) and the rural districts. The issues centred on educational control of language, religion, and the preservation of cultural values.[68] The inspector was responsible for ensuring compliance with the provisions of the Public School Act and the regulations of the Department of Education; compliance with the curriculum was indeed a major issue. Like most teachers in ethnic homogeneous areas in Manitoba (Franco-Manitobans and Mennonites, amongst others), the Sisters tailored their teaching to the community values. The written reports of the inspectors from the Department of Education suggest satisfaction with the public school in Fannystelle.

Dunrea, Couvent de la Nativité

In 1912 Father Norbert Bellavance, the priest of Saint Felix parish in Dunrea, Manitoba, asked Archbishop Langevin to establish a convent of Missionary Oblate Sisters and a parochial school. At the time Dunrea belonged to the diocese of St Boniface but after 1916 it became part of the diocese of Winnipeg. Thanks to local donations four Sisters moved to Dunrea in late August and opened a private elementary school. The Sisters agreed to teach without salary, and by September 1913 the school had thirty-eight children.

The unusually colourful convent journal records that the four Sisters left for Dunrea by train on 26 August 1912, accompanied by Mother St Viateur and another sister. When the train arrived at Somerset, two students who had been boarders in St Charles came to greet them, as well as a young man (also a former student) who came to greet Mother St Viateur. When they stopped in Ninette (a village in the Pembina Hills), the writer of the journal took care to record the Sisters' exclamations at the beauty of the place. When they finally arrived in Dunrea the priest, Norbert Bellavance, and a crowd were waiting to welcome them. The priest showed the Sisters his rectory, the new church, and the old church, which would be used as a school, and finally took the Sisters to the convent, their new home. It was a small two-storey red brick

Convent of the Nativity in Dunrea, Manitoba. The Sisters are relaxing after their first school year is over. Picture taken in the summer of 1913.

Convent of the Nativity in Dunrea, Manitoba. A retreat in the summer of 1929 for young women who came to the convent from surrounding areas.

house surrounded by a garden, rows of trees, and approximately three acres of land, which had been leased from a parishioner.

The school admitted both boys and girls and the convent offered boarding facilities for a few students. The journal moves the reader into a world of neighbours who helped to harvest grain for the Sisters' cows and chickens, Sisters gathering gooseberries and blackberries from their garden, a member of the community asking the Sisters to make a wedding cake, Sisters whitewashing the stable, quarantines (in one case due to scarlet fever) at the school, catechism for the school children, parents at the convent and the school, and visits from Archbishop Langevin. Langevin's visits had a tone of informality, as he sat in the kitchen to chat with the Sisters, "a real father amidst his daughters."[69] The local priest had a strong presence in the life of the convent and the school, and there are many lines referring to his extending a table to accommodate the new boarders, participating in supervising the French exams on a Saturday morning, organizing auction sales at the school with parents' and children's participation to increase revenues, and bringing visitors from the Association d'Education.[70] The priest and members of the village discussed the big question of the village school, a public school that the priest wanted the Sisters to take over.[71]

One of the entries in the journal, 20 June 1917, is revealing of the citizenship formation process in that school:

> The oral exam [under the Association] was presided over by Father Curé Amédée Roy and Fr Heynen with many parents attending. Between the classes there were oratory performances by students followed by awarding of prizes. Both priests addressed the group. Fr Heynen (pastor of the neighbouring village of Mariapolis) had been invited since some children came from his parish to the catholic school in Dunrea. He spoke of the necessity to have this "école libre" and tried to have people understand that we (the Sisters) taught here out of pure dedication, that sometimes, parents might be in the wrong. Addressing us directly he asked us to continue this work, which was one of the "glories of our order" and which we should be ready to maintain at all costs. He said there was no other parish in Manitoba having as much need of a convent as Dunrea. After singing "O Canada" all left satisfied.[72]

The school developed a strong relationship with the association. In 1923 M. l'abbé Adonias Sabourin, the French inspector, visited the Sisters to whom he talked about the Manitoba school question, observed classes, listened to the reading of the examination marks, and expressed

Convent of the Nativity in Dunrea, Manitoba, which opened in 1912. It was leased by a parishioner, Mr Beaupré.

his desire to see the school adopt all the French books chosen by the association. The association provided financial support to the school to the extent that the inspector took proposals of different kinds to the association, for example, the need to have a third classroom.

RESIDENTIAL SCHOOLS

The residential schools have been at the centre of public debate for a long time and they have been the object of outstanding scholarly examination, particularly by Miller, Titley, and Huel.[73] It is not within the parameters of this book to analyze life in the residential schools. Furthermore, the Congregation continues to deal with allegations and claims of abuse. However, it is possible here to explore questions regarding the terms upon which the Sisters worked in the residential schools, and the Sisters' own understanding of the place of the schools in their mission and vision.

The 1906 constitutions set the tone for a broad understanding of the missionary character of the Congregation. The Sisters were expected to go on mission in western Canada where needed, and in the United States if necessary.[74] Thus, the *Chroniques* reveal that the Sisters (under the title "Échos des Missions") included St Charles Convent as well as the residential schools in their reports on the missions. Any assignment outside the Maison-Chapelle was considered a missionary assignment.

Fort Alexander Residential School girls and Sisters (Manitoba). Picture taken in 1916 on the occasion of a visit from Mother St Viateur, after the Oblate Sisters replaced the Daughters of the Cross. Father Geelen, OMI (front row left), was the school principal.

However, the work in residential schools became a substantial component of the Sisters' missions in terms of numbers and human resources. Between 1909 and 1929, the Congregation had missions in six residential schools: Cross Lake (Manitoba), Norway House (Manitoba, between 1910 and 1914), St Philippe (Fort Pelly, Saskatchewan), Fort Alexander (Manitoba), McIntosh (Ontario), and Pine Creek (Camperville, Manitoba).

In the residential schools (unlike in St Charles Convent, any of the Congregation's other foundations, or in public schools) the Sisters did not have the space either to negotiate their own terms of involvement, develop and implement their own views, or even to exercise their own authority without going through an acrimonious process. In 1909, for example, the Congregation started its first mission with the Aboriginal people in Cross Lake. The Oblate provincial, J.P. Magnan, set the conditions. The four Sisters had to teach, take care of the church and the sacristy, keep house, cook, and care for the boarders. The mission paid only for the Sisters' first trip to the school; subsequent travel to and from St Boniface had to be covered by the Oblate Sisters. In addition, since the mission (the Oblate Fathers) assumed the expenses and financial responsibilities, it had the right to claim and retain the salary paid by the government to one of the Sisters who taught at the day school on the reserve. The Sister had to endorse the cheque and send it to the Director of Missions. The Oblate Sisters received seventy-five dollars annually for each of three Sisters; the Oblate Fathers did not cover the expenses of the fourth Sister.[75]

The oral narratives of the Sisters illustrate ongoing difficulties with some of the Oblate principals of the residential schools. Some of these narratives are rather disturbing. For instance, Sister Annie Trohak, a cook at Fort Alexander, complained that the principal, Father Kalmes, either bought the supplies he wanted, or did not buy anything for the kitchen. It was not until he bragged to another priest that he had thrown the shopping list the Sisters had made in the garbage, that the situation reached the ears of the provincial, Father Magnan, who intervened.[76] In spite of such difficulties, there were also instances of joyful social life between the Sisters and the principal and other personnel.

Mother St Viateur had a strong commitment to language and faith. This commitment took the form of a French Canadian nationalism, which was understood as a struggle to survive in the midst of English dominance. She seemed to believe that the residential schools and their work of anglicization were not central to the deepest purpose of the Congregation. However, Mother St Viateur visited all the missions and helped get the Sisters established. Sister Louis de France did not see the work in the residential schools as having a central place in the mission of the community. The Sisters did not articulate Sister Louis de France's reasons but assumed that they had to do with her commitment to education, and with her learner-centred conception of teaching and learning. Mother Marie-Joseph's writings, and her circular letters, show that the work for French Catholic education was at the core of her understanding of the mission of the Congregation. For an example, when requesting the Sisters' service for the "concours de l'Association d'Education," Mother Marie-Joseph wrote: "Despite the additional weight of the work involved in this endeavour [for example, correcting papers for the examination], I consider the task to be an honour for our young congregation, and also an opportunity to work for what is the reason of our own existence as [a] community."[77] In 1939 Mother Marie-Joseph closed her official history of the Congregation, which was sent to Rome, with the following paragraph under the heading Hopes of the Congregation: "Many Indian missions are still waiting for Sisters, but it is especially the country schools where teachers are often without much concern for the religious welfare of students that zealous and dedicated Sisters are needed. The Congregation wishes to direct its efforts toward these. In the Indian missions the demand for Sisters who are nurses is being considered by the Superiors."[78]

The residential schools represented quite a different reality from that of other schools with which the Sisters were involved. The preceding descriptions of school life in Winnipeg, Transcona, Quebec, and in Franco-Manitoban rural communities demonstrate an interconnectedness that was prevalent in private, public, and parochial schools, where Sisters, students, parents, the community at large, and the parish priest all worked together harmoniously. The Sisters' involvement with Native people had an ambivalence generated by the two principles governing the mission there: the epic conquest of souls, which permeated the Oblate Fathers' tradition, and care for the poor, which was central to the spirit of both the Missionary Oblate Sisters and the Oblate Fathers. The conquest of souls, so well analyzed by Choquette, was carried out within the ultramontane context and, as in any conquest, was levied against the Native peoples' will.[79] Schooling was the main medium for the conquest of souls. The references to Fort Alexander in mission journals and letters registered the ambivalence that dominated their complex relations with the children and the communities, mainly with parents and family members residing on the nearby reserve. Instances of resistance (e.g., children running away from schools, at times with tragic consequences), and the use of humiliation as a punitive measure to curb the students' lack of docility are the same as those documented by Miller.[80] There are also tender examples of loving Sisters taking care of sick children, raising orphans and children with physical or cognitive challenges, or grieving over the death of a child. The Sisters recorded picnics, berry picking, and little celebrations, although the notations did not often provide much detail. Sister St Charles was an exception and her writing gives us some glimpses of joyful experiences. For example, she described the trip to St Philippe, Saskatchewan, in 1910 and a picnic that took place a few weeks later:

May 4, 1910, Arrival at Kamsack. As it was impossible to receive Holy Communion this morning, breakfast was eaten on the train, after which Mother Superior [St Viateur] and the Sisters enjoyed the scenery in the vicinity of Kamsack ... Father Provincial conducted all to the Windsor Hotel, a high and shaky-looking building, but on the whole not so bad for a new western town. The owner Mr Sauvé and his sister were very kind. The latter and Mother Superior soon found out they had mutual acquaintances in Montreal. Father

Girls rehearsing a skit about grandmothers knitting mittens at St Phillip Residential School, near Kamsack, Saskatchewan.

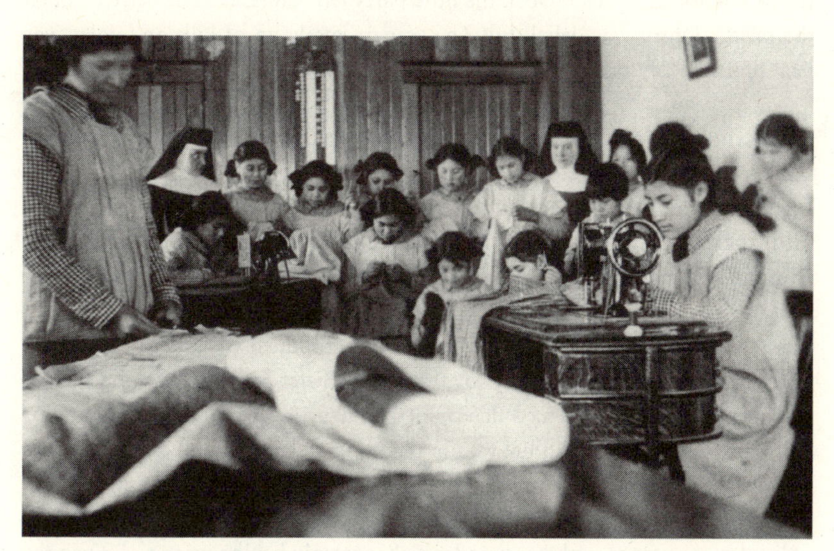

Cross Lake, Manitoba. Sister St-Lucien teaching the girls to sew with Singer sewing machines. Some girls are learning to use a pattern to cut cloth while others are knitting. Picture taken in 1921.

Cross Lake Residential School. Picture taken in 1916. It was built on a scenic peninsula on the Nelson River north of Lake Winnipeg. Sister Marguerite-Marie and thirteen Aboriginal children died in the fire that destroyed the school on 25 February 1930.

Provincial ate breakfast at this hotel and at the same time the Sisters partook of the tea Father ordered. During this time all enjoyed the table-talk relative to the new work ... At ten o'clock the little party left Kamsack. The drive through the open country was delightful. The scenery made up of hills and dales was beautiful, the day bright and clear, houses far apart and travellers few.[81]

An outing on 25 May 1910 gave the writer an opportunity to describe what she felt had been a happy day. The eagerness to enjoy nature, as evidenced in the account below, contrasted with the seclusion and sacredness that permeated convent life in urban settings like Maison-Chapelle:

The morning was a busy one as everybody had to finish work before dinner in order to be ready to leave early for the picnic. Sister St Andrew had difficulty with her bread which seemed determined to deprive her of a half-holiday. At half past one, Father had a big wagon ready for the Sisters and girls. The boys ran on ahead. Mother climbed upon the high seat with facility and laughed heartily at Sister St Charles' inability to do the same. Sister St Andrew was obliged to stay alone with her bread which was only beginning to rise. Even the children felt lonely in leaving her at the door where she came to see all off with a wish for our happiness. The drive through the country was most enjoyable and refreshing. It seemed like a great park for the grass and the trees with their delicate new leaves bordered the road as if planted by man purposely.[82]

Colonization had many sides and poverty was a prominent one. Through the dispensary the Sisters acted as nurses or doctors when necessary and there were cases, narrated with emotion, of a large number of people going to the school for some medical attention, especially in times of epidemics. There were instances when the Sisters made bread to distribute or accompanied children to their homes to help a family that was in distress or stricken with illness. In the Sisters' view, poverty and disease went together.[83] The Oblate Sisters, however, were not alien to the ultramontanism that permeated the Oblate Fathers' mindset and the Catholic church in general. The conquest of souls had epic dimensions in the fight against the forces of evil. The *Chroniques* reflect this approach in the language used. When announcing the opening of a residential school in McIntosh, Ontario, the chronicler wrote: "Most of the children who will benefit from the new school belong to the first missions founded by the Oblate Fathers in the West. After three quarters of a century the good Fathers pick up the work of the brave missionaries of former times. May the Lord bless their new labours and render them fruitful for the good!"[84]

The Sisters, even in their role as auxiliaries to the Fathers, and with limited theological formation, shared in the same theological background. The *Chroniques* include a long article entitled "L'Oeuvre des Religieuses dans L'Ouest," written by an Oblate priest. The article, originally published in *Les Cloches de Saint-Boniface* in 1909, candidly reveals the Oblate Fathers' perception of the Aboriginal people that underlined the missionary work in the nineteenth and early twentieth centuries. The Aborigine is described in purely negative terms that include the following characterizations: "unfortunate natural being," "sad offspring of an ignored race," and "dreadful mixture." The article stated that the Aborigine did not possess an intellectual culture, a comforting religion, or human morals.[85] The Aborigines in these regions, the article continues, lived "a useless, barbaric and often harmful life."[86] Redemption was brought by the Oblate Fathers and then by the Sisters from various congregations.[87] The stage that was set very early for a tragic process of cultural deprivation is well described by the author of this article. The Oblate Sisters joined the Oblate Fathers in their efforts at "regeneration" and "salvation."

The Sisters' subordination to the Oblate Fathers in the residential schools was direct and without the possible mediation created by broader networks framing the interaction. The very visible power of the Oblate Fathers generated tensions and many instances of resistance and

Sister Marie-Estelle (Véronique Chartrand), a Métis from St-Laurent, Manitoba, spent many years in Cross Lake, Manitoba. She spoke Cree and Ojibway and taught catechism in Cree to the beginners.

even contestation, situations that were experienced not only by the Oblate Sisters.[88] Mother Marie-Joseph very early in her mandate advised Sister St Charles, directress of the Sisters at Fort Alexander, to take "a firmer stand" with the principal.[89] The references to the residential schools reflect a difficult and painful reality for the Aboriginal children and parents, and for the Sisters. They also show that the Sisters had very little latitude in making their own decisions and in exercising their own judgment. The ethnocentric character of the missionary work with the Native people and the prisonlike character of the residential schools contrasted with the Sisters' counterhegemonic stand in the Franco-Manitoban communities. For example, the devotions created a layer of common identity in Franco-Manitoban areas but became enforced meaningless exercises for the converted Aboriginal children. The *Chroniques* registered children's mandatory confessions, first Friday devotions to the Blessed Sacrament, and conversions that were not always readily accepted by parents.

In the period analyzed in this book, apostolic work can be construed as a contentious space. Indeed, Langevin conceived the original mission of the Congregation as a way to deal with the consequences of the aftermath of the Manitoba school question. However, as an Oblate, he

Sister St Bonaventure (Marie Ducharme), a Métis from St-Laurent, Manitoba. Picture taken in 1988 on her one hundredth birthday. She taught catechism in Ojibway to the beginners in Fort Alexander and in McIntosh, Ontario, from the 1920s to the 1950s. The children loved her dearly and called her "coucoum" (grandmother).

also wanted them to support the Oblate Fathers in their missions. He infused the new Congregation with Oblate principles such as work with the poor. The Sisters' apostolic work was a reflection not only of the initial inspiration or of their own search for new meanings but also of the complex relationship with the Oblate Fathers as evidenced in the work in Quebec, in collaboration with the Fathers on the Jardins de l'Enfance, in the changes in the 1931 constitutions, and also in the auxiliary work in the residential schools. The Sisters' way of construing their official memories and writing the narrative of their foundation and their changing roles is worthy of analysis. Their omissions and inclusions and their disputatious interpretations are also important components of the historical process.

PRIEZ ENCORE (POUR LA PAIX)

Vous qui pleurez sur les souffrances
Dont saignent tous les cœurs humains,
Vous dont les saintes espérances
Ont foi en d'autres lendemains,
Courbez vos fronts dans la prière
Devant le Maître des mortels,
Et dites-lui : Pardon, ô Père
À genoux devant ses autels.

Pardon pour la France infidèle
Et pour la terre impie;
Au nom de votre peuple fidèle
Et des justes de la patrie.
Au nom des frêles têtes blondes
Dont les regards tournés vers Vous
Vous implorent, Maître des mondes,
Pour apaiser votre courroux.

Puis à genoux sur les dalles
Du temple saint, nous attendons
Au sifflement lointain des balles
Avec espoir, votre pardon.
Pardonnez-nous! Que cette guerre
Meure dans un dernier effort.
Peuples à genoux sur la terre,
Priez, priez, priez encore.

Brise de France (a novice's pen name)
L'Écho 2, no. 3 (25 December 1918).

VI

Establishing Bonding Memories through The Myth of Foundation and Returning to the Past in the Search for Renewal

The Congregation of the Missionary Oblate Sisters construed its official memories as a means of building cohesion, group identity, and solidarity. In that process, particular events in the Congregation's myth of foundation became central to the narrative while others remained invisible, were not included, or appeared only in a marginal manner. This chapter analyses the discursive components involved in the Sisters' interpretation of their own foundation and understanding of their own history. Alongside the official record of memories that are located in written texts, rules, oral accounts, symbols, rituals, social life, and public events, there is also a parallel set of memories that, in contrast, reveals a warm, subjective, and even transgressive quality centring around Sister Louis de France, who had a flair for individual growth and independence.

The tension between such official and unofficial memories becomes part of the discussion in the second part of the chapter, which examines the process of renewal among the Oblate Sisters and their desire "to live" as a community. From the 1970s through the 1990s, within this framework and heeding the mandate of Vatican II, the Congregation (as a community) confronted its memories and its interpretation of the past. The process of looking into the past set new parameters from which that past and the myth of foundation could be scrutinized, making it possible to reconstitute the meaning of spiritual life in the present.

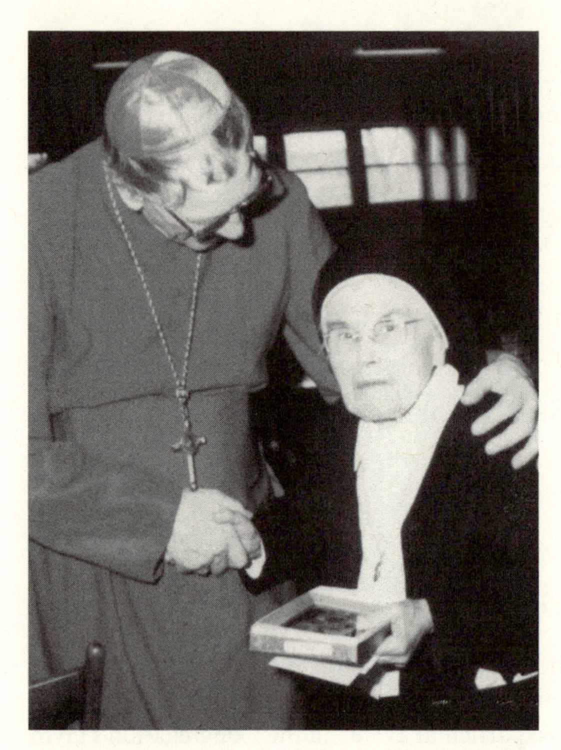

Sister Marie-Gertrude (Elizabeth Storozuk) first came to the Maison-Chapelle at age fifteen in January 1903, intending to become a Sister in the new Congregation. She is seen here in 1976 with Archbishop Maurice Baudoux of St Boniface who presided over the celebration of her seventy years of religious profession of vows.

ESTABLISHING OFFICIAL MEMORIES

Archbishop Langevin wanted the Sisters to record everything regarding the life of the small Congregation in a quarterly publication, *Les Chroniques des Missionnaires Oblates du Sacré-Coeur et de Marie Immaculée*. The first issue was published in 1911. Such established memories would help to generate a family spirit and a bond of communal charity, to gather support among relatives, friends, and members of the Church, and to recruit young women for the Congregation.[1] The early memories contained the stories about the foundation, forming what is now known in religious communities as the myth of foundation. The myth is constituted of rituals, events, and symbols commemorating the treasured facets of the foundation, merged in a sort of sacred memory.[2] In 1939 Mother Marie-Joseph (Alma Laurendeau), second general superior and considered one of the cofounders by the community, wrote an official history of the Congregation, "Rapport Historique de la Congrégation des Soeurs Missionnaires Oblates du S.C. et de M.I.,"

Mother St Viateur (front row right) in Fannystelle. During the 1950 flood in Manitoba, the sick and elderly Sisters were evacuated from the Mother House.

which, as noted earlier, was sent to Rome. In the 1950s she compiled articles from the *Chroniques*, letters, and oral testimonies and prepared a document (later translated into English) entitled "First Attempts at Organizing the Congregation of the Missionary Oblate Sisters." It was only in 1967 that the Congregation produced the biography of Mother Saint Viateur (Ida Lafricain), 1871–1957, first general superior, who was also considered a cofounder by the community.[3]

An understanding of the historical circumstances surrounding the foundation of the Congregation became an essential component of its identity. It is not surprising that from early on, the Sisters saw the foundation in connection with the Manitoba School Question and its unjust solution. One Sister wrote in 1917 in the *Chroniques*, two years after Langevin died, that the archbishop had understood this injustice to be an offence that burnt into the heart of God, and for this reason God made explicit his will for the foundation. The Oblate Sisters' mission represented an act of reparation in the Sisters' spiritual tradition (making amends to God and to fellow human beings for sin or wrongdoing and restoring equity).[4] The tradition also implied an element of protestation, or a denunciation of the ecclesiastical politics of the Manitoba school question. The changes in direction and aims, in particular those expounded in the 1931 Constitutions, did not take root in the collective identity.

The reference to the French Canadian question was strong in the narrative developed under Mother St Viateur but lost strength from the 1930s onwards. In a text written for posterity around 1921, Mother St Viateur was described as being as committed as Langevin to the Catholic cause and to the conservation of "our French language and our rights." The text reads: "The boiling blood of French Canadians that circulated in the veins of our glorious Father and Founder also flows through the whole being of his spiritual daughter, Sister Saint-Viateur."[5] Sister Louis de France, a Franco-American, related the issue of justice to Langevin's Catholic zeal. She made clear that it was the controversial question of the schools of Manitoba that had brought the Oblate Sisters into being. She emphasized, however, that the Sisters were not simply a French Congregation. The article of the first Constitutions that requested that the Sisters learn English, French, and if possible a third language should, in her words, "lay aside forever the ghost of the French foundation. It showed the catholicity of the Archbishop."[6] Yet in the official versions of this component of the foundation, reference to Franco-Manitoban issues and to the French Canadian question parallels discourse with work in all other cultural communities.[7] It is interesting to note that the religious names Louis de France and Saint-Jean-Baptiste, given by Langevin to the two American sisters from North Dakota (whose family was originally from Quebec), seem to confirm the archbishop's efforts to have them endorse his plan of reparation and his struggle against the government by appealing to their francophone roots.

The dissonant memories had roots in the origins, composition, and lived experience of the Congregation. It seems obvious that these were negotiated memories. The Quebec mentality and Québécois understanding of Manitoban reality and religious life often conflicted with the mentality and the cultural and social experiences of the Sisters from the West and the Sisters of French background who had come from the United States. The portrait of Mother St Viateur quoted above is related to her idea of the French Canadian national community across the country and is in line with Langevin's dual vision of Canada. However, Mother St Viateur did not truly understand the West, its history, and its changing nature, which was due largely to the impact of immigration, so she was unable to deal with the contradictory messages given her by Langevin. Emblematic of Mother St Viateur's lack of understanding was the failed attempt to transform the Congregation's private school, the St Charles Convent, into an elementary school modelled on Quebec convent lives, for Mother St Viateur chose to ignore the Manitoba curriculum. The experience at St Charles became part of the oral memory that grew along with a counterculture inspired by Sister Louis de France, who had strongly opposed the changes. She later rebuilt the school program and reputation in ways that honoured the regional Manitoban psyche.

The Manitoba school question embodied an early collective memory for the Manitoban Sisters. This memory was sustained by their work with the Franco-Manitoban communities well into the 1950s, and also by the identity of many of the Sisters. Mother Marie-Joseph, considered by the Sisters to be one of the cofounders, had been a teacher in Franco-Manitoban rural communities for seven years before entering the prospective Congregation in 1903. She included a powerful comment in the "Rapport Historique," an official document written in 1939, in relation to the Sisters' direction and teaching in a public school administered by a local school board in Fannystelle, Manitoba: "This school in the midst of a majority of French-Canadians was the kind which Archbishop Langevin had mostly in mind when he dreamed of new foundations for the Missionary Oblates."[8]

The move of Ida Lafricain, the future Mother St Viateur, from Montreal to Winnipeg was memorialized as a "forced transplantation" and as her "sacrifice."[9] However, it was Divine Providence that made possible both her encounter with Délia Tétreault in 1893 (her spiritual friend and later founder of the Soeurs Missionnaires de l'Immaculée-Conception in 1902) and the sacrifice of their separation in 1904. In the myth, this sacrifice is construed as nourishing the respective missions led by these two women. Thus, as a way of explaining the breaking of Lafricain's early call to religious life, the Sisters firmly incorporated in their common memory the idea that Lafricain, who had worked with the poor in Montreal, dreamed of a mission in a local place, while Tétreault dreamed of missions in the entire world. The discourse concealed the fact that Lafricain and Tétreault had shared a common call, and that Lafricain was committed to Tétreault's project. The myth also obscured the profound spiritual and personal relationship between the two women. It obliterated any possibility of referring to the forceful intervention of Archbishop Langevin and Lafricain's spiritual director in separating her from the École Apostolique in Montreal. Further, the myth ignored Lafricain's drawn-out resistance to the move even after she was established in Manitoba. Instead, Ida Lafricain's relocation to

Mother Marie-Joseph enjoying outdoor exercise, hoeing the gardens and picking onions. Picture taken circa 1940.

Manitoba was construed as the "triumph of grace," and Lafricain's spiritual director was seen as the man she had found at the right time to allow her to enter into the plans God had for her. Grace was also effective, again according to the myth of foundation, because of the confidence Lafricain had in her spiritual director.[10] In this case, Sister Léa Boutin asserted, "the myth portrayed a history of deception rather than a history of fidelity to grace."[11]

The community incorporated in their myth the image of Mother St. Viateur (Ida Lafricain) described by Langevin in later years as "being of perfect obedience,"[12] even though it is noted in her biography that she found it hard to obey when she did not understand the reasons. She projected the image of a strong, intelligent woman. She was also described as having a "virile character" and an acute sense of authority. However, the biography stresses that she was obedient, and that she abandoned herself to God's will. In other words, obedience made her womanly and virtuous.[13]

The community emphasized over the years the spiritual legacy of faith, devotion, docility, and obedience of Mother Marie-Joseph (Alma Laurendeau), the other cofounder. In contrast to Ida Lafricain, Alma was often described as an introvert who had a docile heart and a placid character. In her biography she was portrayed as profoundly oriented towards the love of God and ready to endure the pain and sacrifices arising from the circumstances surrounding her.[14] The notion of co-foundation (Langevin, the Founder, and Mothers St Viateur and Marie-Joseph, the two Cofounders) that appeared in the 1930s became the cohesive element of the myth and provided an underlying idea of co-operation and mutual support.

Another component of the myth of foundation was the suffering Archbishop Langevin endured in the process of establishing the Congregation. In 1915, not long before his death, Langevin shared with the Sisters the anguish and humiliations he suffered when early attempts at founding the Congregation failed. He was certain, however, that the foundation was God's will. He told the Sisters: "It was not I who did the work, but it was the work of God (le bon Dieu)."[15]

Several years later Mother Marie-Joseph referred to the way the Sisters who personally heard Langevin's words about his suffering had interpreted them in relation to their own historical presence. "[The Sisters] had the intimate conviction that the little tree of our religious family, had, itself, its divine seal because its roots were irrigated by the blood from the heart of our venerated Founder."[16] The memorialization of Langevin's struggle and pain became part of the spiritual tradition and an inspiration for sanctification. There was little room left to integrate Ida Lafricain's own suffering beyond the language of grace, providence, sacrifice, and, in particular, obedience. The harder the sacrifice, the more pleasing it would be to God. The redeeming value of suffering and denial of the self were major contributing theological concepts; self-denial would bring spiritual fruitfulness, an abundance of fruits for the apostolate as the work of God.[17] The place of women as subordinate in the spiritual scheme was concealed in such language. As Léa Boutin, MO, and former general superior, said, "It seems there was in the Sisters' minds a confusion between the workings of patriarchy on the one hand, and the work and will of God on the other."[18]

In "First Attempts at Organizing the Congregation,"[19] written several years later, Mother Marie-Joseph explained the early recruitment of representatives from "foreign ethnic groups" by quoting an article written by Langevin in 1902. Langevin summarized the needs of his diocese by using a metaphor, that of numerous outcries echoing in his ears. First of all, he wrote, it was the voices of many thousands of Catholic children who had migrated recently from Galicia, in the Austrian empire. These children would be condemned to grow in ignorance or even worse, be threatened with a Protestant education. The cry was for Catholic teachers. He then mentioned the Indians, some of them pagans, some Methodists, and their cry for help; and then there were the needs of the new settlements made up of Catholics who came from other parts of Canada, the United States, France, Belgium, Poland, and Ireland. Langevin concluded with a call for new foundations, Catholic parishes, and especially, Catholic francophone parishes.[20] Langevin's article, written before the actual founding of the Congregation, is used in the narrative to explain the presence of eastern European Sisters in the Missionary Oblate community (who in fact had to use French as their daily language) and to deal with the catholicity of Langevin as the Sisters understood it.

The contradictions and tensions between lived experiences, in particular in the missions, and the rigidity of the rules were expressed in a parallel memory of a counterculture. This memory questioned the faithfulness to the Rule/rules over personal spirituality, and it claimed a degree of autonomy. Such memory encompassed simple instances of transgression, wisdom, savvy, common sense, a sense of plurality, and a strong faith in education as a form of empowerment for the Sisters. It kept alive the spontaneity of early years. Humorous memories of transgression against the rules are traceable through personal interviews and conversations with the Sisters. As noted earlier, this unofficial memory centred around Sister Louis de France (Albina Laberge), the American Sister who died in 1993 when she was 101 years old. She was known for her reasonableness and down-to-earth approach to life in the community and its problems.

The official collective memory, as recorded in the *Chroniques* and other documents, remained rather static for many years; it became a safe point of reference during the 1950s and early 1960s when changes seemed inevitable. By then, the official memory had taken a regressive character. It was a time of holding back and of faithfulness to the parameters set in the era of the Founders. There was a sense of duty to the official past and attempts were made to stem change while other congregations were organizing themselves at the national level to respond to the signs of a new era. Meanwhile, the Congregation under the influence of Sister Louis de France developed a culture of study. It was not until after the crisis and breakdown that took place between 1963 and 1973 that the sisters started interrogating, as a community, their own understanding of the past.[21] This examination of the past was prompted by the junctural combination of developments motivated by Vatican II, the situation generated by the previous denial of change, and the national political changes affecting the Congregation's mission and vision. The latter included the closing of residential schools for Native children and was accompanied by serious questioning of the missionary work. It also included the process of redefining identity in the French Canadian communities outside Quebec as a result of the break-up of the collective identity of French Canadians in 1967. At that time, Quebec nationalists moved to self-determination and asserted that Quebec was the "national territory" and the "basic polity" of French Canada.[22]

INTERROGATING THE PAST: CRISIS AND RENEWAL

In the 1970s the Missionary Oblate Sisters examined their own memories in a systematic way from the standpoint of their existential crisis in an attempt to found themselves anew. The Congregation had survived defections, loss of identity and mission, and difficult changes in their communal life.[23] Internally, the reformers had built a subtle line of continuity with Albina Laberge, the lone early prophetic voice. There was an institutional movement away from faithfulness to the Rule to the primacy of charity, to meditation and inner life. These changes were encouraged by the Church after Vatican II. The image of a free and responsible woman religious timidly began to emerge, as evidenced in the circular letters of the 1960s under the leadership of Jeanne Boucher, and more clearly in the following decade. Sister Jeanne Boucher was instrumental in ushering in what is known as the "therapeutic" phase in the history of congregations, by opening the doors to a new freer lifestyle and allowing changes in the regulations regarding obsolete customs and traditions that encouraged immaturity and inequality. In 1967 a number of Sisters were also eager for greater grassroots participation in the affairs of the Congregation. The questionnaires regarding what changes should be implemented in the upcoming General Chap-

Picture taken after the election of the sixth general superior, Sister Lea Boutin, in 1973. From left to right with her are Sisters Marie Gertrude (1903), François-Xavier (1907), Marie-de-l'Immaculée-Conception (Léontine Béchard from Quebec, 1907), and Marie-Bernadette (Marie Martel from St Paul, Minnesota, 1907). In parentheses are their dates of entry into the Congregation. Notice the change in habit after Vatican II and the option to wear it.

ter of Aggiornamento of 1968–1969 offered a golden opportunity to voice views and desires regarding every aspect of their lives for the updating of the Constitutions.

In the 1970s the Congregation, led by General Superior Léa Boutin (1973–81) and her assistant Dora Tétreault (1973–77), started to explore the Missionary Oblates Sisters' origin and its own spirituality in the light of Vatican II.[24] It focused on the Founder, Archbishop Langevin. There was a strong sense of history, a desire for refounding grounded in Langevin's vision. Sister Léa Boutin sent a circular letter to the community in 1974 in which she paraphrased Edward Farrell, SJ, by saying that a community reaches its maturity when it owns its history and believes in its future.[25] She did not feel able to judge the degree of maturity of the Congregation, but she perceived in it a profound desire to return to its origin: the gospel and the spirit of the Founder.[26] In the

Senior Sisters' panel, organized by Sister Dora Tétreault (standing) in 1974. From left to right: Sister Elizabeth-de-Hongrie (Juliana Trohak, from Stockholm, Saskatchewan, 1909), born in Hungary; Sister St-Henri (Cécile d'Amours, from Montreal, 1914); Sister François-Xavier (Eugénie Vanier); Sister Marie-Gertrude; and Sister Marie-de-l'Immaculée-Conception.

same circular she referred to "Monseigneur Langevin: son Charisme de Fondateur," a document prepared by Sister Dora Tétreault, and to other studies, to reflect on the spirit of the Founder through personal meditation.[27] The Sisters turned to the past to imagine a future.

Sister Dora Tétreault researched Langevin's life, and more importantly his spirit of faith in an attempt to rediscover the original inspiration for the Congregation (a mandate from *Perfectae Caritatis,* Vatican II).[28] In her view, his spirit of faith was revealed in the Congregation's first Constitutions of 1906, which were written by Langevin. At first the search in the 1970s seemed to be guided by the need (i) to find some indication that the community would emerge from the crisis, and (ii) to have a retrospective look at God's will. The place of women religious and their experience was not articulated in the writings at this point, but by the late 1970s the spiritual interrogating point

The first four generals superior. Seated is Mother St Viateur; to her left, Mother Marie-Joseph and to her right, Mother François-Xavier. Standing in the middle is Mother Jean-de-la-Croix (Marie-Jeanne Arcand), the newly elected general superior. Picture taken in 1951.

of reference was the community's past understanding of the spiritual principles. The writings show great difficulties in revising the understanding of the past (the collective memories) and in sifting through the hagiography.

There was a delicate balance between questioning the understanding of the Congregation's past and acknowledging the legacy that legitimized its own existence. As Dora Tétreault explained, the Sisters tried to make sense of the traditions and memories to find out what they had meant in the past, and to connect them to their living faith. There was a shift from a language of mortification and grace to a language of social justice. The search was on for a renewed spirituality that might be in relation to the Founder and to the spirituality he gave them. Thus, Tétreault analyzed the signification of their name as explained by Langevin. Further, she examined the meaning of religious oblation and reparation for the Oblate Sisters by tracking the writings of Mother Marie-Joseph as published in the *Chroniques* in the 1910s. Tétreault even explored the theological foundation of oblation and reparation. She asked if in the context of the 1970s the original understandings of reparation had been surpassed because its meaning was attached to the mentality of another time. She moved away from a language of pain, which she defined as masochistic, and instead asserted that "before repairing the neighbors' houses we should repair ours first."[29]

While General Superior Léa Boutin's efforts had been directed towards the internal rebuilding of the congregational house and moving towards a more participatory style of leadership, her successor, Sister Alice Trudeau, continued to emphasize the work of human growth and spirituality, "wanting the Sisters to become free themselves."[30] But her main thrust as general superior between 1981 and 1989 was external, directed towards the mission and a repositioning of the leadership at the interface with society and the Church. In accord with the signs of the time, she moved women strongly to the forefront of an interrogation of the past, while Dora Tétreault provided supporting research.

The relation with the Oblate Fathers had always been a sensitive one, but Trudeau even more so than her predecessors did not hesitate to question oppressive practices of the past. The Founder, Langevin, was an Oblate and the Sisters' spirituality and charism were nourished by Oblate spiritual traditions. The Congregation general council's documents and letters show many instances of resistance to and negotiation with the Oblate Fathers, who were in charge of residential schools. However, the work in the residential schools became over time a very important component of the Sisters' work.

Still, many Sisters did not feel ownership of the residential school project, and some, like Sister Louis de France (who was deeply committed to furthering children's education) and Mother St Viateur (who was committed to the place of French Canadians in Canada), seemed to believe that teaching in residential schools was not their deepest purpose as a congregation. It would not be until 1983 that the Sisters would unravel their memories of the relationship with the Oblate Fathers in the residential schools. Alice Trudeau made a presentation to the Oblate Fathers' congress in which she characterized the Sisters' role as missionary educators and auxiliary to the clergy as one of subordination. The Sisters, she said, were in a disadvantageous and, in some cases, abusive situation. "The Sisters," Trudeau told the Fathers, "saw themselves as inferior, as not being motivated to develop their autonomy, or to show initiative and assume responsibilities. Immaturity was encouraged and many felt used." She continued, "Some of the Sisters kept memories of resentment because they felt exploited but they did not have the courage to confront and make their needs known."[31]

In the 1980s and 1990s, the Aboriginal people's testimonies of painful experiences in residential schools and their desire to assert their identity placed the Sisters at the centre of a historical debate concerning cultural genocide. Furthermore, in the mid-1990s accusations regarding the improper behaviour of some priests and brothers in Fort Alexander (and in other residential schools) and the emergence of legal cases generated a degree of sorrow and confusion in some Sisters, and a desire for understanding in others. The interviews with older Sisters conducted by Sister Dora Tétreault and myself produced a defensive historical narrative and a rosy picture of the missions. Important questions emerge. How were the Sisters to interpret that hurting past when the work in the residential schools (missions) had been conceived of as God's will? How were they to deal with their own role when they had served as auxiliaries to the Fathers as stipulated in their 1931 Constitutions? These are questions that have not been entirely resolved. The legal cases have not facilitated open exploration; moreover, nor have the ecclesiastical structure and the place of women in that structure encouraged questioning.

Since 1989 and through the 1990s the leadership of the Congregation reflected the contradictions and fears emerging from the process of change. In a way the leadership represented a challenge to renewal, a move to look for protection in the security of the memories that had made the congregation a growing community. But it was also a period of great grassroots movements with visionary insights that questioned memories and historical narratives, traditionalism, spiritual dualism, and patriarchy, and that searched for new spiritual meanings. The General Chapter of 1993 exemplified the characteristics of that decade. The theme of the chapter, "Rebuild the House," was taken from the book of Haggai 1:8,[32] a theme used by Tétreault in her writings. It reflected the influence of Sisters working for change. The chapter called for "a new collective paradigm to open a way towards an integral transformation" addressing (i) the integration of the Sisters' identity as Oblate women; (ii) the refoundation of the community; (iii) the creation of diversified types of communities; (iv) an understanding of the vows as "elements of transformation for the world"; and (v) the ecological dimension of spirituality. In practice, it was a time of negotiation with a leadership distrustful of change.[33]

In 1990 I became involved with the Congregation as a historian who was willing to question the hagiographic baggage and the entire tradition that had been built up over the years. The process became particularly challenging in 1995 when I presented "Lifting the Veil: The Foundation of the Missionary Oblates of the Sacred Heart and Mary Immaculate in Manitoba" to the symposium on the history of the Oblates in western and northern Canada.[34] The reaction to my paper revealed two major currents in the community: a prophetic-visionary one, and another that feared losing the original meaning, as the Sisters had understood it. That tension remains to this day although the community as a whole has moved dramatically to new understandings. It also became evident that at the time a major part of the community (including the leadership) was not fully interested in a disciplined study of the past. The situation is now changing.

In 1996 Sister Dora Tétreault made a comparative historical analysis of the 1906 constitutions written by Langevin and the 1931 revised constitutions written, in compliance with the 1917 code of canon law, under the guidance of Oblate chaplain Father Péalapra.[35] As explained in chapter 3 of this book, she found that the 1931 constitutions had altered the mission of the Oblate Sisters by subordinating their educational mission to their role of supporting the priests (Oblates). The very vision of the congregation was affected by eradicating the womanly aspects of spirituality and by emphasizing love for the Church and placing respect for the priesthood to the fore. In a way, Tétreault's historical analysis provides a reason, an explanation, for the Sisters' lack of psychological autonomy, independence, and communal apostolic creativity, as well as for institutional spiritual stagnation. It also helps to make sense of the Sisters' relationship with the Oblate Fathers. The textual analysis of the constitutions, however, does not attack the roots of the Congregation's identity or the charism given by their Oblate founder. Rather, it vindicates them.

Tétreault moved ahead to articulate the community's spirituality in a new way by preparing discussion documents for the 1997 General Chapter.[36] She questioned the spiritual dualism still dominant in the Church, which has a hierarchical and patriarchal view of the sacred. She used the 1983 constitutions as a starting point in her argument. These encouraged a renewed spirituality with a biblical and theological basis that was in line with the signs of the time. She imbued the vision of the vows and principles with a dimension of justice, with ecological awareness, and with a sense of personhood.[37] In the process of refounding and in the search for life and relevance, Tétreault's efforts served to recreate and integrate the Congregation's understanding of the heritage of the Founder and Cofoundresses. She used a triangle to articulate this understanding. Alma Laurendeau (Mother Marie-Joseph) represents the interior dimension of the spirituality and of the Mission: relationship to God through the Word and Contemplation. This is in line with the historical memory of her as being profoundly oriented towards the love of God. Ida Lafricain (Mother St Viateur) represents the exterior dimension of spirituality and of the mission: commitment to the poor in the world and through action. Tétreault's interpretation rescues Ida's personal history before she joined the Oblates, yet it is still linked to the original myth of foundation. However, in the same text the reference to Ida's heroic obedience reflects a traditional reading of her induction into the Congregation, using the old language. Archbishop Langevin, the Founder, represents concern for justice, faith, and culture, while maintaining a difficult balance between contemplation and action. Such an interpretation relates to the very origin of the Congregation and to Langevin's quest to repair the injustice to Catholics in Manitoba as a consequence of the resolution of the Manitoba School Question.[38]

The Aulneau Renewal Centre, founded in 1979 at the mother house, 601 Aulneau Street in St Boniface, was turned in the 1990s into a flourishing counselling service centre mainly for low-income people. The centre became the avenue for channelling a renewed commitment to justice. In the rereading of the charism, the Holy Spirit (love) is seen as the link that holds in communion relationship to God, commitment to the poor, and justice. The charism statement paid particular attention to womanhood as a source of life in line with the direction taken by General Superior Alice Trudeau between 1981 and 1989. However, the leaders of the Congregation did not fully address the impact of ecclesiastical power on the community's development.

GOING FULL CIRCLE

The collective memory in its official version helped the Sisters to make sense of their everyday life. The past had always been present in the form of rituals, practices, and routines. Daily language construed and represented a world that the Sisters internalized as a given. The official memories were construed with and through the church language of the time, and they included concepts such as submission, humility, mortification, sinfulness, and providence. They centred from the beginning around Langevin, the Manitoba school question, and the issue of injustice in relation to Catholics and to Franco-Manitobans. The roles of Ida Lafricain and Alma Laurendeau, the first two mothers superior, are placed initially within that context.

The unofficial memories were oral recollections of small acts of transgression that were passed off as amusing stories of challenges to the rules, but that revealed a desire for autonomy. They helped many Sisters to deal with contradictions and feelings. The unofficial memories broke the rigidity of daily life and eventually brought issues such as education, personal autonomy, and womanhood to the forefront of Oblate community life. These memories were reflected in the powerful presence in the community of Sister Louis de France (Albina Laberge), the dissonant early voice, and her influence on the Sisters' educational formation in the 1950s and 1960s.

In an attempt to recreate the meaning of the Congregation, the interrogation of past memories, first motivated by Vatican II, went back to Langevin's Oblate spirituality and the components of the charism he gave to the community. The thread in the construction and reconstruction of the past was the need to develop historical relevance, group solidarity, and cohesion with a thrust towards the future. The community and Dora Tétreault kept Langevin's concern with justice, although it was reframed in a contemporary context. The school-teaching component that was originally central to the mission of the Congregation is not present in the refounding, for now the emphasis is on justice, integral growth and holistic living, healing and ecological restoration, education as empowerment, and spiritual direction. The Sisters identify themselves in the renewal process as educators of the faith.

The Oblate Sisters have been guided by insightful generals superior, namely Sisters Léa Boutin and Alice Trudeau, and inspired by the work of Sister Dora Tétreault, along the renewal journey. These leaders vindicated nonofficial memories (the counterculture), rescued their transformative potential, and articulated, within their own existential parameters, the experiences of their cofoundresses. The interrogation of the past was done in light of the process of refounding or of imagining a future, and this process was understood as life-giving (rather than as death to the Congregation). The pieces of the puzzle have been reaccommodated to the demands of a new world. In this process, the past is infused in the present but couched in a new language.[39]

The contradictions emerging from rereading the charism and the historical interpretative problems may be of concern to scholars like me, but they are of little relevance to the community. The past, as the Sisters understand it, has been part of the process of living a religious life as a community with a degree of cohesion and meaning. A disciplined study of the past would have jeopardized the continuity of memories and tradition that the Sisters were not ready or willing to question or abandon at that point.[40] However, the renewal process opened an inquiry process and a desire to explore meanings and identities. Léa Boutin, Alice Trudeau, and Dora Tétreault are no longer viewed as subversive Sisters but as trusted voices for the ongoing renewal process in the Congregation.

APPENDIX A

Tables

TABLE 1

Missionary Oblate Sisters Who Took Vows 1904–2004: Membership by Province or State of Origin

PROVINCE	
Manitoba	194
Quebec	138
Saskatchewan	34
Ontario	10
Alberta	7
British Columbia	1
New Brunswick	1
STATE	
Massachusetts	3
Maine	1
Minnesota	2
New York	1
North Dakota	3
Vermont	1
Total	396

Source: Archives of the Missionary Oblate Sisters (AMO)

TABLE 2

Membership Profile (1904–2004): Oblate Sisters Who Took First Vows, Left the Mission, or Died

Period (Years) Vows	New Member/1st Temporary Vows	Attrition During Final Vows	Attrition After	Deaths
1904–1915	69	3	–	2
1916–1927	62	6	2	13
1928–1939	82	10	–	11
1940–1951	75	9	–	12
1952–1963	88	13	2	13
1964–1973	17	7	19	19
1974–1981	1	–	11	36
1982–2004	2	1	10	81
Total	396	49	44	187

Source: Archives of the Missionary Oblate Sisters (AMO)

TABLE 3
Membership Profile (1904–2004): Oblate Sister Candidates Entering from Quebec

Period (Years)	New Members/First Vows	Candidates from Quebec	Quebec Members (%)
1904–1915	69	46	66.7
1916–1927	62	30	48.4
1928–1939	82	29	35.4
1940–1951	75	13	17.3
1952–1963	88	17	19.3
1964–2004	20	0	0.0

Source: Archives of the Missionary Oblate Sisters (AMO)

TABLE 4
Father's Occupation Listed for Missionary Oblate Sisters Who Took Vows

Father's Occupation	Oblate Sister Member (#)
Farming	245
Business (commerce)	35
Contractor (building)	13
Labour (journeyman)	25
Trades	35
Office Work	11
Professional	14
Public Services	8
Fishing/Lumber (Primary Industries)	4
Unknown	6

Source: Archives of the Missionary Oblate Sisters (AMO)

TABLE 5

Languages Spoken by Oblate Sisters Prior to Entering the Mission

Period	French Only	English Only	French/ English	English/ Cree	French/ English/ Ojibway	English/ Ojibway	Polish/ English	Hungarian English
1904–1915	27	–	40	–	1	–	1	–
1916–1927	23	–	33	–	3	–	–	3
1928–1939	26	–	50	1	–	1	1	3
1940–1951	14	–	56	–	–	2	1	2
1952–1963	12	–	75	–	–	1	–	–
1964–2004	2	2	16	–	–	–	–	–
Total	104	2	270	1	4	4	3	8

Source: Archives of the Missionary Oblate Sisters (AMO)

APPENDIX B

Maps

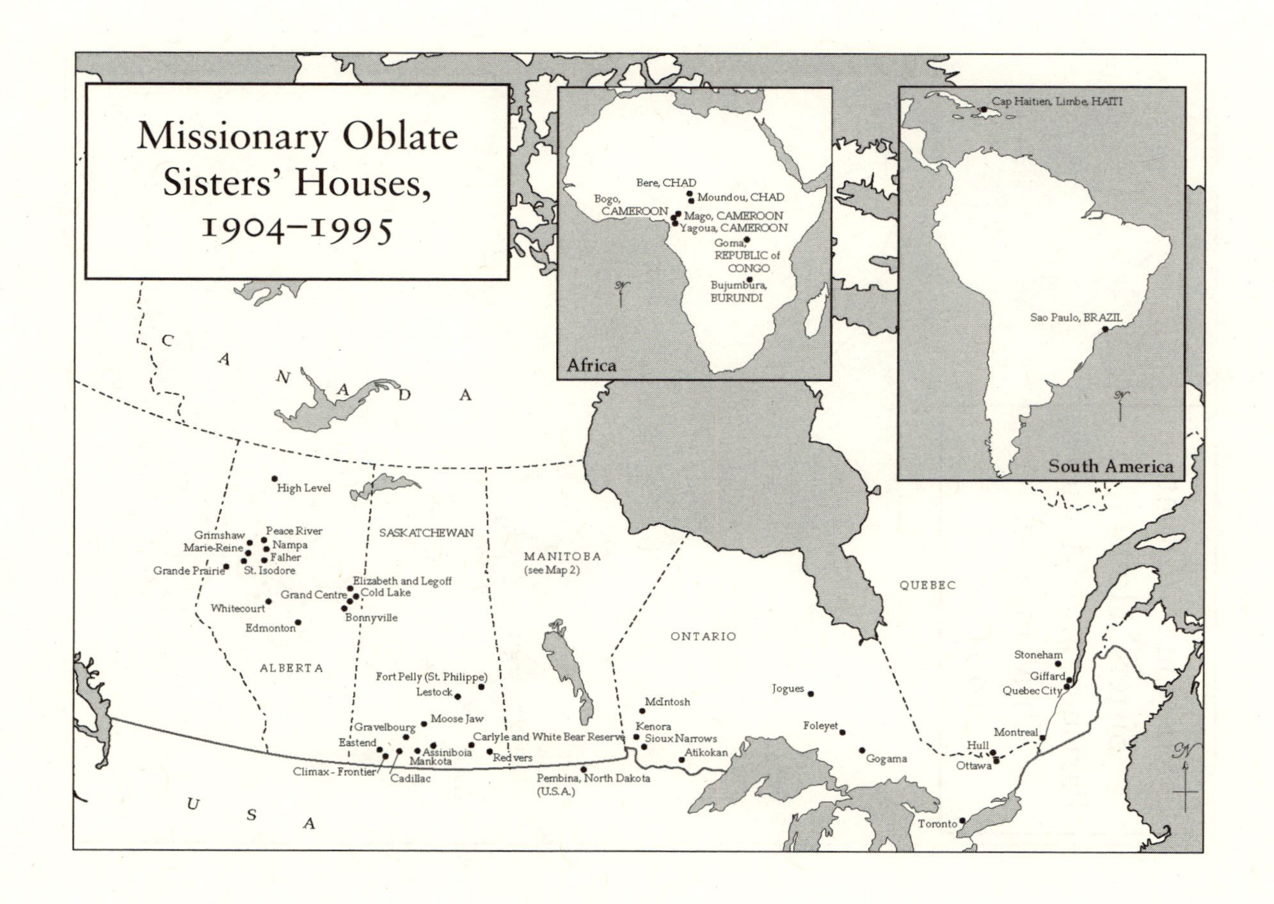
Missionary Oblate
Sisters' Houses,
1904–1995
C A N A D A
U S A
ALBERTA
SASKATCHEWAN
MANITOBA
(see Map 2)
ONTARIO
QUEBEC
High Level
Grimshaw
Marie-Reine
Grande Prairie
Peace River
Nampa
Falher
St. Isodore
Whitecourt
Edmonton
Grand Centre
Elizabeth and Legoff
Cold Lake
Bonnyville
Fort Pelly (St. Philippe)
Lestock
Moose Jaw
Gravelbourg
Eastend
Assiniboia
Mankota
Carlyle and White Bear Reserve
Red vers
Climax - Frontier
Cadillac
Pembina, North Dakota
(U.S.A.)
McIntosh
Kenora
Sioux Narrows
Atikokan
Jogues
Foleyet
Gogama
Toronto
Hull
Ottawa
Montreal
Stoneham
Giffard
Quebec City
Africa
Bere, CHAD
Moundou, CHAD
Bogo,
CAMEROON
Mago, CAMEROON
Yagoua, CAMEROON
Goma,
REPUBLIC of
CONGO
Bujumbura,
BURUNDI
South America
Cap Haitien, Limbe, HAITI
Sao Paulo, BRAZIL

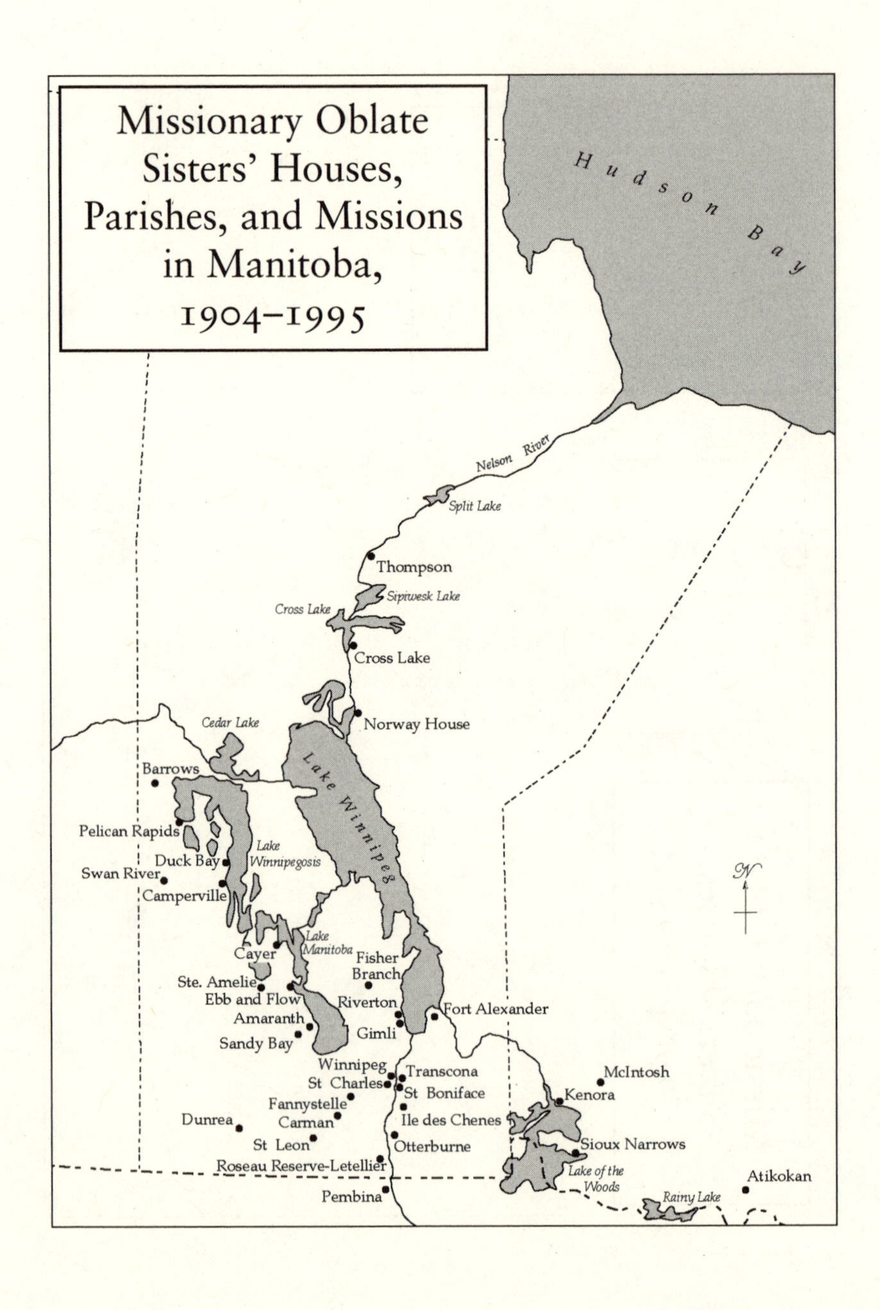
Missionary Oblate
Sisters' Houses,
Parishes, and Missions
in Manitoba,
1904–1995
Hudson Bay
Nelson River
Split Lake
Thompson
Sipiwesk Lake
Cross Lake
Cross Lake
Norway House
Cedar Lake
Lake Winnipeg
Barrows
Pelican Rapids
Lake Winnipegosis
Duck Bay
Swan River
Camperville
Lake Manitoba
Cayer
Fisher Branch
Ste. Amelie
Ebb and Flow
Riverton
Amaranth
Fort Alexander
Gimli
Sandy Bay
Winnipeg
Transcona
St Charles
St Boniface
Fannystelle
McIntosh
Kenora
Dunrea
Carman
Ile des Chenes
St Leon
Otterburne
Sioux Narrows
Roseau Reserve-Letellier
Lake of the Woods
Atikokan
Pembina
Rainy Lake
N

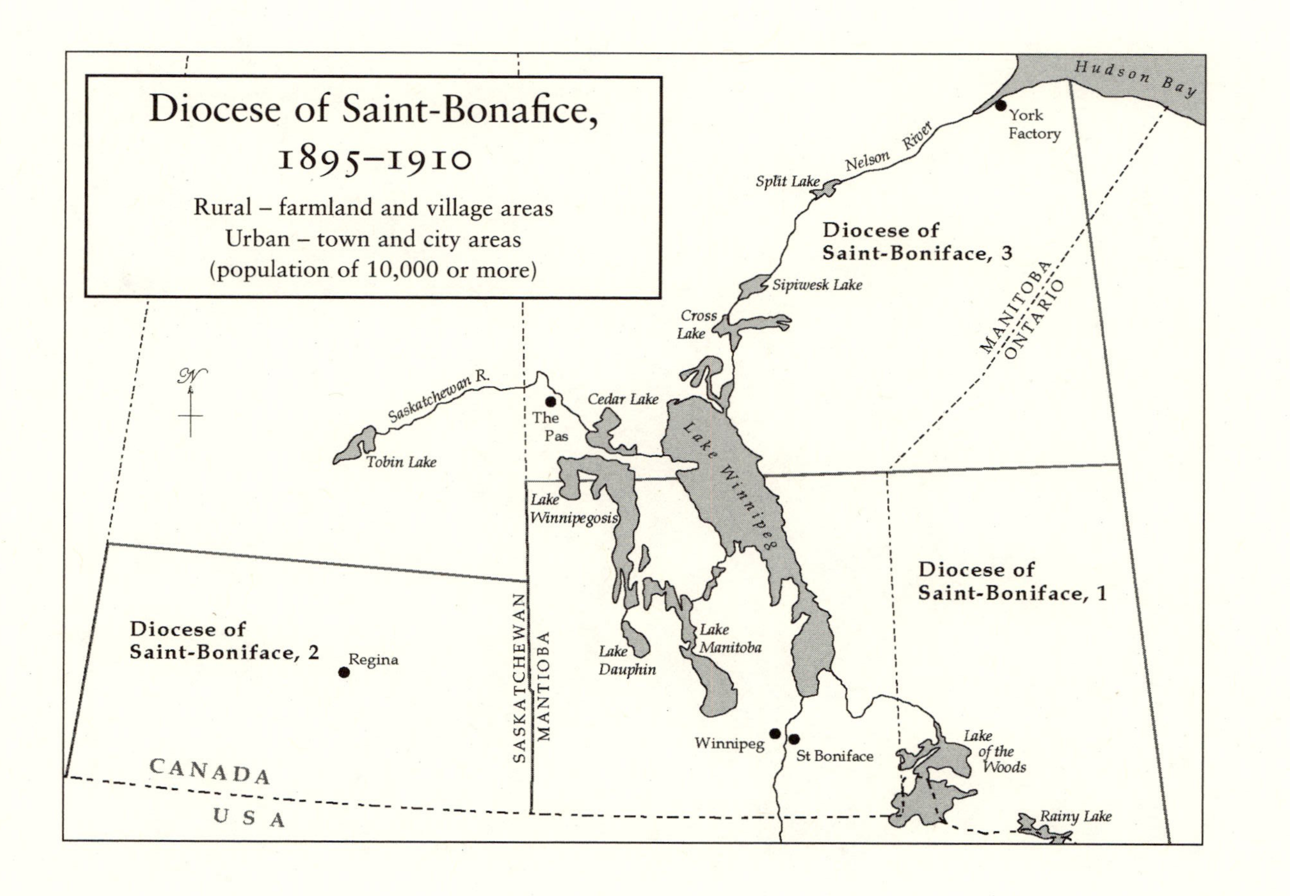

Diocese of Saint-Bonafice,
1895–1910
Rural – farmland and village areas
Urban – town and city areas
(population of 10,000 or more)
Hudson Bay
York Factory
Nelson River
Split Lake
Diocese of Saint-Boniface, 3
Sipiwesk Lake
Cross Lake
MANITOBA
ONTARIO
Saskatchewan R.
Cedar Lake
The Pas
Tobin Lake
Lake Winnipeg
Lake Winnipegosis
Diocese of Saint-Boniface, 1
Diocese of Saint-Boniface, 2
Regina
SASKATCHEWAN
MANTIOBA
Lake Dauphin
Lake Manitoba
Winnipeg
St Boniface
Lake of the Woods
Rainy Lake
CANADA
USA

APPENDIX C

Missionary Oblate Sisters' Houses

	Date opened	Name of House	Location/Diocese	Function
1	1902	Maison-Chapelle	St Boniface, Manitoba Diocese: St Bonifice	Mother house and novitiate
2	1906	St Charles Convent/Academy (In 1985 St Charles Retreat Centre opens in the Sisters' new residence)	323 St Charles Street St Charles, Manitoba Diocese: Winnipeg (1916)	Private, boarding (till 1969) and day school, grades K-12 (10–12 till 1973) Retreats and spiritual direction
3	1909	Cross Lake Indian Residential School (Oblate Fathers in charge)	Cross Lake I.R. Manitoba Diocese: Keewatin-Le Pas	Residential school, (closed 1969) Same work in all residential schools: teaching, child care and supervision, nursing and domestic work. Day school (till 1972)
4	1909	Jardin de l'Enfance Langevin	St Boniface, Manitoba Diocese: St Boniface	Private boarding/day school for boys, grades K-6, closed 1973
5	1910	St Philippe Indian Residential School (Oblate Fathers) (see no. 15)	Fort Pelley I.R. Saskatchewan Diocese: Regina	Residential school (closed 1913, lack of personnel and resources)
6	1911	Couvent St-Joseph	Fannystelle, Manitoba Diocese: St Boniface	Public school, grades 1 to 11 day students/boarders, closed 1984

	Date opened	Name of House	Location/Diocese	Function
7	1912	Couvent de la Nativité	Dunrea, Manitoba Diocese: Winnipeg	Parish school (to 1953/ boarders till 1960) Public school 1942–73
8	1913	Mary Immaculate Academy	Pembina, North Dakota, USA Diocese: Fargo	Parish day and boarding school (closed 1915, lack of resources and students)
9	1914	Fort Alexander Indian Residential S. Replaced Sisters of the Cross (Oblate Fathers in charge)	Fort Alexandre I.R. Manitoba Diocese: St Boniface	Residential school (till 1970) day school (till 1973), pastoral work (till 1995)
10	1915	Maison St-Joseph (Clerics of St Viateur in charge)	Otterburne, Manitoba, Diocese: St Boniface	Domestic care of Maison St-Joseph, a boys' orphanage (till 1920)
11	1918	Collège Mathieu (Oblate Fathers in charge)	Gravelbourg, Saskatchewan Diocese: Regina	Domestic care of Collège Mathieu (till 1921)
12	1921	Jardin de l'Enfance ND du Rosaire (1 Sister returned to Gravelbourg for Pastoral and Youth Ministry in 1999)	Gravelbourg, Saskatchewan Diocese: Regina (Gravelbourg 1930)	Private boarding and day school for boys, grades K-7 (1924–1964)

	Date opened	Name of House	Location/Diocese	Function
13	1921	Jardin de l'Enfance St-Joseph	Giffard, Quebec Diocese: Quebec	Private boarding school for boys grades K-6 (till 1944)
14	1924	École de l'Assomption	Trancona, (Winnipeg) MB Diocese: St Boniface	Parish bilingual day school, grades K-8 (till 1973)
15	1925	McIntosh Indian Residential School (Oblate Fathers in charge)	McIntosh, Ontario Diocese: St Boniface (Thunder Bay 1952)	Residential school (till 1969)
16	1925	Stoneham school (parish school subsidized by a lumber company)	Stoneham, Quebec Diocese: Quebec	Parish day and boarding school (till 1930, under a 5-year contract)
17	1928	St Philippe Indian Residential School (Oblate Fathers in charge)	Kamsack, (Fort Pelley) Saskatchewan Diocese: Regina	Residential school (till 1952)
18	1928	Camperville Pine Creek Residential School. Replaced the Benedictine Sisters (Oblate Fathers in charge)	Pine Creek I.R. Camperville, MB Diocese, Winnipeg	Pine Creek I.R. School (till 1969) Day school (1970–84) Pastoral work

	Date opened	*Name of House*	*Location/Diocese*	*Function*
19	1932	Lestock Indian Residential School MO Sisters replaced Grey Nuns (Oblate Fathers in charge)	Lestock, Saskatchewan Diocese: Regina	Musquowequan residential school (till 1979)
20	1936	School on Berens River Reserve Sisters replaced by the Grey Nuns	Berens River, Manitoba Diocese: St Boniface	The Sisters left when the Dept of Indian Affairs opened a hospital instead of a school.
21	1939	Île-des Chênes Convent	Île-des-Chênes, Manitoba Diocese: St Boniface	Public school, bilingual, grades 1–11 (till 1991) pastoral work - 2000
22	1939	Christ the King Convent	Camperville, Manitoba Diocese: Winnipeg	Day school under the official trustee, MB Dept of Ed. (till 1973)
23	1939	École Ménagère Notre-Dame	St Boniface, Manitoba Diocese: St Boniface	Home economics school for girls till 1968 Working girls' residence till 1980
24	1942	Maison Notre-Dame-du-Cénacle	St Boniface, Manitoba Diocese: St Boniface	Hospitality and domestic work for diocesan retreat house (till 1957)
25	1944	École St-Joseph	Quebec City, Quebec Diocese: Quebec	Private day school for boys (till 1985)

	Date opened	Name of House	Location/Diocese	Function
26	1940	St-Amélie Convent	St-Amélie, Manitoba Diocese: Winnipeg	Public school, grades 1–8 (with boarders at the convent till 1970)
27	1943	École Ste-Marie (Sisters resided at Maison-Chapelle, St Boniface)	St Vital, Manitoba Diocese: St Boniface	Parish bilingual school, grades 1 to 8 (till 1968)
28	1944	Residence Nazareth	St Charles, Manitoba Diocese: Winnipeg	Dormitory for senior boarders of St Charles Academy (till 1966)
29	1945	Cayer Convent	Cayer, Manitoba Diocese: Winnipeg	Public school, grades 1-8 under official trustee.(Boarders at the convent till 1957)
30	1948	Missionary Oblate Sisters Infirmary	St Boniface, Manitoba Diocese: St Boniface	For sick and elderly sisters
31	1950	Otterburne Convent	Otterburne, Manitoba Diocese: St Boniface	Public school, grades 1–8 (till 1975)
32	1952	Île-des-Chênes Convent	Île-des-Chênes, Manitoba Diocese: St Boniface	Public school, 2-room rural, grades 1 to 8 (till 1959)

	Date opened	*Name of House*	*Location/Diocese*	*Function*
33	1953	Duck Bay Convent	Duck Bay, Manitoba Diocese: Winnipeg	Public school grades 1–8 under official trustee. (Teaching till 1974; pastoral work till 1998)
34	1956	Assiniboia Convent	Assiniboia, Saskatchewan Diocese: Gravelbourg	Assiniboia RC separate school grades 1–12; teaching (till 2000)
35	1957	Riel School (rural). Sisters residing at Île-des-Chênes Convent	Grande Pointe, Manitoba Diocese: St Boniface	Two-room Public school grades 1–8 (till 1959)
36	1957	Pelican Rapids Convent	Pelican Rapids I.R. Manitoba Diocese: Winnipeg	Day school, grades 1–8 Teaching, nursing, (till 1978)
37	1957	Marie-Reine Convent	Marie-Reine, Alberta Diocese: Grouard-McLennan	Catholic bilingual separate school grades 1-8 (till 1969)
38	1958	St-Isidore Convent	St-Isidore, Alberta Diocese: Grouard-McLennan	Catholic bilingual separate school grades 1–8 (till 1969)
39	1958	Our Lady of the Lake Convent	Cold Lake, Alberta Diocese: St Paul	St Dominic RCS school, grades 1–12 teaching and pastoral work (till 1991)

	Date opened	Name of House	Location/Diocese	Function
40	1960	Joseph the Worker Parish, Residence at Assumption Convent	Transcona, Manitoba Diocese: St Boniface	Anglophone Catholic parish school grades 1–6 (till 1984)
41	1961	Holy Family Convent	Grimshaw, Alberta Diocese: Grouard-McLennan	RC separate school, grades 1-8 teaching, pastoral work (till 1987)
42	1961	Blessed Sacrament Parish Sisters reside at Assumption Convent	Transcona, Manitoba Diocese: St Boniface	Anglophone Catholic parish school grades 1–6 (till1973)
43	1961	St-Emile Parish (1961–66), Sisters commute from the mother house. (In 1966 residence rented from the parish)	St Vital, Manitoba Diocese: St Boniface	Anglophone Catholic parish school grades 1–8 (till 1986)
44	1962	Nampa Convent	Nampa. Alberta Diocese: Grouard-McLennan	Catholic separate school grades 1–8 (till 1987)
45	1962	MO Sisters with the St Boniface Missionary Pastoral Team in Brazil	San Paulo, Brazil Diocese: San Paulo	Pastoral and religious ed. work in two favella parishes to 1966
46	1963	Assumption RC separate school with Sisters commuting from Cold Lake	Grand Centre, Alberta Diocese: St Paul	Assiniboia RC Separate School grades 1–9 then 10–12 (till 1987)

	Date opened	Name of House	Location/Diocese	Function
47	1963	Whitecourt Convent	Whitecourt, Alberta Diocese: St Paul	Catholic separate school, grades 1–9 and social work (till 1975)
48	1965	Sioux Narrows Convent	Sioux Narrows, Ontario Diocese: Thunder Bay	Father Moss Public school grades 1–9 (till 1970)
49	1965	Holy Cross Parish Sisters commuting from other houses	Winnipeg, Manitoba Diocese: St Boniface	St Boniface Diocesan High School sisters teach till 1970
50	1965	Mankota Convent	Mankota, Saskatchewan Diocese: Gravelbourg	Catholic separate school grades 1–8 (till 1981)
51	1967	St Patrick Parish Convent	Atikokan, Ontario Diocese: Thunder Bay	St Patrick Catholic separate school grades 1–9 (till 1976)
52	1967 (1975)	Manitoba school for the Deaf Sisters commuting from St Boniface in residence at Deaf Centre Manitoba	Winnipeg, Manitoba Diocese: Winnipeg	Religious Ed. (Sign language) board member, pastoral ministry, parish administration (till 2001)
53	1969	Our Lady of Peace Convent	Peace River, Alberta Diocese: Grouard-McLennan	Catholic separate school, grades 1–6 and 7–12, nursing (till 1975)

	Date opened	Name of House	Location/Diocese	Function
54	1969	Lestock Convent	Lestock, Saskatchewan Diocese: Regina	2 public schools, grades 1–6 and 7–12 (till 1979)
55	1969	Ebb and Flow Convent	Ebb and Flow , Manitoba Diocese: Winnipeg	Public school, grades 1–8 (till 1974)
56	1969	Barrows Convent	Barrows, Manitoba Diocese: Winnipeg	Public school, teaching grades 1–8 (till 1993) and pastoral work
57	1969	Sisters commuting from St Boniface	John Bosco Centre/Kateri Tekakwitha, Winnipeg, Manitoba	Religious education, pastoral work with aboriginals (till 1992)
58	1970	Kenora residence	Kenora, Ontario Diocese: Thunder Bay	Catholic separate school and Confederation College (till 1972)
59	1970	Sisters commuting from St Charles	Stony Mountain, Manitoba Diocese: Winnipeg	Visitation, music ministry Liturgy, chaplaincy (till 1994)
60	1971	Elphinstone-Crystal City residence	Elphinstone / Crystal City Diocese: Winnipeg	Teaching and pastoral work (till 1978)

	Date opened	*Name of House*	*Location/Diocese*	*Function*
61	1971	Swan River Convent (See reopening in 1993)	Swan River, Manitoba Diocese: Winnipeg Religious	Education and pastoral work (till 1983)
62	1971	Moundou Residence	Moundou, Chad, Africa Diocese: Moundou	Catholic girls' school, teaching and training of teachers (till 2000)
63	1972	Béré Convent	Béré, Chad, Africa Diocese: Moundou	Promotion of women: literacy, health, social, and parish work (till 1993)
64	1974	Riverton and Gimli residence	Riverton and Gimli, Manitoba Diocese: Winnipeg	Evergreen school Division, teaching and coordination of special services (till 1977)
65	1974	St Francis Assisi / St Louis Monfort parish residence	Ottawa, Ontario Diocese: Ottawa	Pastoral work (till 1992)
66	1974	Sister commuting from St Charles to John XXIII Parish	Winnipeg, Manitoba Diocese: Winnipeg	Coordinator religious education pastoral work (till 1993)
67	1976	L'Arche (Jean Vanier Homes for adults with intellectual disabilities	Edmonton, Alberta Diocese: Edmonton	Manager-coordinator of L'Arche Enterprises, women's section (till 1982)

	Date opened	*Name of House*	*Location/Diocese*	*Function*
68	1976	Middlegate Apartment	Winnipeg, Manitoba Diocese: Winnipeg	Misericordia Hospital Chaplaincy (till 1989) PRH Formation
69	1976	Sisters Commuting from St Charles to Grace Hospital	Winnipeg, Manitoba Diocese: Winnipeg	Nursing and pastoral work at Grace Hospital (till 1997)
70	1976	Elizabeth Residence	Elizabeth & Legoff, Alberta	Pastoral work and religious education Cold Lake First Nation (till 1981)
71	1980	Falher Residence	Falher, Alberta Diocese: Grouard-McLennan	Co-ordination of diocesan religious education and audio-visual resource centre (till 1988)
72	1981	Emmaus House (Balmoral Street) and Galilee Residence at Arnprior, Ontario (till 1985)	Diocese: St Paul Winnipeg, Manitoba Diocese: Winnipeg	Formation for candidates and youth ministry (till 1986) Intercommunity formation team
73	1982	High Level Residence	High Level, Alberta Diocese: Grouard-McLennan	Elementary Catholic separate school and pastoral work (till 1985)
74	1982	Hull - Fournier District Residence	Hull, Quebec Diocese: Hull Pastoral	Pastoral work (till 1989)

	Date opened	*Name of House*	*Location/Diocese*	*Function*
75	1982	Carman Residence	Carman, Manitoba Diocese: St Boniface	Pastoral work, religious education, and nursing (till 1985)
76	1983	Roseau - Letellier Residence	Roseau I. Reserve Diocese: St Boniface	Pastoral work (till 1987)
77	1983	St Leon Residence	St Leon, Manitoba Diocese: St Boniface	Elementary public school (till 1990)
78	1984	Cadillac Residence	Cadillac, Sakatchewan Diocese: Gravelbourg	Parish administration and pastoral work (till 1986)
79	1984	Oakwood Residence	Oakwood Street, Winnipeg, Manitoba Diocese: Winnipeg	House of formation for candidates (till 1992)
80	1984	Cap Haitien Residence	Cap Haitien, Haiti Diocese: Limbé	Nursing at Hôpital St-Jean (till 1987)
81	1985	Sandy Bay Residence	Amaranth/Sandy Bay, Manitoba Diocese: Winnipeg	Religious education at Sandy Bay First Nation school and pastoral work (till 1999)

	Date opened	Name of House	Location/Diocese	Function
82	1985	Résidence Père Marquette	Québec, Québec Diocese: Québec	Teaching at École Jean-Berchmans Pastoral ministry with immigrants
83	1985 1986	Mission de Guémé Yagoua Centre	Guémé, Cameroun, Africa Yagoua, Cameroun, Africa Diocese: Yagoua	Pastoral work with SND sisters Co-ordinator at Yagoua Diocesan Missionary Centre (till 1988)
84	1986	Mission de Maga	Maga, Cameroun, Africa Diocese: Yagoua	Parish founding/administration Pastoral work/teaching at high school/women and youth (till 2000)
85	1986	Mission de Bogo	Bogo, Cameroun, Africa Diocese: Maroua-Mokolo	Teaching, pastoral work, promotion of women (till 1996)
86	1986	Point North Project	Argyle Street, Winnipeg, Manitoba Intercommunity	Ministry project with prostitutes (till 1991)
87	1985	Toronto Residence	Eglinton Street, Toronto, Ontario Diocese: Toronto	Counselling at Southdown (till 1992) Teaching at Loretto Academy

	Date opened	Name of House	Location/Diocese	Function
88	1986	Bonnyville Residence	Bonnyville, Alberta Diocese: St Paul	Co-ordination of religious education, Lakeland Catholic school division (till 1994)
89	1986	Grande Prairie Residence St Joseph Parish	Grande Prairie, Alberta Diocese: Grouard-McLennan	Teaching and pastoral work (till 1994)
90	1986	Carlyle Residence	Carlyle, Saskatchewan Diocese: Regina	Religious education and pastoral work at Carlyle and White Bear Mission (till 1992)
91	1987	East End Residence	East End, Sakatchewan Diocese: Gravelbourg	Parish administration and pastoral work (till 1990)
92	1987	Frontier Residence	Climax, Saskatchewan Diocese: Gravelbourg	Parish administration and pastoral work (till 1994)
93	1987	Thompson Residence	Thompson, Manitoba Diocese: Keewatin-Le Pas Parish	Administration, pastoral work at Wabowden and Thicket Portage
94	1988	Colony-Balmoral Inner City Project	Winnipeg, Manitoba Diocese: Winnipeg	Community development and family assistance (till 1994)

	Date opened	*Name of House*	*Location/Diocese*	*Function*
95	1989	Les Enfants d'Amour Project	St-Anselme, Quebec Diocese: Quebec	Home for 20 adoptees with handicaps of Louise Brissette, MO Associate
96	1989	Rue de la Roche Apartment	Montreal, Quebec Diocese: Montreal	Nursing home caregivers; spiritual and human growth counselling
97	1989	Fisher Branch Residence	Fisher Branch, Manitoba Diocese: Winnipeg	Pastoral work at Arborg, Peguis Reserve, hospital and nursing home
98	1990	Moose Jaw Residence	Moose Jaw, Saskatchewan Diocese: Regina	Teaching at St Margaret Mary separate school, pastoral work (till 2000)
99	1991	Carman Rectory	Carman, Manitoba Diocese: St Boniface	Parish administrator and pastoral work at Carman and Elm Creek (till 1997)
100	1991	Redvers Residence	Redvers, Saskatchewan Diocese: Regina	Pastoral work (till 1994)
101	1992	St-Joachim Rectory	Edmonton, Alberta Diocese: Edmonton	Parish administration and pastoral work at St-Joachim French Parish

	Date opened	*Name of House*	*Location/Diocese*	*Function*
102	1992	Maison Langevin	Langevin Street, St Boniface, Manitoba Diocese: St Boniface	Counselling at Aulneau Renewal Centre
103	1993	Swan River Convent	Swan River, Manitoba Diocese: Winnipeg	Religious education, pastoral work at Swan River, Pelican Rapids, Belsite Barrows, Mafeking
104	1993	St Andrew's -West St Paul	St Andrew's, Manitoba Diocese: Winnipeg	Pastoral and music ministry at St Theresa Parish
105	1993	St Mary's Road Apartment	Winnipeg-St Vital, Manitoba Diocese: St Boniface	Pastoral work at St-Eugene Parish (till 1999)
106	1993	Setter Street Apartment	Winnipeg, Manitoba Diocese: Winnipeg	VON - WHRA, nursing and palliative care
107	1994	Kenaston Rectory	Kenaston, Saskatchewan Diocese: Regina Parish	Parish administrator and pastoral ministry (till 1995)
108	1995	Gogama Residence	Gogama, Ontario Diocese: Hearst	Parish administration and pastoral work at Gogama, Shining Tree, Westree and Mattagami Reserve (till 2001)

	Date opened	Name of House	Location/Diocese	Function
109	1995	Foleyet Residence	Foleyet, Ontario Diocese: Hearst	Parish administration and pastoral work at Foleyet, religious education at Chapleau (till 1996)
110	1995	Goma Residence for ARP Rwanda Project (Aid to Reconstruction of Persons), with IFHIM (Institut de Formation Humaine) and TSF (Terre sans frontières) of Montreal, and Oxfam Canada Goma,	Goma, Republic of Congo, Africa Diocese: Goma	Counselling and training of professional people among the Rwanda refugees to empower the others to overcome their trauma, rebuild their lives and communities (till 1997)
111	1997	Bujumbura Residence (similar project with same partners as 108 above: IFHIM and TSF)	Bujumbura, Burundi, Africa Diocese: Bujumbura	Similar work as 104 above (till 2002)
112	2000	Bujumbura Project École New School with TSF	Bujumbura, Burundi, Africa Diocese: Bujumbura	Direction of project (till 2002)
113	2002	Goma Residence for a continuation of project ARP-Goma (# 104) in the aftermath of the volcano eruption	Goma, Rwanda Diocese: Goma	A two-year ARP project helping people rebuild their lives and homes (extended till 2006)

	Date opened	*Name of House*	*Location/Diocese*	*Function*
114	1996	Mattice Residence	Mattice, Ontario Diocese: Hearst Parish	Administration and pastoral work (till 1998)
115	1998	Regina Residence	Regina, Sakatchewan Diocese: Regina	Director of diocesan pastoral ministries (till 2000) Volunteer work at Visitation House, Correctional Centre (2001–)
116	2001	Alexandre de Sève Residence	Montreal, Quebec Diocese: Montreal	Pastoral work at Paroisse du Sacré-Coeur
117	2001	Good Shepherd Convent, Project with Scarboro Missions and the Sisters of the Good Shepherd	Pattaya, Thialand, Asia Diocese: Pattaya	Work at Fountain of Life Centre with women and children, victims of the sex trade and poverty
118	2002	Residence and work with Holy Cross Sisters	Cap Haitien, Haiti Diocese: Limbé	Work in a program of educational development among the poor

Notes

FOREWORD

1 Rosa Bruno-Jofré and Sybil Shack (compilers), "Recollections, Reminiscenses and Reflections," in *Issues in the History of Education in Manitoba: From the Construction of the Common School to the Politics of Voice*, edited by Rosa Bruno-Jofré (Lewiston, NY: Edwin Mellen Press, 1993), 627–33.

2 Rosa Bruno-Jofré, "Lifting the Veil: The Founding of the Missionary Oblate Sisters of the Sacred Heart and Mary Immaculate in Manitoba," *Historical Studies in Education* 9, no. 1 (Spring 1997): 1–21.

3 Ibid.

CHAPTER ONE

1 Adélard to My Dear Daughters, Rome, House of the Oblates of Mary Immaculate, 29 September 1906, Archives of the Missionary Oblate Sisters (henceforth, AMO), St Boniface.

2 "La Province Ecclésiastique de Saint-Boniface," *Les Cloches de Saint-Boniface* 1, no. 1 (15 January 1902):3. See also Josaphat Magnan, OMI, "I Remember Archbishop Adélard Langevin, OMI," brochure for the exclusive use of the Congregation (no date), 32, translated by Patricia Leahy for the Missionary Oblate Sisters, 1985. *Oblate Fathers Manitoba Monthly Review*, 1958.

3 For the Manitoba school question see Robert Perin, *Rome in Canada: The Vatican and Canadian Affairs in the Late Victorian Age* (Toronto: University of Toronto Press, 1990), ch. 5, 127–57; Tom Mitchell, "Forging a New Protestant Ontario on the Agricultural Frontier: Public Schools and the Origins of the Manitoba School Question 1881–1890," *Prairie Forum* 2, no. 1 (1986): 33–51; Gilbert Comeault, "The Politics of the Manitoba School Question and Its Impact on L.-P.-A. Langevin's Relations with Manitoba's Catholic Minority Groups, 1895–1915" (Master's thesis, University of Manitoba, 1977).

4 J. Ad. Sabourin, DD, *En face de la persécution scolaire au Manitoba*, brochure (St Boniface, Manitoba: Arthur, Archbishop of Saint-Boniface, 1922), 131.

5 See for example, J. Ad. Sabourin, DD, *La religion et la morale dans nos écoles*. Brochure (St Boniface, Manitoba: Arthur, Archbishop de Saint-Boniface, 1925).

6 Gérard Jolicoeur, *Les Jésuites dans la vie Manitobaine, 1885–1922* (St Boniface, Winnipeg, Manitoba: CEFCO, 1986), 91–4.

7 Marguerite Jean, CCIM, *Evolution des communautés religieuses de femmes au Canada de 1639 à nos jours* (Montreal: Fides, 1977), 151–6.

8 Archbishop Langevin was often portrayed as intransigent, as unable to find negotiated solutions, and as a person who was eager to have absolute, all-or-nothing, solutions.

9 Adélard, OMI, Archbishop of Saint-Boniface to Dr Jacques (Montreal), 10 October 1900; Adélard to Allen Guasco (General Secretary for the Propagation of the Faith), 30 March 1902; Adélard to Georgina White (Montreal), 22 March 1902; Adélard to Gravel, 30 March 1902; Adélard to the Mother General of Les Soeurs des Saints Noms de Jésus et Marie, 22 April 1902, AMO. See also Adélard, OMI, Archbishop of Saint-Boniface, "Appel en faveur des oeuvres catholiques du diocèse de Saint-Boniface, Manitoba," *Les Cloches de Saint-Boniface* 1, no. 2 (15 February 1902): 25–8, AMO.

10 Adélard to Guasco, 30 March 1902; Adélard to Georgina White, 22 March 1902; Adélard to Gravel; Adélard to the Mother General, 22 April 1902, AMO.

11 Adélard to J. Emile Foucher (Montréal), 18 December 1902, 11 January 1903, 27 March 1903, 31 January 1904, AMO.

12 "Premières constitutions des Soeurs Missionnaires Oblates du Sacré-Coeur et de Marie Immaculée" (1906), copy of the manuscript, St Boniface, Manitoba, 3 July 1968, ch. 1, D9, 8, AMO.

13 "Monseigneur Langevin," Quelques extraits des notes de notre Soeur St-Charles, Edith Hennesey, MO, décédée le 10 décembre 1945," manuscript, AMO.

14 Jean Séguy, 'Pour une sociologie de l'ordre religieux," *Archives des sciences sociales des religions* 57, no. 1 (January-March 1985): 64–5.

15 Robert Perin, *Rome in Canada,* 127.

16 1 Timothy 6:20.

17 For an account of early efforts at recruiting see "Les Débuts de la Congrégation des Missionnaires Oblates du SC et de MI," in *Chroniques des Missionnaires Oblates du Sacré-Coeur et de Marie Immaculée* 1, no. 1 (June 1911): 19–21, AMO.

18 Mère Marie-Joseph, MO, "First Attempts at Organizing the Congregation of the Missionary Oblate Sisters," 2, translated by Sister Suzanne Boucher, manuscript, AMO.

19 Elizabeth Storozuk (Sister Marie-Gertrude). Oral history of the beginnings of the Missionary Oblate Sisters, as told in 1974 when she was eighty-four years old. AMO

20 The Congregation used in their letters the term "recrue" (recruit) and the verb "recruter" to refer to the candidates who had been interested in being admitted, in particular.

21 "Journal de la Maison-Chapelle," 29 July 1903, AMO.

22 The scapular of the Sacred Heart of Jesus is a piece of white flannel cloth embroidered with the emblem of a red bleeding heart circled with thorns and surmounted with golden flames. It is said that from 14 February to 8 December 1876, the Virgin Mary, calling herself "mother all merciful," appeared to Estelle Faguette, in Pellevoisin, France. Estelle Faguette (1843–1927) was a thirty-year-old woman dying of tuberculosis and peritonitis. She was miraculously cured. She spent the rest of her life spreading Mary's message: love of Jesus through prayer, conversion, penance, and reparation and by making scapulars of the Sacred Heart of Jesus. Monastère des Dominicaines, *Pellevoisin, Un centenaire: Estelle nous parle* (Pellevoisin, France: Imprimerie Laboureur, 1976).

23 Mère Marie-Joseph, MO, "First Attempts," 10–11. This is the only source of information regarding the first two attempts to create the Congregation and it is based on oral accounts.

24 Mère Marie-Joseph, MO, "First Attempts," 18.

25 Ibid., 21–3.

26 Ibid., 14–19.

27 Adélard to Foucher, 11 January 1903, 27 March 1903, 16 October 1903, 6 November 1903, 10 December 1903, 31 January 1904, 25 February 1904, AMO.

28 Sister Gabrielle Viau, MO, *Elles étaient deux, vol. 2, Mère Marie-Joseph du Sacré Coeur, MO, 1879–1958* (St Boniface, Manitoba, n.p., 1989), 31.

29 "Journal de la Maison-Chapelle," Opening Note, March 1904; also 15 and 24 March 1904, AMO.
30 According to Yves Raguin, SJ, Father Pichon founded Bethany House. Yves Raguin, SJ, *Au-delà de son rêve ... Délia Tétreault*, 49 (Montréal: Fides, 1991). However, according to the "Notes of Père Léon Pouliot, SJ," the house was founded by Madame Poitou. Archives ASJCF, St-Jérome BO-51, 1 Pichon (RP)
31 Sister M. Francois-de-Sales, MO, "Notes recueillies sur notre chère Mère M. Saint-Viateur," under the title "Petits faits," n.d., written before 1922, manuscript, AMO. For an account of Délia Tétreault's life and her relation with Father Pichon and the clergy see Yves Raguin, SJ, *Au-delà de son rêve*, chs. 2, 3, and 4.
32 Gisèle Villemure, MIC, *Qui est Délia Tétreault? Mère Marie du Saint-Esprit, 1865–1941* (Bibliothèque nationale du Québec, 1983), 23.
33 Sister M. François-de-Sales, MO, "Notes recueillies," 8–9, AMO. In a letter addressed to Délia Tétreault dated 15 August 1905, Ida wrote a post scriptum saying: "You will receive shortly the ring that you have given me. Here we will wear a silver ring. Therefore, I am sending it back as I had promised with best thanks." Sister St Viateur to Ma bien chère amie (Délia Tétreault), 15 August 1905. Archives, Missionnaires de l'Immaculée-Conception (hereafter AMIC), Montreal, Quebec.
34 Gisèle Villemure, MIC, *Qui est Délia Tétreault?*, 25.
35 "Journal de la Maison-Chapelle," 29 July 1903, AMO.
36 Adélard to Foucher, 6 November 1903, AMO.
37 Foucher to Adélard, 11 November 1903, AMO. Also reproduced in Mère Marie-Joseph, MO, "First Attempts," 19.
38 Gustave Bourassa to Délia Tétreault, 8 August 1902, AMIC. This letter leads us to believe that Ida did not hide her feelings of disagreement, as became clear later during her first years in St Boniface.
39 Sister M. François-de-Sales, MO, "Notes recueillies," 10, AMO.
40 Ibid. A novena is a devotional prayer recited during nine consecutive days usually to obtain a special favour from God.
41 Adélard to Foucher, 31 January 1904, 25 February 1904, 6 March 1904, AMO.
42 Sister M. François-de-Sales, MO, "Notes recueillies," 10–11, AMO.
43 Mère Marie-Joseph, MO, "First Attempts," 28.
44 "Les débuts de la Congrégation," *Chroniques des Missionnaires Oblates*, 1, no. 1 (June 1911): 21. AMO.
45 Sister M. Francois-de-Sales, MO, "Notes recueillies," 11–12, AMO.
46 "Les débuts de la Congrégation," 24.

47 Hermenegilde Charbonneau, OMI, "Les pauvres et les âmes abandonnées d'après Mgr de Mazenod," in "Actes du congrès sur le charisme du fondateur aujourd'hui, Rome 24 April – 14 May 1976," edited by Marcello Zago, OMI, *Vie Oblate*, 36 (March-June 1977): 131.

48 Since the Second Vatican Council, the term "charism" has been associated with the identity and integrity of religious congregations. It refers to the founder's spirit and special aims. See Margaret Susan Thompson, "Charism or Deep Story? Towards Understanding Better the 19th Century Origins of American Women's Congregations," *Review for Religious*, 58 (May–June 1999): 230–1.

49 The Oblate Fathers had authority over the Missionary Oblate Sisters in the residential schools and the missionary work with the Aboriginal peoples.

50 Ida Lafricain to Foucher, 28 March 1904, AMO.

51 Adélard to Mes chères filles, 24 April 1904, AMO.

52 Sister St Viateur to Foucher, 1 May 1904, AMO.

53 Ibid.

54 Sister St Viateur to Foucher, 7 August 1904, AMO.

55 Ibid. See also Sister Gabrielle Viau, MO, *Elles étaient deux*, vol. 2, *Mère Marie-Joseph du Sacré-Coeur,* MO, 36. After Langevin returned from Europe in October 1904, he dismissed Father Trudel and replaced him with Father J. Camper, OMI.

56 Sister St Viateur to Foucher, 7 August 1904, AMO.

57 Sister St Viateur (Ida Lafricain) destroyed the first letters she received from Délia Tétreault. Later on the letters they exchanged on special occasions were formal and devoid of any personal sentiments.

58 Sister St Viateur to Ma chère amie (Délia Tétreault), 23 August 1904, AMIC.

59 Ibid.

60 Adélard to Foucher, 18 February 1905, AMO.

61 Ibid.

62 Ibid.

63 Sister St Viateur to Foucher, 19 February 1905, AMO.

64 Sister M. Francois-de-Sales, MO, "Notes recueillies," 12, AMO.

65 Sister St Viateur to Foucher, 19 February 1905, AMO.

66 Sister M. Francois-de-Sales, MO, "Notes recueillies," 12, AMO.

67 Adélard to Foucher, 19 April 1905, AMO.

68 Ibid.

69 Ibid. Father J.C. Camper, OMI, was appointed jointly by his provincial superior and Langevin as chaplain of the Maison-Chapelle, 31 October 1904.

70 Sister Gabrielle Viau, MO, *Elles étaient deux*, vol. 1, *Mère Saint Viateur,* MO, (St Boniface, Manitoba, n.p., 1967), 22.

71 Sister Marguerite Viau, MO, former archivist, reported that both Sister St Viateur and Sister Marie-Joseph destroyed the letters they had written to Langevin when these were returned to them after Langevin's death. Sister St Viateur also destroyed some of the letters from Foucher.

CHAPTER TWO

1 The Rule of St Augustine refers to a rule or plan of life after the spirit of the gospel ascribed to St Augustine, bishop of Hippo, Africa (354–430). It is used by those whose special object required a somewhat less strict form of government than that of the Rules of St Basil or St Benedict. The Fourth Council of the Lateran (1215) refused to recognize any religious institutes that did not observe a rule approved by the Holy See. Consequently, the founders chose a rule already accepted by the Church. *Catholic Encyclopedia*, vol. 12, S.V. "Religious Life." (New York: The Grilinary Society, 1911).

2 The Sacred Heart refers to Jesus who gave his life out of love to save humanity. "Premières Constitutions des Missionnaires Oblates du Sacré-Coeur et de Marie Immaculée" (1906), copy of the manuscript, St Boniface, Manitoba, 3 July 1968, AMO.

3 Ibid. "Constitutions de la Congrégation des Missionnaires Oblates du Sacré-Coeur et de Marie Immaculée, St-Boniface, Manitoba," 1931, ch. 1, article 3: 2, 4, and 6, AMO.

4 A mendicant order is an order of friars or nuns, such as the Franciscans or Dominicans (both founded in the thirteenth century), that combines monastic life and outside activities and that originally owned neither personal nor communal property.

5 "Monseignor Langevin," "Quelques extraits de notes de notre Soeur St-Charles, MO, Edith Hennesey, décédée le 10 déc. 1945," AMO.

6 Adélard to My Dear Daughters, St Boniface, 6 October 1905, AMO. Parmélie Comeau, a schoolteacher from Quebec whose brother, Ambroise Comeau, was an Oblate priest, was the fourth woman to join the community after March 1904.

7 Ibid.

8 Sister Louis de France (Albina Laberge), recorded interview by Rosa Bruno-Jofré and Dora Tétreault, 3 July 1990.

9 Adélard to My Dear Daughters, Rome, Oblate College, Via Polveriera, 19 September, 1906, AMO.

10 "Mémoire en faveur de la fondation récente de la Congrégation des Oblates

du Sacré-Coeur et de Marie-Immaculée," 19 September 1906, *Chroniques des Missionnaires Oblates du Sacré-Coeur et de Marie Immaculée* 1, no. 6 (September 1912): 93–4.

11 "Premières constitutions" (1906), AMO. "Constitutions de la Congrégation," 1931, ch. 1, article 3:3 and 6, AMO.

12 For an analysis of French Canadianism see Marcel Martel, *French Canada: An Account of Its Creation and Break-up, 1850–1967*, The Canadian Historical Association, Canada's Ethnic Group Series, booklet no. 24, 2–4.

13 Adélard to Sister St Charles, 17 October 1909, AMO.

14 Adélard to Sister St Charles, 5 November 1909, AMO.

15 Adélard Langevin to Sister St Charles, Grey Nun, Ottawa, 4 April 1896, AMO. Mme de Staël (Germaine Necker, Baronne de Staël, 1766–1817) was an influential French writer whose liberal tendencies incurred the hostility of Napoleon.

16 Ibid.

17 Adélard to My Dear Daughters, St Boniface, 6 October 1905, AMO.

18 Adélard to My Dear Daughter (Sister St Viateur), First Council of Bishops, Quebec, 14 October 1909, AMO.

19 Adélard to My Dear Daughters, Canadian Pacific Railway, 12 May 1910, AMO.

20 "The Subject and Power," in Michel Foucault: *Beyond Structuralism and Hermeneutics*, edited by Hubert Dreyfus and Paul Rabinow (Brighton, UK: The Harverster Press, 1982), 214.

21 "Journal des novices à l'étude à St-Charles, pour leur Mère-Maîtresse," 11 June 1909, AMO.

22 Adélard to My Dear Daughters, Liége, 24 August 1904, AMO.

23 Adélard to My Dear Daughters, Rome, Oblate College, 19 September 1906, AMO.

24 See for example, Adélard to My Dear Daughter (Sister St Viateur), 20 January 20 1908 and 5 June 1905, AMO.

25 Adélard to My Beloved Daughters, Notre Dame de Lourdes, Hautes Pyrénées, 6 July 1908, AMO.

26 Capital sin refers to evil inclinations in human nature, such as pride, gluttony, greed, sloth, envy, anger, or impurity.

27 "Premières constitutions" (1906), ch. 3, D4. AMO.

28 Archbishop Langevin, Sermon to the Sisters, 17 November 1912. Notes taken by Sister Marie-Joseph, AMO.

29 See for example, "Journal des novices à l'étude à St-Charles, pour leur Mère-Maîtresse," 11 June 1909, AMO.

30 Éva Dégagné, "Mémoires written at the age of ninety-three at the request of Sister Alice Trudeau, in 1988–89, AMO. "Danser le petit bonhomme" means skipping from one foot to the other in a crouched position.

31 Father Albert Lacombe, OMI (1827–1916), became a legend in Alberta. He was born in the parish of St Sulpice near Montreal, son of Agathe Duhamel, descendent of a maiden carried off into captivity by the Iroquois in their seventeenth-century wars against the French. Father Lacombe, who made his perpetual vows as an Oblate in 1856, worked in Alberta from 1852 until his death in 1916. He served the white and Métis settlements at Lake St Anne, St Albert, and Saint-Paul-des-Cris on the Saskatchewan River, itinerated to evangelize the 1,100 Aboriginal people of the surrounding area, and visited the Peace River country and the satellite mission of Lesser Slave Lake, 260 kilometres away. He developed ties of friendship and trust with the Cree, Blackfoot, and Chipewyan. Robert Choquette, *The Oblate Assault on Canada's Northwest* (Ottawa: University of Ottawa Press, 1995), 43-5.

32 Juniorists were high school girls interested in becoming Sisters who were enrolled in an informal formation program intended to prepare them to enter the Congregation.

33 Adélard to My Dear Daughter (Sister St Viateur), Personal letter 125, 4 January 1909, AMO.

34 Adélard to My Dear Daughter (Sister St Viateur), Archbishop's Residence, 5 January 1909, AMO.

35 Adélard to Sister Marie-Joseph, maîtresse des novices, Archbishop's Residence, 17 May 1909, AMO.

36 See note 20 in chapter 1 with reference to the use of the term "recruitment."

37 Adélard, À tous les membres de la Congrégation des Missionnaires Oblates du Sacré-Coeur et de Marie Immaculée. "Lettres du Fondateur," 174, [no day], January 1910, AMO.

38 Langevin to My Dear Daughter (Sister St Viateur), Archdiocese of St Boniface, 3 January 1910, AMO.

39 Adélard à toutes les Missionnaires Oblates du Sacré-Cœur et de Marie Immaculée à la Maison-Chapelle, St-Charles, Corss Lake, Fort Pelley, 12 May 1910, AMO.

40 Henri Bernard to Sister Marie-Joseph, 29 July 1911, AMO. Also, in 1913, Sister Marie-Joseph was sent as directress to open a new convent in Pembina, North Dakota, thus distancing her from Mother St Viateur.

41 Langevin to My Dear Daughter (Sister St Viateur), Archbishop's Residence, St Boniface, 24 March 1910, AMO.

42 Adélard to Henri Bernard, 19 December 1913, AMO.

43 For comparisons with other congregations' experiences with the Rule see Micheline D'Allaire, *Vingt ans de crise chez les religieuses du Québec: 1960–1980*, "La Règle qui tue l'esprit," ch. 6, (Québec: Éditions Bergeron, 1983), 181–222. Also, Mary Ann Hinsdale, I.H.M., "'The Roughest Kind of Prose': IHM Socialization, 1860–1960," in *Building Sisterhood: A Feminist History of the Sisters, Servants of the Immaculate Heart of Mary*, edited by Sisters, Servants of the Immaculate Heart of Mary, Monroe, Michigan (Syracuse, NY: Syracuse University Press, 1997), 119–49.

44 Adélard to Rev. Mother St Viateur, 15 September 1913, AMO.

45 Adélard to the Missionary Oblate Sisters of the Sacred Heart and of Mary Immaculate, 8 September 1914, AMO.

46 Henri Bernard to Rev. Père A.J. Morice, Saint-Pierre, Montréal, 20 November 1915, 5–7, AMO. The acceptance of Henri Bernard by Langevin was obviously important. He had been threatened with prison as a consequence of his battles against the Freemasons. He appeared in a pictorial history entitled "Monseigneur Langevin: L'Archevêque patriote, 1855–1915," Les Contes Historiques de la Société Saint-Jean-Baptiste de Montréal, 1920, AMO.

47 Henri Bernard to Sister St Viateur, 16 October 1909, letter 14, AMO.

48 H. Bernard to Adélard Langevin, 25 December 1911, AMO.

49 "La mort de notre bien-aimé Fondateur et Père," *Chroniques des Missionnaires Oblates* 2, no. 4 (June 1915): 1; emphasis in the original.

50 "Journal de la Maison-Chapelle," AMO. Also quoted in Dora Tétreault, "Monseigneur Langevin: Son charisme de fondateur," presented at the meeting of Oblate directresses, 20 August 1974, AMO.

CHAPTER THREE

1 Lawrence Cada, SM, Raymond Fitz, SM, et al., *Shaping the Coming Age of Religious Life* (New York: The Seabury Press, 1979), ch. 2. Sister M. François-de-Sales, MO, "Notes recueillies sur notre chère Mère St-Viateur," under the title "Petits faits," n.d., written before 1922, manuscript, 28, 34, AMO.

2 Mother St Viateur to Henri Bernard, 30 June 1915, AMO.

3 Sister M. François-de-Sales, MO, "Notes recueillies," 28, 34, AMO.

4 Code of canon law (approved in 1917 and published in 1921).

5 Sisters Servants of the Immaculate Heart of Mary, eds. (Munroe, Michigan), *Building Sisterhood, A Feminist History of the Sisters, SIHM*, (Syracuse, NY: Syracuse University Press, 1997), 179.

6 Minutes du Conseil, 2 August 1921, AMO.

7 Minutes du Conseil, 28 July 1916, AMO.

8 See Sören Kierkegaard, *The Journals of Kierkegaard*, translated by Alexander Dru (London: Collins, 1967), and Jean-Paul Sartre, *Being and Nothingness*, translated by Frank and Hazel Baines (London: Methuen, 1957), 112. See also Micheline D'Allaire, "Le Coutumier des religieuses – Codificateur de vie?", in *Religion Populaire Religion de Clercs?*, edited by Benoit Lacroix et Jean Simard (Quebec City: Institut Québecois de Recherche sur la Culture, Bibliothèque Nationale de Québec, 1984), 235–56. D'Allaire also noticed the different approach that men took to the rules.

9 Ibid.

10 Sister M. François-de-Sales, MO, "Notes recueillies," 35, AMO. Already in 1902 Ida Lafricain had been assigned by Délia Tétreault the responsibility of purchasing the furniture, sewing machines, and other items for the École Apostolique in Montreal and had been commended by the chaplain, Father Bourassa, for her abilities in that regard.

11 Ibid.

12 Ibid.

13 Sister M. François-de-Sales, MO, "Notes recueillies," AMO.

14 For example, Henri Bernard relates to Mother St Viateur the contents of a letter that a discontented Sister sent him after she left the community (apparently she was not considered a suitable member). There are also sympathetic narrations from older Sisters. For example, Annie Trohak, interviewed by Dora Tétreault.

15 "Journal of St Philippe," 18 and 28 June 1910, AMO.

16 Father Louis Péalapra to Archbishop Béliveau of St Boniface et al., Document entitled "In View of a Foundation by the Oblate Sisters in Quebec to Promote their Recruitment," written sometime in 1919, AMO.

17 Mother St Viateur to Péalapra, 7 September 1919, from St-Sauveur, Quebec, AMO.

18 *Chroniques des Missionaires Oblates du Sacré-Coeur et de Marie Immaculée* 3, no. 9, (June 1920): 143. See also ibid. 3, no. 12, (June 1920): 184.

19 L. Péalapra to Father Lortie, 4 June 1919, AMO.

20 L. Péalapra to Father Lortie, 12 April 1920, AMO.

21 Mother St Viateur to Péalapra, 7 September 1919 from St Sauveur, AMO.

22 "Giffard, Qué." *Chroniques des Missionnaires Oblates* 5, no. 4 (December 1924): 58–60.

23 Mother St Viateur to Péalapra, dated from Quebec, 1 September 1922, AMO.

24 Minutes of the General Council of the Missionary Oblate Sisters, 29 January 1927, AMO.

25 *Chroniques des Missionaires Oblates* 2, no. 6 : 103–4.

26 Letter to Sister St Charles, Grey Nun of Ottawa, 18 December 1907, AMO. She was principal of a girls' high school in Ottawa where Langevin had been chaplain.

27 Henri Bernard to Mère St-Viateur, 24 December 1915, AMO.

28 Minutes of the General Council, 8 November 1919, AMO. The exhortation of the Founder "Vous qui élevez l'enfance ..." seems to refer to that kind of school. "Premières constitutions des Soeurs Missionaires Oblates du Sacré-Coeur et de Marie Immaculée" (1906), copy of the manuscript, St Boniface, Manitoba, 3 July 1968, ch. 1, pt. 5, 15–16, AMO.

29 Ibid.

30 "Journal de St-Charles," 1920, AMO.

31 Sister M. François-de-Sales, MO, "Notes recueillies," 27, AMO.

32 Sister Louis de France herself had taken courses with the University of Manitoba from 1936 to 1938 and obtained her Bachelor of Arts degree from the University of Ottawa in 1941.

33 Jeanne Boucher and Léa Boutin, recorded interview by Rosa Bruno-Jofré and Dora Tétreault, Mother House, Winnipeg, Manitoba, 26 October 1994, AMO.

34 Zélia Auger, recorded interview by Dora Tétreault, Mother House, Winnipeg, 13 March 1994.

35 Evelyn Woodward, *Poets, Prophets and Pragmatists: A New Challenge to Religious Life* (Notre Dame, IN: Ave Maria Press, 1985), 24.

36 Sister Louis de France to Mother Marie-Joseph, 10 January 1949, AMO. Was Sister Louis de France going through what Elizabeth Kubler-Ross calls the bargaining stage in her book *On Death and Dying* (New York: Macmillan, 1969) or was she simply trying to reconcile her behaviour with the strictness of the rule and struggling to find peace with herself?

37 Bessie Donaldson-Maguet, recorded interview by Rosa Bruno-Jofré and Dora Tétreault at her home in St Boniface, Manitoba, 18 November 1993, AMO.

38 Robert Choquette, *The Oblate Assault on Canada's Northwest* (Ottawa: University of Ottawa Press, 1995), 2.

39 Sister Marie-Anne Fillion, recorded interview by Sister Dora Tétreault, 16 October 1994.

40 Sister Gabrielle Viau, MO, *Elles étaient deux*, vol. 2, *Mère Marie-Joseph du Sacré-Coeur, MO 1879–1958* St Boniface, Manitoba, n.p., (1989), 10.

41 The second constitutions of the Missionary Oblate Sisters received diocesan approbation in 1930 and were published in 1931. "Constitutions de la Congregation des Missionaires Oblates du Sacré-Coeur et de Marie Immaculée," St Boniface, Manitoba, 1931, AMO.

42 "Constitutions de la Congregation," 1931, ch. 1, article 2:3, AMO. Compare with the "Premières constitutions" (1906), ch. 1, section 2:2.

43 Sister Dora Tétreault, "Document de travail sur la spiritualité des Missionnaires Oblates," August 1996, translated by Sister Dora Tétreault under the title "Working Paper on the MO Spirituality," 7–8. AMO. She refers here to the "Constitutions de la Congregation," 1931, ch. 11, article 1, and to the "Premières constitutions" (1906), ch. 1, section 3: 3–8.
44 Sister Dora Tétreault, "Document de travail."
45 Ibid.
46 Interestingly, Rev. Henri Bernard, benefactor and friend of the Congregation, had expressed concerns that the clergy could dominate the Sisters after Langevin's death.
47 Father L. Péalapra to Mother St Viateur, 6 February 1926, AMO.
48 *Explications des constitutions et circulaires du R.P. Péalapra*, OMI, Maison Chapelle, St Boniface, 1963. This book produced by the Oblate Sisters contains notes of Father Péalapra's presentations on the 1931 constitutions between 1939 and 1944.
49 Ibid., 31–5.
50 Ibid., 36.
51 Ibid., 38.
52 Ibid., 27.
53 Sister Dora Tétreault, "Document de travail sur la spiritualité des Missionnaires Oblates," 7, AMO.
54 Sister Marie-Joseph du Sacré-Cœur, "First Attempts at Organizing the Congregation of the Missionary Oblate Sisters," 38, translated into English by Sister Suzanne Boucher, MO, manuscripts, AMO.
55 Sister Evelyne Brodeur, recorded interview by Dora Tétreault and Rosa Bruno-Jofré, Mother House, St Boniface, Manitoba, 14 December 1993. Sister Evelyne recalled that she was taking grade 10 (1924–25) in St Charles when she noticed that Mother St Viateur could not remember certain things anymore.

CHAPTER FOUR

1 Sister Marguerite Viau, interviewed by Rosa Bruno-Jofré, 10 March 1994, Mother House, St Boniface, Winnipeg, Manitoba.
2 Mother St Viateur, Circulaire no. 1, Manuscript, 25 July 1927, Maison-Chapelle, St Boniface, Manitoba, AMO.
3 Ibid.
4 Mother St Viateur, Report to the General Chapter, August 1927, AMO.
5 Mother Marie-Joseph to Révérende Soeur Laurendeau, Couvent de Sainte-Anne-des Chênes, 4 October 1927, AMO.
6 Actes du Chapitre, manuscript, 1927, AMO.

7 Ibid.
8 See for example, Minutes du conseil des Missionnaires Oblates du SC et de MI tenu à la Maison-Chapelle le 11 août 1928, AMO.
9 Information provided by Sister Dora Tétreault.
10 Mother Marie-Joseph, Circular no. 3, 19 April 1928, AMO.
11 Louis Philippe Adélard Langevin to the Missionary Oblate Sisters of the Sacred Heart and of Mary Immaculate, Archbishop's Residence, St Boniface, 8 September 1914, AMO.
12 Sister Marie-Joseph, St Charles, Manitoba, to Father Péalapra, 15 July 1921, AMO.
13 Sister Marie-Joseph, St Charles, Manitoba, to Father Péalapra, 23 December 1920, AMO.
14 Mother St Viateur, St Charles, Manitoba, to Sister St Charles, Fort Alexander, Manitoba, 30 October 1927, AMO.
15 Mother St Viateur, St Charles, Manitoba, 30 October 1927, also 1 May 1929 and 28 October 1930, to Sister St Charles, Fort Alexander, AMO.
16 Mother St Viateur, St Charles, Manitoba, to Sister St Charles, Fort Alexander, May 1929, AMO.
17 Mother Marie-Joseph, Maison-Chapelle, St Boniface to Rev. L. Péalapra, OMI, Superior Noviciat de Marie Immaculée, St Laurent, Manitoba, 7 September 1927, AMO.
18 Ibid.
19 Mother Marie-Joseph, Maison-Chapelle, St Boniface to Rev. L. Péalapra, OMI, Superior Noviciat de Marie Immaculée, St Laurent, Manitoba, 16 November 1927, AMO.
20 Mother Marie-Joseph, Maison-Chapelle, St Boniface to Henri Bernard, 5 October 1931 and 12 November 1931, AMO. The letters provide an account of the events that took place in the summer of 1931.
21 Henri Bernard, St Boniface, to Father Péalapra, July 1931, AMO.
22 A reference to the prayer "Praised be the Sacred Heart and Mary Immaculate" that Langevin had given the Sisters and that they repeated as a constant refrain during the day. On 15 November 1908 Langevin wrote to Mother St Viateur: "I am sending you a very important paper that has been signed by the Pope, thanks to Bishop Grouard (OMI). It is 300 days of indulgence for the invocation you so often say: 'Praised be the Sacred Heart and Mary Immaculate.'" AMO.
23 Father Henri Bernard to the Community of the Maison-Chapelle, 1931, AMO.
24 Minutes du Conseil des Missionnaires Oblates du SC et de MI, tenu à la Maison Chapelle, 27 avril 1929, AMO.

25 Mother Marie-Joseph, Maison Chapelle, St Boniface to Ma chère Mère, 4 July 1929, AMO.
26 Questions résolues en Chapitre comme devant faire partie du directoire ou du coutumier, 1929, manuscript, AMO.
27 Mother Marie-Joseph, Circular no. 12, 24 December 1932, AMO.
28 Mother Marie-Joseph, Circular no. 17, 29 September 1933, AMO.
29 Mother Marie-Joseph, Circular no. 18, 21 December 1933, AMO. "Dépot" (the sacred gift entrusted to the Oblate Sisters) is a reference to Archbishop Langevin's motto: Depositum custodi (Garde le dépot – Keep the trust), 1 Timothy 6: 20.

CHAPTER FIVE

1 Sister Germaine Cinq-Mars, recorded interview by Sister Dora Tétreault, 27 October 1993, AMO.
2 "Journal des Novices à l'étude à St Charles pour leur Mère-Maîtresse," 17–18 December 1908, AMO.
3 Annie Trohak, interviewed by Sister Dora Tétreault, at age ninety, 11 November 1993, AMO.
4 It is a theme in the various interviews conducted by Sister Dora Tétreault or by Rosa Bruno-Jofré.
5 Sister Gisèle d'Amour, recorded interview by Sister Dora Tétreault, 1994, AMO.
6 Sister Marie-Anne Fillion, recorded interview by Sister Dora Tétreault, 16 October 1994, AMO.
7 Annie Trohak, interviewed by Sister Dora Tétreault, at age ninety, 9 November 1993, AMO.
8 "Journal des Novices à l'étude à St-Charles pour leur Mère-Maîtresse," 23 September 1908 to 11 April 1909, AMO.
9 Annie Trohak, recorded interview by Sister Dora Tétreault.
10 Personal communication from Sister Dora Tétreault.
11 Eva Dégagné, "Mémoires written at the age of ninety-three at the request of Sister Alice Trudeau, in 1988–89," AMO. Sister Eva Dégagné recalled the negative aspects of the novitiate as she experienced them between 1913 and 1916.
12 Ibid. The "rendement de compte" was a personal encounter in which the novice would inform the directress regarding her work, health, and compliance with regulations.
13 Ibid.

14 Ibid.

15 Personal communication from Sister Dora Tétreault.

16 *L'Écho*, a periodical magazine, written by the novices from 1916 to 1921, AMO.

17 See for example, the sections "Actualités" or "La guerre" in *l'Écho*, 1, no. 1 (1916): 1; *l'Écho* 2, no. 1(1917):1

18 Annie Trohak, recorded interview by Sister Dora Tétreault, at age ninety, 11 November 1993, AMO.

19 Zélia Auger, recorded interview by Sister Dora Tétreault, 13 March 1994, AMO. Interjections by Dora Tétreault.

20 Ibid.

21 Marguerite Viau, Conversation with Rosa Bruno-Jofré, 15 August 1994.

22 Marta Danylewycz, *Taking the Veil; An Alternative to Marriage, Motherhood and Spinsterhood in Quebec, 1840–1920* (Toronto: McCelland and Stewart, 1987), 106. See also The Clio Collective (Micheline Dumont, Michèle Jean, Marie Lavigne, and Jennifer Stoddart), *Québec Women: A History*, translated by Roger Gannon and Rosalind Gill (Toronto: The Women's Press, 1987).

23 Sisters Zélia Auger, Laurette Salvail, and Mélina Choquette, recording of a memory circle with Rosa Bruno-Jofré and Dora Tétreault, Mother House, St Boniface, March 1994, AMO.

24 Lettres du Vénéré Fondateur à ses filles Les Missionnaires Oblates du Sacré-Cœur et de Marie Immaculée 1903–1915. Archevêché de St-Boniface, À la Révérende Mère St-Viateur, 8 July 1911, 107, AMO.

25 Expression used by Langevin in "Premières constitutions des Missionnaires Oblates du Sacré-Coeur et de Marie Immaculée." (1906), copy of the manuscript, St Boniface, Manitoba, 3 July 1968, AMO.

26 "Premières constitutions" (1906), ch. 5:15.

27 Ibid.

28 No author. "Notre vocation d'éducatrice," a summary of talks to the Sisters at St Charles by Rev. D.M. Beauregard, parish priest from 1921–1928. *Chroniques des Missionnaires Oblates du Sacré-Coeur et de Marie Immaculée* 4, no. 3 (December 1921): 41.

29 Ibid, vol. 4, no. 3 (December 1921): 40–2; no. 4 (March 1922): 57–9; no. 5 (June 1922): 68–71; no. 7 (December 1922): 108–10; vol. 5, no. 10 (September 1923): 108–57.

30 "In Memoriam, Révérende Soeur Saint-Jean-Baptiste, Assistante générale," *Chroniques des Missionnaires Oblates*, 5, no. 2 (June 1924): 17–22.

31 Compositions et journal des élèves, Couvent Saint-Charles, September 1911–1912 to 17 October 1913, AMO.

32 "Congrès pédagogique, les 16, 17, 18 et 19 août 1921." *Chroniques des Missionnaires Oblates* 4, no. 2 (September 1921): 19–21.

33 For a general historical overview see Brian Clarke, "English-Speaking Canada from 1854," in Terrence Murphy and Robert Perin, eds., *A Concise History of Christianity in Canada* (Toronto: Oxford University Press, 1996); 280–3.

34 J.H. Thompson has argued that "the problems with regard to education that beset other minorities directly involved French Canadians." He goes on to say that "including French-Canadians among those regarded by English-Canadian Westerners as 'foreigners' also seems to illustrate the prevailing opinion that the French, far from being 'partners' in Confederation, were simply another ethnic group speaking another foreign language." John Herd Thompson, *The Harvests of War: The Prairie West, 1914–1918* (Toronto: McClelland and Stewart, 1981), 74.

35 Robert W. Milan, "Education and the Reproduction of Capitalist Ideology: Manitoba, 1945–1960" (Master's thesis, University of Manitoba 1980), 62. Jean-Marie Taillefer, "Les Franco-Manitobains et l'Éducation 1870–1970: Une Étude quantitative" (PhD thesis, University of Manitoba, 1987), 262.

36 Ibid. , 263. See also Yvette T. M. Mahé, "Official and Unofficial School Inspection as Hegemonic and Counter-Hegemonic Struggle in Prairie Districts Before 1940," *Canadian Ethnic Studies* 33, no. 2 (2001): 31–51.

37 Taken from Rosa Bruno-Jofré, "Citizenship and Schooling in Manitoba, 1918–1945," *Manitoba History*, (Autumn/Winter 1998–99): 33–5.

38 Ibid.

39 Adélard, OMI, to Soeur Saint-Viateur, document I, St Charles, J.P. Magnan, OMI, Provincial for the Oblate Fathers to Mgr Langevin, St Mary's, Winnipeg, OMI.

40 Adélard, Oeuvre du Couvent de St-Charles, Archevêché de St-Boniface, September 1907, AMO.

41 Adélard, Mémoire pour la Révérende Soeur Directrice du Couvent de St-Charles, Archevêché de St-Boniface, 21 November 1906, AMO.

42 Adélard to Sister St Viateur, on the train, Station Wolfe, August 1906, AMO.

43 Adélard à Mes bien chères filles, Archevêché de St-Boniface, 22 August 1906. Also Adélard to Ma chère fille, St-Laurent, 9 September 1907, AMO.

44 Mother St Viateur, Report to the General Chapter, August 1927, AMO.

45 Mother St Viateur, Report to the General Chapter, August 1927, AMO.

46 Sister Louis de France, interviewed by Rosa Bruno-Jofré and Dora Tétreault, AMO.

47 "Journal de St-Charles," 1911–1915, AMO.

48 "Compositions et journal des élèves," Couvent de St-Charles, 13 April

1911, AMO. The students' journal covered from September 1911–1913 inclusively.

49 Ibid., Couvent de St-Charles, 16 April 1911, AMO. The style and content of the journal varied with the different writers.

50 Constance Franzmann, manuscript, no date. Provided to the author during an interview with Connie in Elm Creek in 1992.

51 Ibid.

52 Bessie Donalson-Maguet, recorded interview by Rosa Bruno-Jofré and Dora Tétreault at her home in St Boniface, Manitoba, 18 November 1993, AMO.

53 Zélia Auger, recorded interview by Dora Tétreault, 13 March 1994, AMO.

54 Sister Louis de France, interviewed by Rosa Bruno-Jofré and Sister Dora Tétreault, Mother House, St Boniface, Manitoba, 3 July 1990, AMO.

55 Mother Marie-Joseph du Sacré-Coeur, "Historical Report on the Congregation of the Missionary Oblate Sisters of the Sacred Heart and Mary Immaculate of St Boniface, Manitoba, Canada," 1939. Translated by Sister Simone Ruest, MO, in 1985, AMO. Original manuscript sent to Rome in 1939.

56 "Transcona, Manitoba" *Chroniques des Missionnaires Oblates* 5, no. 7 (September 1925).

57 Father Péalapra to Mr J.B. Morissette, President of the Schools Boards, Quebec, 2 June 1919, AMO.

58 Until 1909, the boys, mostly from families that were far from school and from a church, were taught at St Charles. They slept in the church rectory but had their meals at the convent. However, there were problems of space and difficulties emerging from the need to separate the boys from the girls since the Church strongly opposed co-education. The Oblate Sisters' Jardins de l'Enfance for boys was a practical solution.

59 Mère Marie-Joseph, MO, "First Attempts at Organizing the Congregation of the Missionary Oblate Sisters," translated into English by Sister Suzanne Boucher, MO, AMO.

60 Sister M. François-de-Sales, MO, "Notes recueillies sur notre chère Mère St-Viateur," under the title "Petit faits," n.d., written before 1922, manuscript, 24. Father L. Péalapra to Archbishop O.M. Mathieu, 23 April 1919; Father L. Péalapra to Father A. Lortie, OMI, 23 April 1919; Archbishop O.M. Mathieu to Father Péalapra, OMI, 10 May 1919, AMO.

61 Mother St Viateur to Péalapra, Quebec, 1 September 1922, AMO.

62 "Journal de Giffard," December 1921 and onwards, AMO; "Giffard, Que.," *Chroniques des Missionnaires Oblates* 5, no. 4 (December 1924): 58–9; "Quebec, École Sainte-Marguerite-Marie," Ibid. 5, no. 5 (Mars 1925): 71–4, among others.

63 Mother Marie-Joseph du Sacré Coeur, "Rapport historique de la Congrégation des Soeurs Missionnaires Oblates du SC et de MI de Saint-Boniface, Manitoba, Canada," typewritten manuscript, 10 July 1939, 9, AMO. This manuscript was sent to Rome.

64 Réouverture des classes, *Chroniques des Missionnaires Oblates* 1, no. 10, 164, AMO.

65 "Journal du couvent St-Joseph," Fannystelle, 1911–1915, AMO.

66 Constance Franzmann, manuscript, memoirs written upon request by the author in 1992.

67 Ibid.

68 Rosa Bruno-Jofré and Colleen Ross, "Decoding the Subjective Image of Women Teachers in Rural Towns and Surrounding Areas in Southern Manitoba: 1947–1960," in Rosa Bruno-Jofré, *Issues in the History of Education in Manitoba: From the Construction of the Common School to the Politics of Voice* (Lewiston/Queenston/Lampeter: Edwin Mellen Press, 1993), 586–7.

69 "Journal du Couvent de Dunrea," 8 September 1912, AMO.

70 Ibid., 1912–1924, AMO.

71 Ibid., 14 June 1924, AMO.

72 Ibid., 20 June 1917, AMO.

73 J.R. Miller, *Shingwauk's Vision: A History of Native Residential Schools* (Toronto: University of Toronto Press, 1996); R. Huel, *Proclaiming the Gospel to the Indians and the Métis* (Edmonton: University of Alberta Press and Western Canadian Publishers, 1996), ch. 8; B. Titley, "A Troubled Legacy: The Catholic Church and Indian Residential Schooling in Canada," in *The Colonial Experience in Education*, edited by A. Novoa, M. Depapepe, and E.V. Johanningmeier, Paedagogica Historica, Supplementary Series 1, 1995.

74 "Premières Constitutions" (1906), ch. 1, article 3.

75 Letter from J.P. Magnan, OMI (Provincial) to Révde Soeur Saint-Viateur, Winnipeg, 24 August 1909, OMI.

76 Sister Annie Trohak, interviewed by Sister Dora Tétreault, 9 October 1993, OMI. She was in Cross Lake from 1926 to 1930 and during the 1950s.

77 Sr Marie-Joseph, General Superior, Maison Chapelle, Circular Letter, 19 April 1928, AMO.

78 Mother Marie-Joseph, "Rapport Historique," AMO.

79 Robert Choquette, *The Oblate Assault on Canada's Northwest* (Ottawa: University of Ottawa Press, 1995). See in particular chs. 10 and 11.

80 J.R. Miller, *Shingwauk's Vision: A History of Native Residential Schools*, 151–343.

81 "Journal de la mission de St-Philippe," 4 May 1910, AMO.

82 Ibid., 25 May 1910.

83 "Echos des Missions. Lac La Croix, Manitoba, École Indienne Saint-Joseph," *Chroniques des Missionnaires Oblates* 5, no. 6 (June 1925): 89.

84 "Nouvelle Fondation à McIntosh," *Chroniques des Missionnaires Oblates* 5, no. 5 (March 1925): 67–8.

85 "Oeuvre des religieuses dans l'ouest," *Chroniques des Missionnaries Oblates* 2, nos. 1 and 2 (September-December 1914): 5–11. Reproduced from R.P. Lewis, OMI, *Les Cloches de Saint-Boniface* 8, no. 22 (15 November 1909): 279.

86 Ibid.

87 Ibid.

88 See for example, Margaret McGovern, SP, "*Perspective on the Oblates: The Experience the Sisters of Providence*," in R. Huel, ed., *Western Oblate Studies* 3, Proceedings of the Third Symposium on the History of the Oblates in Western and Northern Canada, Faculté Saint-Jean, Edmonton 14–15 May 1993 (Edmonton: Alberta, Western Canadian Publishers, 1994), 91-108.

89 Reference in the letter written by Sister St Charles to Mother Marie-Joseph, 26 May 1931. The letter refers to a conflict-ridden relation between Sister St Charles and the principal at Fort Alexander, Father Kalmes, AMO.

CHAPTER SIX

1 Sister Gabrielle Viau, MO, *Elles étaient deux: vol. 2. Mère Marie-Joseph du Sacré Coeur,* MO (St Boniface, Manitoba, n.p., 1989), 22, 49. Elizabeth Smyth provides an interesting analysis of the historical writing of the Sisters of St Joseph of Toronto in "'Writing Teaches Us Our Mysteries': Women Religious Recording and Writing History," in *Creating Historical Memory: English-Canadian Women and the Work of History*, edited by Beverly Boutilier and Alison Prentice, (Vancouver: University of British Columbia Press, 1997), 101–28.

2 Lawrence Cada, SM, Raymond Fitz, SM et al., *Shaping the Coming Age of Religious Life* (New York: The Seabury Press, 1979), 55.

3 Rosa Bruno-Jofré, "Lifting the Veil: The Founding of the Missionary Oblate Sisters of the Sacred Heart and Mary Immaculate in Manitoba," *Historical Studies in Education* 9, no. 1 (Spring 1997): 17.

4 "En Esprit de Réparation," *Chroniques des Missionaires Oblates du Sacré-Coeur et de Marie Immaculée* 2, 13 (September 1917): 201–3; Rosa Bruno-Jofré, "Lifting the Veil," 17.

5 Sister M. Francois-de-Sales, MO, "Notes recueillies sur notre chère Mère M. Saint-Viateur," under the title "Petits faits," n.d., written before 1922, manuscript, 14, AMO.

6 Sister Louis de France, MO, "Archbishop Adélard Langevin," manuscript, February 1977, 2, AMO.

7 See for example, Sister Gabrielle Viau, MO, *Elles étaint deux: vol. 2, Mère Marie-Joseph*, MO, 22, 28; Sister Dora Tétreault, MO, "Monseigneur Langevin: Son charisme," manuscript, 20 August 1974, AMO. Mère Marie-Joseph, "Rapport historique de la Congrégation des Soeurs Missionaires Oblates du S.C. et de M.I. de Saint-Boniface, Manitoba, Canada," manuscript, 10 July 1939, AMO.

8 Ibid. In 1911, the community accepted the direction of the school in Fannystelle, a public school administered by a local school board. After the 1916 legislation, the Sisters found ways to teach French and to maintain the Catholic faith; they even hired a special teacher to teach French in a separate room.

9 Expressions used in Mère Marie-Joseph, MO, "First Attempts at Organizing the Congregation of the Missionary Oblate Sisters," translated into English by Sister Suzanne Boucher, MO, AMO. Ida Lafricain's early call to religious life was contextualized in the new project with Délia Tétreault to which Ida felt strongly attracted. She had to force herself to accept and fit in with Langevin's project, which involved a different charism and mission.

10 Sister Gabrielle Viau, MO, *Elles étaient deux: vol. 1, Mère Saint-Viateur, MO*, (St Boniface, Manitoba, n.p., 1967), 10.

11 Comment made by Sister Léa Boutin, MO, when she read the manuscript version of this paper, October 2003.

12 Sister Gabrielle Viau, MO, *Elles étaient deux: vol. 1, Mère Saint-Viateur, MO*, 22.

13 Ibid. The biography was written by a Sister with traditional views who stressed obedience as a religious virtue. Also, Sister Eva DeGagné, MO, "Mémoires écrits en 1988–89," manuscript, AMO.

14 Sister Gabrielle Viau, MO, *Elles étaient deux: vol. 1, Mère Saint-Viateur*, 8. (Contains a description of Mère Marie-Joseph.) This is also part of the oral tradition of the Congregation. Sister Gabrielle Viau, MO, *Elles étaint deux: vol. 2, Mère Marie-Joseph du Sacré Coeur*, MO, 45, 110–19. Notice that this biography was written in 1989; it shows changes in the way of interpreting Mother Marie-Joseph's spirituality.

15 "Journal de la Maison-Chapelle," 16 May 1915, quoted in Sister Dora Tétreault, MO, Monseigneur Langevin: Son charisme de Fondateur, manuscript, 20 August 1974, AMO.

16 Ibid.

17 The relation of the myth of foundation was taken from Rosa Bruno-Jofré, "Lifting the Veil," 17–20.

18 Sister Léa Boutin, MO, October 2003, comment made when she read the manuscript version of this chapter.

19 Mother Marie-Joseph, MO, "First Attempts." Self-denial inasmuch as it removes the self-seeking obstacles to a full spiritual life can be fruitful. It could also mean abdication of personal freedom and responsibility, and excessive attachment to the rules.

20 Adélard Langevin, "Appel en faveur des oeuvres catholiques du diocèse de Saint-Boniface," *Les Cloches de Saint-Boniface* 1, no. 2 (15 February 1902): 25–8.

21 Between 1963 and 1973, the Congregation went through a rapid and uneasy process of change affecting daily life as a response to Vatican II and larger societal changes. The Sisters took back their secular names; the requirements for the trousseau and objects for personal use changed; the habit was dropped in favor of secular clothes; regulations regarding use of the telephone, correspondence, travels, visits, holidays, and swimming were drastically changed. Lettres circulaires de Soeur M. Jeanne-d'Arc (Soeur Jeanne Boucher) MO, Supérieure Générale, of 24 August 1968, 27 March 1969, 21 February 1969, 25 April 1969, 8 August 1969, among others, AMO.

22 Marcel Martel, *French Canada: An Account of its Creation and Break-up, 1850–1967,* The Canadian Historical Association, Canada's Ethnic Group Series, booklet no. 24, 1–4.

23 Already in 1963 the outgoing superior general reported that over the last six years out of sixty-two aspirants, eleven left during the postulancy; eight of the fifty-one Sisters who pronounced vows became secularized. Sister M. Jean-de-la-Croix, MO, General Superior. This was the situation in all religious communities in North America. See Micheline D'Allaire, *Vingt Ans de Crise Chez les Religieuses du Québec: 1960–1980* (Montreal, QC: Éditions Bergeron, 1983); Sisters, Servants of the Immaculate Heart of Mary, eds. (Monroe, Michigan), "*Building Sisterhood: A Feminist History of the Sisters, Servants of the Immaculate Heart of Mary*" (Syracuse, NY: Syracuse University Press, 1997); Anita Caron, *Femmes et pouvoir dans l'église* (Montreal, QC: VLB Éditeur, 1991).

24 Boutin and Tétreault were influenced by Lawrence Cada, SM, Raymond Fitz, SM, et al., *Shaping the Coming Age of Religious Life* (New York: The Seabury Press, 1979).

25 Edward Farrell, SJ, *Disciples and Other Strangers* (New Jersey: Dimension Books, 1974), 33.

26 Sister Léa Boutin, MO, Supérieure générale, Lettre circulaire aux Missionnaires Oblates du SC et de MI, manuscript, 24 October 1974, AMO.

27 Sister Dora Tétreault, MO, "Monseigneur Langevin; Son charisme de fondateur," presented to the meeting of directresses, 20 August 1974, AMO.
28 Decree on the up-to-date renewal of religious life, Vatican II, *Perfectae Caritatis*, 28 October 1965, in *Vatican Council II. The Conciliar and Post Conciliar Documents*, edited by A. Flannery, OP, rev. ed. (Grand Rapids, Michigan: William B. Erdmans Publishing, 1992).
29 Sister Dora Tétreault, MO, "Notre oblation et l' esprit de réparation," manuscript written and presented to the Congregation in February 1977; revised and corrected in January 1978. Also Sister Dora Tétreault, "The Spirit of Oblation and Reparation of the Missionary Oblate Sisters," 1981, AMO.
30 Sister Alice Trudeau, recorded interview by Rosa Bruno-Jofré and Sister Dora Tétreault, Winnipeg, Mother House, 21 October 1994.
31 Sister Alice Trudeau, MO, "Une religieuse interpelle les Oblàts," manuscript, 1983, AMO.
32 Jerusalem Bible.
33 Missionnaires Oblates du Sacré-Coeur et de Marie Immaculée, "Montez à la montagne: rebâtissez ma maison" (Aggée 1: 8), manuscript, 1993. Actes du quinzième Chapitre Général, 7–21 juillet 1993, St Boniface, Manitoba, AMO.
34 Fourth Symposium on the History of the Oblates in Western and Northern Canada, Collège Universitaire de Saint-Boniface, 25–26 August 1995.
35 "Premières constitutions des Soeurs Missionnaires Oblates du Sacré-Coeur et de Marie Immaculée" (1906), copy of the manuscript, St Boniface, Manitoba, 3 July 1968, AMO; "Constitutions de la Congregation des Soeurs Missionnaires Oblates du Sacré-Coeur et de Marie Immaculée, St-Boniface, Manitoba," 1931, AMO
36 Sister Dora Tétreault was inspired by the work of female theologians like Barbara Fiand, *Living the Vision: Religious Vows in an Age of Change* (New York, NY: Cross Road, 1990).
37 Sister Dora Tétreault, MO, Comité de la Spiritualité, "Document de Travail sur la Spiritualité MO," manuscript, 1 August 1996, and "Rereading our Charism for Today," presented to the General Chapter, manuscript, 1997, AMO.
38 D. Tétreault, MO, "Rereading Our Charism for Today," AMO.
39 For a discussion of memory see Kerwin Lee Klein, "On the Emergence of Memory in Historical Discourse," *Representations* 69 (Winter 2000): 127–47; Pierre Nora, *Realms of Memory: The Construction of the French Past*, translated by Arthur Goldhammer (New York: Columbia University Press, 1996); Chris Lorenz, "'You Got Your History, I Got Mine': Some Reflections on Truth and Objectivity in History," *Österrichische Zeitschrift für Geschichtswissenschaften* 10, no. 4 (1999): 563–84.
40 See J.H. Plumb, *The Death of History* (London: MacMillan, 1969).

Index